Eriskay Where I Was Born

Eriskay Where I Was Born

ANGUS EDWARD MACINNES

MERCAT PRESS
EDINBURGH

First published in 1997 by Mercat Press
James Thin, 53 South Bridge, Edinburgh EH1 1YS

ISBN 1873644 760

Set in Palatino at Mercat Press
Printed and bound in Great Britain by
Athenæum Press Ltd., Gateshead, Tyne & Wear

To my wife, Mary,
who typed and helped me with the English
and many other things

Contents

❧

Illustrations

Chapter 1

The island of Eriskay where I was born lies to the south of the Uists in the Outer Hebrides and is separated from South Uist by a stretch of water known as the Sound of Eriskay. The island is only three miles long and two miles wide with one road running from north to south. The village where all activity takes place is known as the Haun, a Viking name which means 'Haven'.

To look at, Eriskay is a rocky outcrop, its redeeming features being its silvery sands and crystal-clear waters. There are only three trees on the island but it is covered with lush, green grass where sheep graze, with purple and white heather growing in abundance together with many wild flowers such as poppies, fragile harebells the colour of cornflowers, wild primroses, wild roses and clover, as well as buttercups and daisies, to mention but a few. There is also the attractive pink flower which was planted by Prince Charles Edward Stewart during the time he remained on Eriskay in 1745. The bay where he came ashore is also named after him. The reason he landed on Eriskay was to summon aid from MacDonald of Boisdale but MacDonald refused any help and advised the Prince to return to France. The Prince however did not take this advice, preferring to carry on to the mainland where he raised his standard at Glenfinnan. It was after the Battle of Culloden when the Prince and his men were defeated that MacDonald of Boisdale was helpful in hiding the Prince from the English soldiers as he crossed the Minch to the islands until he found his way back to France.

There are two hills of note on Eriskay, namely Ben Scrien to the north and Ben Stack to the south. The effort of climbing to the top of Ben Scrien is amply rewarded by the view across the Minch to the surrounding islands of Coll, Tiree, Mull and Skye, especially on a clear, sunny day when the mainland hills of Morven and even Ben Nevis and the island of St Kilda can be seen.

The three trees in Eriskay

Eriskay ponies, a few of which remain today on the island, are a hardy, sure-footed breed being able to carry creels filled with peat or seaweed. Some were exported to various parts of the country. It is hoped that their numbers will increase.

The island's church of St Michael is built of stone and stands at the top of the brae up from the Haun village and overlooking the sea. The story attached to the altar in the church is one which will always be remembered. A lifeboat was washed overboard from an aircraft carrier which was on manoeuvres to the west of the Hebrides. It was when the lifeboat was washed ashore at the south end of South Uist that Father Calumn MacNeil, who was resident priest on Eriskay at the time, came to hear about it and what better use to put it to than into the altar for the church. The bow of the lifeboat was fashioned as the centre piece, an anchor on either side support-ing it and the altar slab secured on top. This was done in 1967 by Father Calumn MacNeil himself, a man of fine artistic ability.

Eriskay at one time belonged to the MacNeils of Barra who sold it to the MacDonalds of Clanranald of South Uist. After their estates went bankrupt it then passed into the hands of the Gordons, an Aberdeenshire family who put Eriskay to good use as they could land anybody there, that is anyone whom they could not tie up and banish to the colonies. But it was while it was in the hands of the MacNeils of Barra that one of them built a tower on Stack Island which was used for piratical expeditions on passing ships. At last he must have gone too far as soldiers were sent to put a stop to him but when he saw them coming he made off with his boat to the mainland of Ben Stack. The chase with the soldiers after him lasted until he was cornered in a hollow called Lag na Chreache or Killers' Hollow, where the soldiers killed him. So that was the end of 'Breabadair Stache', which was his Gaelic name meaning 'weaver of stack', as he must have done some weaving when not engaged in his piratical practices.

There must be some truth in the legend that there is gold buried around the Stack Islands for it is more than likely that these piratical raids of his were beneficial to him in some way and any loot which he commandeered must have been sold to somebody, gold being the only currency in circulation around this part of the world in these days. I heard an old man say once that seven pony skins full of gold are buried somewhere on these Stack Islands. Anyway Breabadair Stache's wife, a St Kilda woman, and his family were staying with him there, and a boy of his must have survived his father's killing as by the time he was a grown man, and making his way in the world, he was once in some place in America in company when the talk was about some various heroic deeds ones in the company did during their lifetime. This man said, showing his hands, that these were the hands that killed the Stack Island pirate. The son told him who he was and they challenged each other to a duel, which was a common occurrence these days when people wanted to settle their arguments. The duel was fought, the Stack Island pirate's son being the winner, killing his opponent.

The main industries of the island are crofting and fishing. The younger people born on the island today, if not employed in fishing, must needs leave their home to seek employment on the mainland. Those wishing further education must also leave for universities and technical colleges, returning only at holiday times. Some marry and settle down after a while on the mainland where they raise their families and are happy to go visiting the island whenever a holiday time comes around. Many on retiral return to the place of their birth having been left a house or a croft by their relatives.

The home industry of hand-knitted Eriskay jerseys is still carried on by some of the island's women folk. The Prince and Princess of Wales each received a gift of one of these jerseys when they visited the island during the early eighties. They landed by helicopter above the bay where Prince Charles Edward Stewart landed in 1745. After leaving the helicopter they were driven to the Community Hall where they met and shook hands with the island population.

Eriskay is an ideal place for a caravan site or for camping. The beaches are out of this world for cleanliness, for swimming and for roaming among rocks at low-water spring tide. Sands with plenty of shellfish, namely cockles, razor-fish, winkles, also crabs and lobsters, are all there for the picking on its west side. On its east side it is an angler's paradise right along from Rosinish to Ben Stack, especially at the Cleat which is at the foot of Ben Scrien. For anyone keen on shooting—another sport for which no permit is needed—just fire away at rabbits, sea and land birds anywhere you choose.

There is a fine football pitch where teams from other islands meet the loyal local team when they are playing at home, while in another field I have seen ones playing golf—although no golf course exists there is plenty of open space to enjoy the sport.

Jogging is also another sport which is prevalent on the island, mostly up around the common grazing, where again there is abundant space and no one to stop you as the crofts are no longer being worked there. Today all milking cows have gone. The milk is now bought in the shop together with all other commodities, just the same as in the towns. The slavery of the croft has gone long ago. All that is planted now are a few potatoes. The sheep are on the crofts or behind fences on common grazing.

There is always accommodation available for anyone wishing to stay on the island. All of the croft houses have been renovated and modernised. Also in 1969 the first six council houses were built with another few being added afterwards in 1979. Some of the islanders have had modern houses built, aided by grants and loans which can be applied for through the Highlands and Islands Board.

The house where I was brought up was one where visitors stayed and we always had a full house during the summer months. I have seen the same people come to grandmother's house year after year. Only peace and quiet they were looking for. Many came from the south of England.

Calvay, a small island, can be reached on foot when the tide is out. No one ever stayed on this island, but it belonged to South Glendale hill grazing and was used at one time to keep rams there, so isolating them from the ewes until mating season began, when they were let loose among the ewes for breeding. When the tack was broken up and the place crofted, Calvay was then leased to a man who had kept shop on Eriskay and who would fill it with sheep at the beginning of summer, taking a few off Calvay at a time in order to keep his customers in meat. However with all sorts of regulations about butchering nowadays this way of life has disappeared long ago.

Calvay would make an ideal place for picnics, also the Sound between it and Uist used to be teeming with fish. The biggest flounder I have ever seen was caught in that Sound, nine inches thick she was at her mouth. A boat's crew of six men could not eat all of her. It was off the end of this island of Calvay that the famous *Politician* of *Whisky Galore* fame went ashore. A toast was always given when drinking to the one that did not see Calvay, as she struck the rocks in pitch darkness when it was impossible to see anything.

My childhood days on the isle of Eriskay were spent at the small village called the Haun. This village was made up of a few houses, two shops, a small church which stood high up on the brae and a school which was nearby at the foot of the brae. The harbour was very exposed to any wind from the north as the only shelter came from the Uist shore which was a mile away. The ferry and mail carrier ran from this harbour as it was central for the

Auntie Bella, auntie Mary Kate and sister Catriona, with daughter Caorsdith and niece Mary Ann, outside the house where I was born at Haun

whole island. Anyone visiting or leaving the island boarded and left the ferry here. The MacIsaac family who ran the ferry were our next-door neighbours and almost everyone travelling between Barra, Eriskay and Uist had to journey in their boats. It was through Polochar in Uist that the mails for Eriskay were delivered as there was no road to Ludag in these days.

I was brought up in my grandparents' house as my father and mother lived there more or less for the first six years of their married life. It took them this length of time between putting up a temporary place then pulling it down and going back to the grandparents' house while they built a permanent home. And so when they moved for the second time to the new house they must have forgotten to take me or else they were glad to see the last of me. By this time my grandparents' house was empty as all the unmarried members of the family were away from home. My parents had four children on that second flitting with a baby arriving every second year for about twelve years, and where they built the new house there were also large families. The house on one side of us had ten in the family while the house on the other side had fourteen, so I was not much missed out of that crowd.

My earliest memories of my grandparents was of my grandfather travelling for a Glasgow firm, Hamilton, Murray & Co., who were food suppliers for the north and west of Scotland. Almost every stranger visiting the island came to stay with us.

There was a quarter of a mile between my parents' and grandparents' homes, a good distance when I had to run for it after falling out with the

Our own family, taken in 1936. From left to right, back row: myself, Angus John, John, who died through accident aboard ship in Auckland, New Zealand, and Mary. Front row: Ronald, who died while serving aboard ship at Greenock, John Joseph, and part of Roderick, who is sitting down.

crowd. There was an old woman, MacLellan by name, who lived half way between the two houses, and many a day I was glad to get inside the safety of her door when being chased by a dozen kids and every one ot them holding a stone and demanding that she send me outside to face my desscrts. She would get on to them, threatening to tell the schoolmaster or anyone else holding office on the island. This same old woman had a brother who at one time was an officer in the Japanese navy. He was seen one day by another man from Eriskay who was standing on the street in Sydney, Australia, watching Japanese navy men marching by. A Japanese man of war had come into port and at this time the Jap navy had some British officers teaching them the know-how. This Eriskay man spied an officer leading the crowd of Japs and was sure he had seen him somewhere before. So he followed them until he got a chance to speak to the officer and found to his amazement that the officer was this old woman MacLellan's brother.

There was another man, Donald Macintyre, who was brought up just a stone's throw from this old woman's house. He commanded the loch's sailing vessels. It was a marvel how these men managed to achieve these positions having left home with little schooling, as compulsory education had not been introduced at this time. Getting a Master's Square Rigged ticket must have been a bit trying for the best, but for someone who did not have other than basic learning it must have been a hard struggle. These loch sailing vessels would have been about the last sailing vessels out of Glasgow. They were on the go right up until the First World War. There used to be one of them as a coal hulk in Adelaide after the Second World War. I remember being aboard her once when she was alongside us with bunkers. The *Loch Tay* she was called, and as I was scouting around her with other members of our crew and landing under her fo'c'sle head I was surprised to read on one of her beams, 'Certified to accommodate twenty-seven seamen', and

6

a windlass for hauling the anchors placed right in the middle of the fo'c'sle. We were only an old tramp but she was a palace compared to the *Loch Tay*.

The island in the early thirties had a population of five hundred. It was a lovely sight to see the boats in Haun Bay during the summer but as it was very exposed here the boats had to be moved to the harbour at the south east end of the island for the winter. If the harbour had been where the highest hill was it would have been more central for everybody. Where the harbour was there were only a dozen houses, which meant that it was hard work on Saturdays carrying home wet, torn nets to have them mended. The same carry-on had to be gone through on Mondays but this time at the beginning of the week men were refreshed and the nets were dry.

To look at the island you would wonder how it ever managed to support a population with nothing to be seen but rocks staring you in the face, especially when you were told by older folks that eighty years before that time the island was populated by only a few families. There were people still living on the island who were not born there and the sufferings and hardship these people went through from the time they were cleared out of their land in South Uist and Barra until they were finally settled in Eriskay and survived thereafter is a tale of hardship, toil and want.

The people who were cleared from the Bornish area of South Uist to make way for the big farms when the kelp industry collapsed were the ones worst hit, as they had to undergo two more clearances in ten years before they arrived in Eriskay. First of all they were moved to the back of Ben Mhor around the Hushinish area. I remember an old man telling me they had to get up at three o'clock in the morning when the cockerel started to crow in order to travel to Bornish in time for mass, the Bornish and Eocher churches being the only ones in South Uist and Barra at that time. I can also remember my grandmother saying that they would go from the Barra Head islands to Bornish, a distance of fifty miles, for a priest if anyone was dying.

After a few years, having cleared some land and built some houses, they were again moved out because the new farms wanted more grazing land for sheep. This time they were settled in Bun Struth and Bha Hartabhagh. One wonders how they managed to survive but the truth is some of them did not. The second clearance was worse than the first because they were placed twenty miles further away from the church and the people they knew. I used to hear old Angus Cumming tell how his mother carried a baby all the way from Bun Struth to the church in Bornish to be baptised and how afterwards the same baby, now a grown man, was being called by the nickname of 'Sinker'.

There was another woman named MacCuish who I think might have some grandchildren, MacEachan, still around Oban. She found a half-drowned Dutch seaman in a cove known to this day as Dutchman's Cove. She must have been a very strong woman as she carried him to her own home, a distance of half a mile.

Their years of toil and breaking-in of land all went for nothing as they had to move again, this time to Eriskay, where some of their descendants are to this day. Eriskay must have been a heartbreaking sight for them after all the suffering they had endured during these clearances, but it was the one place that was going to be their saviour, as the sea would be kinder to them than the land. There must have been a breaking up of families on this third trek, because in my young days people going over to Uist for corn or seed had relations they would visit on these expeditions.

I remember one night drinking in the Dalton Hotel in Vancouver when this fellow came over to the table. Hearing from someone that I was from Eriskay he began to talk about his relations there. It took me a while to figure out the McIntyre family he was talking about, as the name had died out and any relations he had there were under another name. His own name was Ian McIntyre and his grandfather Ian Mhor had been sent to Garnamonie while Ian Oig, his grandfather's brother, had been sent to Eriskay, so these two brothers must have separated on this third trek. Maybe there was a method in the madness of separating relations. Perhaps it was to take out some of the fight that was left in them, but this fellow had left Uist in his teens along with the emigrants, then went back to fight for us during the war and was on full disability pension, having been badly injured during the fighting.

It is easy to blame the estate owners for all of this suffering but there are two sides to every story. The kelp industry had collapsed after the Napoleonic wars, the reason being that there was no money in it for the estate owners, who had over-populated estates on their hands with nothing for the people to do. There was a big emigration from the mainland to the islands during the kelp bonanza, and I think every surname in Scotland must have been there. In my young days on Eriskay there were about twenty surnames altogether. There were only a few surnames native to the islands, the rest being from mainland clans. How they got as far as Skye can be anybody's guess but they must have crossed the Minch under very primitive conditions. It was by the shortest sea route that people went over in these days. It is strange after being without a service for a long time that people today are crossing on the same triangular route as their forebears.

The ferrying of cattle then was done with more or less open boats called 'packets'. All cattle coming from the south islands had to be ferried over from Lochmaddy. Three grand uncles of mine had one of these packets and it was while aboard this vessel that all of them were drowned. Their surname was Campbell and after the disaster only my great-grandmother and an orphan boy were left. My great-grandmother lived on in Eriskay but the orphan boy Dougal, who was in fact her nephew, was brought up in South Lochboisdale.

Before the clearances, when there was plenty of work for everybody, the estate owners were able to maintain a good lifestyle, living it up in their big houses in London. It was only when the bonanza stopped they had no other option but to turn nasty. The question was what could these estate owners do as they were on the verge of banruptcy themselves with no income coming in from their estates. I have heard from people who went into the same land eighty years later when the tack leases had expired and the land given to crofters, that they had some job clearing away old ruins, an average of three to every croft. And so what were these people who had lived there before them to do? Their only qualifications were the gathering and burning of seaweed. The days were long gone when people could be put to whatever work the chiefs deemed fit. But the colonies then were crying out for settlers and that is where some of them went while others were refusing point blank to go. Most of those who went had to be forcibly put aboard the emigrant ships.

Two or three cows would be the most any of them would have had while the kelp was in its heyday, and the patches of land they were given in Eriskay when they went there first would be enough to keep that number of stock before they began to subdivide the land between their families. But there was a difference in Eriskay, where they could keep a boat afloat all the year round, while on the west side of Uist they were lucky to keep her afloat during the summer months. And so people with only two or three cows had to have some other source of income, that being the sea.

Pollachar, at the west end of the Sound of Eriskay, was the hub of activity in the old days. There was always an inn there to cater for people travelling between the Sounds. If you went cadging seeds or corn you had to go through there, then start the round of houses all the way to Boisdale. I can still remember some of their names: Alick Hugh MacRae and Allan Mhuiler (Allan, the son of the miller), so called because his father had a mill at one time. They were the worst pair, calling us for everything. Allan had a boat which he used to fish in the Sound with small lines for flounders. At this time Eriskay boats had started to use trawls for a couple of months during the winter. Allan was always blaming the Eriskay crowd for all the scarcity. If you went to Allan's house and asked him had he caught any flounders the last time he was fishing that was enough to get him riled. He would start off saying, 'You've had them trawled long ago'.

These good people were quite content with their few Highland cattle and with catching lobsters during the summer. They always seemed to have time to sit down and have a yarn. Allan and another character, Ian Brussel, would talk about the times in their young days when they would go as hired hands to the east coast fishing. They were always able to part with something about the spring of the year when things would be very scarce in Eriskay. I do not think they were in need of very much in the way of money, as what they earned from lobsters and the selling of a few calves was keeping the house going. Pollachar with its inn was handy for them, but they did not seem to care all that much for drinking.

Allan had a son, Norman, who I do not think tasted drink in his life. I remember one day Norman was taking a stack of corn up to Pollachar along with his next door neighbour Alick Hugh MacRae. Having taken up the last load Norman left Alick Hugh to do the business of being paid for the corn, but the two MacIsaac boys who were with the *Yawla Mhor*, Shemus and Aoghus Ian, collared Alick Hugh as soon as he got the money and bullied him into buying a round of drinks. The MacIsaac boys were well acquainted with everybody around that area having been on the mail run along with their father since they were born.

After a couple of rounds Shemus started getting on to Alick Hugh saying what a crook he was for charging so much for the stack of corn and to give his father one of the pound notes back. That started Alick Hugh off running down the Eriskay crowd, calling them for everything. He was a great fellow for swearing. He lived with his sister, Flora, who was for many years housekeeper to my great uncle in the church at Daliborg.

I saw Alick Hugh not long after at the cattle sales when I was there with a few-months-old calf. It had been born at a bad time, just after the New Year, and I do not think the poor creature had had a mouthful of milk in its short life. I remember it was white all over and had a couple of prominent horns sticking out. I was trying to hide him from people as best I could, as the folk from Uist were always making fun of the animals coming over from Eriskay, but Alick Hugh spied me anyway and over he came. I was trying my best to go between him and the calf but he managed to get a good look at it, then said, 'It must have been a goat that gave him birth'. However someone who had imbibed rather well offered a pound for him. I received eighteen shillings as they kept two shillings' commission. This was the first time I ever bought a round of drinks, with the result I arrived home with only a few bars of chocolate.

Pollachar was the important place in these days. It is a wonder they did not build a pier there as all the traffic, mails etc. had to pass through, and as a matter of interest it was from there that the sheriff with the big thumbs sailed from. He was going over to serve a bankruptcy summons to MacNeil and was travelling over with the blind man who had six fingers who was going over to collect alms. The Brahan Seer predicted that the day the two of them would be together in Barra, the MacNeils' reign over Barra would come to an end.

Pollachar was not a good place to sail from as even on the best of days the shore was bad, there being no jetty. Gillesbuig, the ferryman, had a bad run when he had to call there every day with and for the mails. Some days he could not manage it and had to walk there from the nearest point he could make in the Sound. The south east wind was the worst as you were lucky with a sail boat to make Eriskay after five tacks. Eriskay women, travelling mostly to the herring gutting in those days, would have one look at the weather when they arrived at Pollachar and if it was from the south east they would say, 'Good God Lingay tack', Lingay being an island half way to Barra that had to be reached go about and go on the other tack. The road to Ludag, which was completed at the beginning of the war, was a godsend to the people in Eriskay, as the crossing could then be made in all but the worst of weathers. Gillesbuig was very lucky. He was a good seaman, being all these years without an accident.

Bobby MacAskill, who was the proprietor of the Pollachar Inn, was a nice man. Many an Ayrshire cow he sent over to Eriskay, getting them home from Oban, where he had land, when they were a year old. All my young days he kept a weather eye out if people were inclined to drink too much and then go out in a boat. Not that he had to worry much, as the Eriskay men in those days were not in any way keen to drink when boats had to be handled. It was Bobby's mother's people, the Fergusons, who had the place from the beginning.

The Fergusons had a couple of tacks in South Uist, also shops owned by Donald at South Lochboisdale and Eriskay. His sister, Annie, was in Pollachar and it was here that Bobby's father got to know her as she was more or less one of his nearest neighbours. He was curing white fish out at a place called Leachach past South Glendale on the Sound of Eriskay, curing white fish being the main industry of the islands at that time. Apart from the shepherd's house at South Glendale and the tack house at East Kilbride, Pollachar was his next neighbour. So being out at Leachach all summer it is more than likely he would have a stroll into Pollachar.

Families brought up in the islands can be lucky, others can be very unlucky. My father's family, four boys and two girls, were one of the lucky ones, none of the boys ever being lost at sea when every penny they ever earned was at sea. The family next door to where they were brought up at Balla, Eriskay, was the opposite. That whole family was nearly wiped out through drowning in the space of four years, the saddest thing being that the mother was drowned along with them. At the beginning of 1914 this family was well off according to our island standards, with a new house and a new boat called the *Mystical Rose*, when the world seemed to crash around them. One of the daughters, Mary, was married and living in Barra, and it was during a trip over to see her that the drowning happened. They were sailing nicely, with just a fine breeze by sailing standards, when out of the blue as they were approaching the Barra side a puff of wind came and capsized the boat. Four were drowned, the mother, one of the boys and another boy and girl from two other families.

But it was Calumn Ian Mhor, my father's neighbour, who was hit the hardest, the mother and son Eoin, a boy of twenty-three, getting drowned. Iagan, the boy who was steering the boat when the disaster happened, lost his life through drowning during the war a few years afterwards. A girl, Effie, who was at home, died of a broken heart caused through all of these drownings. Calumn himself survived for a few years afterwards along with his son, Donald, who was married by this time. He must have been strong to have survived so long after these disasters but he was a tough nut from the clipper ship days. A whole week he was once tied to a bed aboard a sailing ship suffering from smallpox. It was the only cure that was available as he might have torn himself to ribbons as the itch they had to bear was terrible.

Calumn's brother, Angus, who had the boat called the *Virgin* and was a neighbour on the other side was also a tough nut. If he fell into the sea he would not even change, but just shake himself like a dog and carry on. His lifestyle was a bit too much for a human body, as in later life he had a perpetual bend caused by rheumatism, but his heart was as good as new. He met with a bad accident one day while cutting seaweed with the boat. When they left in the morning at half tide it was a lovely day but they were hardly at the rocks when it started to blow from the north east. The boats being high and dry it was not easy for them to make for home. By the time the tide was high enough for them to leave it was blowing a hurricane. Too much seaweed was left in her for ballast, so she did not go very far when she started to sink, going on her beam ends. By the time another crew had reached them the two younger members had lost their grip of the boat and were drowned. Angus and his brother-in-law, Iagan Bheag, were saved in the nick of time as they were exhausted by the time the rescue boat got to them. Angus's son Donald, a boy of fourteen, was found the following day, but try as hard as they could, they were unable to find the other boy. This boy of eighteen was an orphan from the homes and had been brought up by Angus's sister Masag. They lost all hope of finding him until one day in the autumn when they were cutting the corn, word came from north Uist that they had retrieved a body from the sea on their west side. The boat left right away for Lochmaddy to identify the body, and on arrival they saw that he was the boy. The salt water had preserved him well. He had a foot missing but apart from that he was intact, and this after five months in the water.

There were only four years between the disasters, which made it worse. Six people were drowned from a community of ten houses and within sight of their own homes, besides mishaps to ones away from home. In my young days the old women who lived there had plenty to cry about. The same with my mother's parents. They had a lot to cry about with losing two sons during the war, both aged twenty-one, one in 1916 and the other in 1918. But the ones who were left had to carry on. Some of those who survived not getting drowned lived until they were over ninety, my grandfather ninety-four.

There was another cousin of Calumn and Angus, Seonaid, who had her croft next to ours. This old woman coming up to her eighties was still working away on her croft right up until she died. I am sure had she been in the Black Hole of Calcutta the night history was made she would have walked out in the morning and started working on her croft. I never heard her complaining that she was tired. The only one of her near relations who was like her was a nephew of hers, Doondy. He was tough. He had nearly half his bones in a box on the mantlepiece having had them taken out of him after a bad injury aboard a deep-sea vessel. He was landed in Cape Town more dead than alive, having been three days aboard the ship after the accident but he had the heart of a horse and so he survived. By the time I knew him he had settled down at home, fishing.

Making buoys for the herring nets was his favourite hobby. He made them usually from dog and sheep skins. Buoys could be had from a fish salesman but they were not for Doondy, as he liked to make his own. He made a good one from the skin of a pony belonging to his aunt Senoid. It was so good that one evening while they were shooting their nets a herring drifter came steaming up alongside them telling them that they must have lost their dog overboard. They were a bit mystified at first until somebody mentioned that it must be the buoy Doondy had made from the pony. Every buoy he made from some animal skin but Senoid's pony was one of his masterpieces.

He never seemed to be scared of anything. If any wild beast had to be ferried between the islands Doondy would be consulted. It did not matter the size of a horse that had to be ferried—if Doondy said it could be done it was 'go ahead'. Horses were the worst animals to ferry as you had to get them down and lash them well. He used to make a bowline on the bite, put it around the horse's neck, take the two parts under its body, separate the two parts at the hind legs and take a part up on each side to the bowline on the bite. Both parts were then pulled tight, making sure each part was under a hind hoof. Then it was heave away until his hind legs were taken from under him. When he was brought down his front legs would be swinging away in the air, then a running bowline was put on them. After this his feet were lashed and he was ready to be man-handled aboard the boat.

I remember one day in the bar in Lochboisdale we were telling the boys behind the bar about our latest job—a horse brought from Barra to Eriskay. This old farmer was listening and he could not make out how we were not killing the horse by getting him down that way, telling us how tender some parts of the animal's body were and how we Eriskay people were taking a big chance with our carry-on.

Before 1895 the island was served Mass from Dalibrog in South Uist. This parish being such a big responsibility for one person, Father Allan was given Eriskay after his health broke down. There was plenty of work for him to do there, as the old church which had been built with the help of funds from the foreign missions was in such a state of disrepair that it had to be pulled down altogether and the new one built. The building of the new church was difficult in so far as funds were concerned, but as things turned out the money was raised by contributions from various parts of the world, as well as from the island's residents.

13

There were two stonemasons from Benbecula who started off the building of the new church, Eoghain Ruadh and Muldonaich, in 1899. Both of them stayed in my grandfather's house on my mother's side. This house, a two-storey with a shop in it then, is still standing there to this day. These two Benbecula men were not long employed in this until the Boer War broke out and Muldonaich, who was in the reserve, was called up. I still remember my granny telling me how one evening while they were having their meal after the day's work was over, a knock came to the door, but on opening the door there was no-one in sight. The second night at exactly the same time they were having their meal when the knock came again, and when they answered there was somebody with word for Muldonaich to pack his bag, as the reserve was being called up for South Africa. What his thoughts were leaving Eriskay the following morning after these knockings is anyone's guess, but he fought out in the war and lived to a ripe old age in Benbecula. Eoghain Ruadh had to carry on by himself with the building of the church until that terrible day when he was almost killed when the scaffold collapsed. He had to be carried down to grandfather's house. He was in a very bad state, and medical help being unavailable these days, people just had to do the best they could to nurse him. They must have managed to give him some medical aid, for although slightly crippled, he also lived to a ripe old age. However all of this was worrying to Father Allan until he got someone to finish the job. The church was opened in May 1903, but sorry to say, with all the worry, Father Allan only survived for two years afterwards, dying at the early age of forty-six in October 1905.

Priests in the islands always had to be on hand at any death, the death by typhus being the worst, when victims were avoided and sadly sometimes died without anyone coming near them, like the old woman I was told of. She had died of typhus alone in her own home, and this fellow, who was not too bright, after being given a few shots of whisky was sent inside the house with a rope to tie around the old woman's legs, so that the ones outside could pull her out and bury her in a hole they had dug near to the house. It was thought that the typhus all started with people digging around old buildings where boiling water from cooking pots had been poured into the ground.

There were relations of mine at Balla, Eriskay, an old great-aunt, Peggi Mhor, and her brother's wife, Mary, and also a young boy, Ruaridh Mhor MacLeod, was with them for the summer herding of their cows. They were digging around the front of the old house this day when afterwards all three of them went down with typhus. As there was no one to attend to him, Ruaridh Mhor had to be taken home to his father's house on a stretcher. His father and mother cleared the rest of the family out while they looked after him. Ruaridh survived but his father contracted the disease and died. On his death, Iagan Ian Mhor, who stayed with his sister Masag, went to coffin him. After this Iagan also died of the typhus infection. Then Masag with a great uncle of mine, Mhaighter Ian, who was a priest in Eriskay at the time, coffined him and took him outside the house. The typhus seemed to have stopped after this as both Masag and Mhaighter Ian seemed to have escaped it.

Masag was a hardy person. She had to be to survive all the disasters that came her way, as not long after the typhus epidemic the eighteen-year-old home boy, Rob, was drowned when the boat sank full of seaweed.

When I knew Masag she was living on her own, always getting on to her nieces and nephews. She would be crying for the dead one minute, but when it came to the survival side of life she could certainly argue, as one of the loudest arguments I have ever heard was between herself and her brother Angus over repairing the hill fence. This day in uncle Eoin's house the two of them were to the fore, Angus laying down the law about people not facing up to their responsibilities and doing their share of the work of repairing the fence, Masag being one of them. However he was not getting everything his own way as she was facing up to him and shouting him down. She outlived all of her generation and was at the bedside of her brother Angus when he was at death's door. She remarked softly that he would only 'fade away'—saying this whispering—but Angus must have heard her as he retorted '*Tha dhe gilla agaid*'—'Not this boy here'.

Eventually Masag herself died in hospital in Lochmaddy, as she was getting so old she needed caring for at all times. One day before she actually died we happened to be in Lochmaddy with our boat, the *Lady of Fatima*, and so we went to the hospital to see her. Masag was up in arms as usual over ten pounds that had gone missing on her trek between leaving her own house and staying a while with her niece, Mari Doughall, then another while in hospital in Dalibrog before she reached Lochmaddy, and so who better to blame than her niece, Mari Doughall? Mari got to hear of this and came to our house one day demanding to find out what Masag was saying. Mari was there and then going to Lochmaddy to behead her aunt Masag. The truth of the matter was that Mari had given the money to the nuns in the hospital when she left her in their care, but Masag was for looking after her own finances. That ten pounds, I believe, was supposed to go to the person who got everything she ever had to spare, namely Mhaighter Ian, who was around to help her in her hour of need.

There were no more outbreaks of typhus in Eriskay, but there was the red house built for those afflicted in South Uist when there was a bad outbreak there before the turn of the century, in which a number of people, including the priest, died. The priest, Father George Rigg, will always be remembered in South Uist. One of the loveliest songs ever composed there was praising him for his devotion in tending the sick of all denominations. This song was composed not by a catholic but by a protestant, who called his son George, a name that was common around that area in both protestant and catholic families.

With proper housing and sanitation this typhus scourge seems to have been stamped out until there was no need for the red house at last. However my great uncle, Mhaighter Ian, who was priest in Dalibrog at the time, got a few wise heads together to think about buying it, as the parish being so spread out it could be used for a temporary church at Garynomonie, and so the red house was auctioned and bought. The red house was then dismantled and carried with carts and horses to be rebuilt at Garynomonie. This so-called temporary building was put up so well that it served the folks at that end of the island for forty years.

One of my brothers who was home fishing was talked into buying a television set by a dealer in Mallaig. Eriskay had electricity at the time but there was a question as to T.V. reception there as a few over on the Uist side had tried it without success. Anyway, by the time I got home about a year later, reception could be had and the house was like a dock-area New York picture house, where older immigrants who had never mastered English had to have someone with them to translate what was happening on the screen. My own T.V. experience was seeing glimpses of it while ashore in sailors' homes and pubs, but my mother and father thought it was the 'bees knees'. You would have thought they knew the stars on the screen personally, or at least that the women did. It would have been all silent movies with them, as some of them had not been away from home since marrying, and so about forty years of progress had been missed by some of them. During a Cowboy and Indian battle, Mari next door was wondering whether they were the same horses as she had seen in the Lorne picture house fifty years before, when she was working in the Gray Dunn biscuit factory in Kinning Park, Glasgow.

That is one thing the television did for people, it brought them the same recreation as anywhere else, bringing them up to date with world affairs. Whether they are any better-off for it I do not know, but speaking for myself I would just as soon be listening to some old-timer telling of an experience he had met with while travelling the world.

To see some of these worthies working on their crofts you would think, if you did not know any better, that they had never been further than twenty miles from the boundaries of their own crofts in their lives, until you would listen to them telling their tales of happenings in foreign lands. The most hair-raising story was told by one who said he had been an executioner in the Philippines. How he came to hold this position can be anybody's guess, but he sure had an audience around him, mostly children, all eager to find out how he was hanging the victim. 'Hanging—no!', and he would spit out after a puff of his pipe. He was using more modern methods, our country's methods—meaning Britain—were too out-dated and far behind. He had a machine to do the job and he would get the head of the poor geezer who was about to meet his Maker into this gadget, clamp it shut, and start screwing until the victim's eyes popped out. He was then declared dead. I would think so, after going through that lot.

In the long summer evenings, especially Saturday evenings when they were home from the fishing, some outdoor recreation was always in vogue, all the young ones gathering at Tigh Aoghais Ian Bheag or Tigh e Bealaich, as it is known in Father Allan's poem. This certain Saturday a bicycle had arrived on the scene, a few of the boys having clubbed together to buy one. The only person who could ride a bicycle at the time was Ellen Bheag, one of the family who stayed in Tigh e Bealaich. Ellen Bheag learned how to ride a bicycle during the times he worked on the farms in Crieff, a bicycle being a necessity in order to get around the countryside. His sister was married there and so at certain times of the year if shipping was slack around Glasgow he would visit her, getting employment during the harvest times. Ellen Bheag was home in Eriskay showing his skill at riding the bicycle. He would jump on to it and ride around the field, the rest of the boys trying to get onto it and falling all over the place, causing laughter all around. However Ellen Bheag was getting all the attention this Saturday evening, everyone looking at him with admiration, when his brother Ian comes out of the house and probably being somewhat jealous of all the hero-worship given to Ellen Bheag, he started to argue with him saying that he was not teaching the boys to ride the bike properly, and for devilment said that some man was teaching him to ride the bicycle a different way. Once the argument started between Ian and Ellen Bheag there was no stopping them until the boys who owned the bike did a bit of mediation between Ian and Ellen Bheag and decided to give Ian a start with his first lesson. Ian gets on the bike at the top of the brae and off he goes free-wheeling downhill, landing in a muddy ditch, getting splattered all over with mud and slightly hurt, as he was moaning a bit on the way over to the house where sister Peggy was waiting to give him what for! Ian was a great fellow for arguing, being the prince of the family at it. It is a pity he did not have an education to be a lawyer. I think he missed his vocation there.

His sister Peggy was the island's eye specialist, getting herring scales out of eyes with her tongue. She must have had a good nerve when you hear of today's students spending all that time learning how to specialise on parts of the human anatomy. I have seen something of Peggy's nerve once at home while I was fishing in the *Lady of Fatima*. Another character Neuka was aboard with me who one day was doing something around the engine and got a piece of steel in his eye. While walking home from the harbour it was decided to pay Peggy's surgery a visit. Well, without a word of a lie, she got hold of Neuka, made him lie on the bench, got herself spread-eagled on top of him and got her tongue in his eyes. Neuka was shouting at her to get to hell off

Iagan Mhor, whose wife was leader of the waulking gang, and Peggy McMillan, who used her tongue to take herring scales etc., out of eyes

him, but was unable to free himself from her grip until the surgery was over and Peggy had the bit of steel on the tip of her tongue while Neuka was groaning, but fit as a fiddle, with only a small trace of blood showing in his eye. This remarkable family, whom I knew well in my childhood days, were the 'have a go' type both on the entertainment and surviving sides of life. Their house was never without musical instruments and visitors. I believe Ian was the only one I have ever seen playing the bagpipes while sitting on a chair, everyone else playing them while standing.

Where Chapel Road ended was where the island bull was housed. Strangers would get annoyed at Eriskay for putting their old chapel grounds to such a use, but the old church had been built on right-of-way land that people at Balla used to take their cattle and carry their peat between the hill and the houses. The folks at Balla considered it their land, others would say when no one from Balla was around that it belonged to them all. Anyway the bull was kept where the Chapel Road ended, the MacMillans being his nearest neighbours, only a stone's throw away. Having to serve over one hundred cows on the island there was always some cow being served and, after serving, the bull had to be taken away from them, a job all the children around this area used to have a hand in. I was not very interested in learning at school but one thing I was interested in seeing was which dogs were the best for taking the bull away from the cows. There were some dogs would just bark in his face and that was no use, but the MacDonalds next door had a good one called Wallace. He would bite the bull's hind legs.

There was another good black collie in Catriona Mhic Ian's house. He would grab the bull by the tail and twist it away. Then there was Mari's collie, which would go for his horns. If the Board of Agriculture who supplied the bull had seen him being chased like this I believe they might have had second thoughts about giving Eriskay another bull.

The bull had to be herded a day for every cow, a job usually done by the children as they were just following him around, these Highland bulls being very savage. It was all right for some, if they saw the bull walking over where their crops were planted, to start screaming, but nobody had the courage to go and head him off. I think Eriskay folks were more terrified of bulls than others. One of the biggest rows I have ever heard on the island was about the bull tramping over somebody's croft crop. It was between a local character, Domnall Ian Mhac Tailler, and a home boy from one of the orphanages. Domnall Ian had been herding the bull when he encountered this young fellow with a Glasgow twang. Domnall Ian began speaking a form of English he had picked up in east coast herring boats, the orphan boy trying to create an impression on his adopted parents by guarding their property. Anyway it was some entertainment for us children hearing Domnall Ian telling us about the orphans he supposedly had seen being shoved into carts and taken to the orphanage.

Castrating horses was another job that was being done in the field opposite the MacMillan's house. That was more or less a twice-a-year job as there would only be about half a dozen stallions at a time. It was always strangers who did the job, ones from Barra and Uist. They were strangers to us children who were told by older ones that they grew horns and had other peculiarities.

When I think of Eriskay I remember how little we saw of the outside world as children, only people arriving on some business, or hawkers. I was not too badly off for mixing with strangers as where I was staying at Haun with gran was the place where strangers came and went off the island, also lodgers staying in grandfather's house and aunt Bella who was nursing in Barra coming over some Sundays with a crowd from there. I just had to mix with them all, but being terrified at the same time of the Barra folks, having heard stories about them.

Barra with four times the population of Eriskay and its army of strangers during the herring season was like a den of iniquity to us. Auntie Bella would arrive over with a crowd from Barra and you would listen in to all the happenings and the latest scandals, with granny, who knew them from olden days, shaking her head wondering what was blessed Barra coming to, her belonging to there.

By this time their fishing fleet was away, with most of its population scattered over the face of the earth. I think shop-keeping was the latest craze there for the ones left at home, as I heard one of them counting thirty-two shops one day. When asked the reason for somebody going bankrupt the reply would be, 'No more sheep left in the dark glen', or in Gaelic, '*Theirgh na caorich ais e glen dorcha*'. Then somebody would start telling a story about some crooks butchering a ram that was not their own. By this time with sheep going missing, a law was made that anyone bringing a carcass to a shop had to have the head still on, as with most of the sheep branded, these crooks were changing the brand and had a red hot poker in the fire. The dog, which must have been a spectator, was standing in the way of the fellow who was taking the poker out of the fire and got it stuck in his eye. This happening in the small hours of the morning, the dog yelping and howling woke up half of Barra.

So hearing all of these happenings over in Barra made me quite dubious of ever going there until one Sunday these relations of mine at Balla were going over. Domnall Calumn often visited his sister Mary, the last of the family left alive, who resided at Bruernish. This crowd from Balla were the 'baddies' from Eriskay, as every time Father Gillies wanted to vent his anger from the altar, they were always the culprits. Anyway this Sunday they were all in the holiday spirit going to Barra. I was a bit apprehensive about going with them, being only five years of age, and filled with dread after all the terrible happenings in the place I had been hearing about. However my mind was made up for me when Eoin Aoghais Ian Mhor got a hold of me and threw me to somebody in the dinghy, the *Tarbh Bheag*, so that was me shanghaied on my first deep-sea voyage.

I have heard once of a sailing ship leaving San Francisco with the padre from the mission shanghaied aboard. Seemingly he went aboard to lay down the law about shanghaiing sailors when he was knocked out himself. I must have felt the same as this Frisco padre going over to Barra that day on the *Mystical Rose*. I can still see Domnall Calumn manoeuvering the *Mystical Rose* through the narrow channel they call the Caol Bheaga at the Sound of Barra entrance to North Bay, with her nearly scraping the barnacles off the rocks. During my time at sea I was to sail in some of the most dangerous pilotage waters in the world, but the *Mystical Rose* sailing the Caol Bheaga that day still stands out in my memory.

Going ashore in North Bay was another thought, wondering what I was going to meet with once I stepped from the safety of the boat. I was not long ashore when I saw a motor car for the first time, one of the few in Barra then. This was the man known as the Coddie getting into the hiring business in which I would say he was doing well, for along with traffic on the north end of Barra he was getting the Eriskay traffic coming Oban way. I have seen them arriving in daylight hours around the beginning of April when people came home mostly to do the spring work. You got into the Coddie's car on Castlebay pier, drove if the tide was suitable to his small pier beside the road, and jumped into his boat which would be sailing the Sound of Barra at the same time as the mail boat would be passing outside it on the way to Lochboisdale. The Coddie's boat would land you as near as possible to your home. A great organiser he was. I think Barra was just a bit too small for him.

I never arrived in North Bay yet when the Coddie was not outside his buildings to welcome you. He was one of the few I knew in Barra, having seen him over in Eriskay at the Haun. The burning question put to the Coddie at these times would be whether any of these man-eating Boreachs—natives of the west side of Barra—who we heard so much about, were around. The Coddie would reply that we were safe enough as they had had a big feast the day before to celebrate the good crop they had harvested, the year before being the year of short corn when no one was safe from them. At this time the poor Boreachs were the Irish of Barra. Any joke or anything stupid being done in a boat, like not rowing in harmony, the joke was always on them. With the Coddie giving the all clear and his word of honour not to start the car while we were over there, it was decided to go on the short walk to auntie Bella's house. In auntie Bella's lobby was another contraption I had heard so much about, a bicycle! This bicycle was forever in our prayers as every time granny went on her knees to say her prayers, she would mention Bella and her bicycle.

The curse with small islands like Eriskay was that ground was too limited for all families to have a croft there, as a line was drawn that crofts could not be subdivided any more among families. There was only one way and that was to have the houses built around the harbour, leaving the rest as a communal grazing, but ones falling heirs to crofts would not hear of this.

The plan of having the houses around the harbour and leaving the rest of the island as a communal grazing for cattle might have had its draw-backs, but it would have been better than a system that had families fighting feuds, as only one member of any family could claim the whole croft. I am sure it would have worked in the two islands of Scalpay and Eriskay, where land was limited and fish plentiful, and had it been tried at the beginning of the century, when new two-storey houses started being built and crofts could not be subdivided any more. The system they were working under would cause nothing but trouble in the years to come. I am sure fifty of these Ayrshire cows could keep the likes of Eriskay in milk, half of them for the summer and the other half for the winter. The bit of machair on the west side would have been more than adequate for everybody to have a plot in which to plant potatoes. Once new houses started being built on crofts it was too late. Then tacks started being broken up, but that did not solve the problem, it only arrested it for a short while and isolated people from one another. If it had been done before the First World War at the change over from the thatched house, when income from the herring fishing was enough to build new ones without loan or grant, people would have been agreeable to developing the harbour, which would have enabled herring curers to start there. I am sure it would have saved plenty of trouble between families, trouble that has lasted to this day. Everyone would have had the same say in the running of the place. It would have done away with one member of the family having all and driving the rest into the sea. The fodder the cows would need—and that would not be much—the sale of the calves would pay for. Probably one coaster load would have done for the winter.

The system they were working under was like slavery—for the sake of a drop of milk and a few potatoes which they had for only half the year, as these items had to be bought from local shops the rest of the time. These crofts caused only fights and bad blood, with every member of a family sooking up to some old devil who was enjoying this proud position in life, having a rented croft in his name to give to the one who sooked up the most.

My father had to build his two houses with his own money, as he did not qualify for grant or loan, since he did not have a croft but was living temporarily on his father's croft. After the temporary house was up for about three years, he again had difficulty getting permission from the old father of his. I do not think he ever did get permission, but his brother, Iagan, who was the oldest of the family, told him to go ahead and not to listen to his old father. That was the curse of the Highlands, these old devils keeping crofts for whoever they stayed with, usually a daughter. They would drive the rest into the sea if they could. The bit of field he gave us to plant potatoes was the worst bit he had on his machair. The bit he gave for building the house was the biggest ditch he could find on his grazing land. We kept a cow but she never got a mouthful of grass from his croft. All the good he would do us was to steal anything that was not nailed down and take it back to his own place to give to my father's sister who stayed with him.

There was a smart one in Eriskay who had a croft and every year papers came to be filled about how many sheep, cows, etc. that were on the croft and how many acres under cultivation. He had down 'fourteen acres under cultivation', so the ones who the papers were sent to queried this by sending somebody to see this fellow. This man from the Board of Agriculture wanted to see where the fourteen acres he had under cultivation were, and he was told that he did not put down fourteen acres. 'Yes, you did', said the man from the Board, and showed him the paper where he wrote it. 'Oh', he says to the official, 'I forgot to put a stroke between the one and the four, it's a quarter of an acre I have.'

I heard my father saying the plan to build a deep-water berth for Eriskay harbour was shown to him while he was still a schoolboy by Captain John MacInnes, who was Master in the Clyde Shipping at the time. He had the plan drawn in such a way that he would have a loaded ship up to a few thousand tons go in and out of there with plenty of room to cant (turn). The berth was going to be outside the entrance to the inner anchorage on the south side, capable of berthing continental traders who were on the salt herring trade and were mostly loaded from small flit boats in herring ports. The plan was feasible to the ones who were prepared to spend the money on it, as they had enough sense to see that not only would it help the island but would pay its way through time. But no!, the man was nearly mobbed for it and his own nearest relations were the worst. They wanted a break-water in the Haun, as the Kilbride tack was going to be broken up to let the Haun be the hub of activity. This was a place where it took you all your time to keep a dinghy afloat in winter, and was so tidal that after a few feet of ebb you were trapped for the duration of that tide.

The breakwater they wanted for the Haun would not have made sense. The money would have been spent on putting a small breakwater at the southside entrance to the outer harbour, leaving the centre fairway open, but the only ones agreeable were those at the south end of the island, the rest being against it, as to their way of thinking it was no benefit to them, with the result they did not get anything.

For the young ones staying there today these plans do not make much sense, but they do to older ones who remember the difficult times crews had joining boats living miles apart, with the terrible Sound in between. Boats were risked at anchor in Haun so that they could be more central for everybody on both sides, as before roads were built on the Uist side all their business was carried out in boats across the Sound to Eriskay. Thirty years they were staying in Kilbride before a road was built, and I am sure it must have driven half of them to an early grave on either side of the Sound, with the carry-on they had working these bits of crofts which were hardly any asset to anybody.

Even if herring were plentiful, around the middle of August they would have to down tools and start cutting their few straws of corn from amongst the rocks, and potatoes had also to be gathered. All this had to be done quickly, half of it before ripening, to allow that army of horses to be let loose to eat every blade of grass. With corn so scarce there was always some-body's cows having dizzy turns in spring, with the result that all hands would be called for the usual ritual of lifting them up. It was then that the cadging expeditions would start going over to the Uist side for corn, every-one with a tale of woe about their poor, starving beasts.

Somebody went over one day to a local worthy's house, Ian Mac Ruaridh Mhor, and started giving him the usual tale of want. His house would be one of the first, as he was well acquainted with all of them from his sailing days. 'What on earth', says Ian, 'were you giving them before they came to this trancing state?'

'Wind', says the Eriskay man.

'What a feed they must have had the day of the big gale', says Ian.

There was another worthy, Mhac Doughal Bhan, next to him, swearing like a trooper, which was one of his special talents whenever he would see a face from Eriskay, knowing well what they were after. However, his was a good house if everywhere else failed as his wife belonged to Eriskay. I believe the poor soul must have left himself short a few times rather than see them go back empty-handed. So you carried on all the way to Boisdale on these cadging expeditions, some of them for a laugh putting you on a bum steer telling you so-and-so had seeds or corn they were sieving yesterday. On arriving at the house you probably found out to your dismay that the house was on a common grazing and they had no croft. Then kids howling with laughter would start shouting after you, 'Skate worth of corn', skate being an unmarketable fish, as it could not be salted. All this carry-on just to ensure a drop of milk in the tea for about half the year. I think Eriskay would have been better off had they gone in for goats like Switzerland.

My grandfather took a couple of goats home from Kintail when he was travelling for the Hamilton & Co., but there were so many complaints coming in about them always getting into some kind of mischief that we had to get rid of them eventually.

Eriskay folks just could not get away from the idea that not having a croft and stock was considered poor. It took four generations after settling there before they realised that being without a cow or horse was not a reason for thinking that you were poor.

Carrying a load of corn on your back all the way from Boisdale was no mean feat. I remember carrying a bag of seed from Calumn en Aoghais's house in Boisdale to Ludag. I was cadging all the way there. They seemed to have enough for everybody in Calumn's house as there were another few fellows along with me who were also given a share. By these days' standards they were well-off in Calumn's house. His wife gave us a meal which we badly needed. They had a nice engined boat for the lobsters and also a car, which was something rare in Uist at that time.

There must have been big changes in the postal services around the 1880s because I remember my grandfather telling me that he recalled well the Barra mails being delivered between Pollachar and Eoligarry. Up to this time mails used to be delivered from Lochmaddy overland. Not many letters would be arriving to these islands then as not many of the people could read or write. The Free Church school was opened in Eriskay after the Compulsory Education Act was passed. The school, which stands there to this day, was opened in 1878. It was only a one-teacher school run by a Mrs Charlotte Robertson, whose husband was in the lighthouse service in the Mauritius Islands and died there. Being left a widow in these days was quite a worry, especially as she had a small daughter. So she must have had an education to qualify for this post of schoolteacher and she must have been the only grown-up person on the island who could read and write, as she ran the post office when it came to Eriskay in 1885.

The Barra mails, which were delivered from Pollachar by a family called the Portainen, who had their crofts adjacent to Pollachar, became extinct around this time, as a mail boat had started running from Oban. Both jobs must have been too much for Mrs Robertson, because 'crabbed' Dougal got the post office in 1888 and kept it for fifty years until 1938. It must have been a bit of a trying job for Dougal, as ones are inclined to be somewhat cheeky and Dougal was not being in the best of health, suffering from King's Fever. This was a sickness cured only by the healing power of a seventh son whose father was also a seventh son. I heard my grandmother say when she came to Eriskay that Dougal was the only person she knew, having seen him in Mingulay. He was getting healing from a fellow who was the seventh son of the seventh son, and with her residing in Berneray, which was only a stone's throw from Mingulay, it is more than likely there would be communications between the two islands. Poor Dougal never did get properly cured but he still held on to his job for fifty years. The telegraph coming there in 1902 would also have added to his responsibilities and ill-humour.

The mails to and from Eriskay were delivered through Pollachar for the small sum of ten shillings, not much when the wear and tear of boat and engine had to come out of it after 1927, that is, up to the beginning of the war. There were six crossings a week; Monday, Wednesday, Friday—mails going away; Tuesday, Thursday and Saturday—mails coming to the island.

The family MacIsaac, who used to run the mails, would never have kept going if they had not added to their income by being handy with repairing the boats themselves and also with repairing boats for other people and building houses. They were never idle, ones in the family being better than others at doing certain things. It is the waters between Barra and Uist which are plagued with the most dangerous rocks in the Western Isles. Crossing in the dark with no aid to navigation, that was the menace in their job, and was a common occurrence when they had to pick somebody up in North Bay. They would have to come out of there in pitch darkness, head for Pollachar through these dangerous rocks, land the passengers and then head back to Eriskay. All this would sometimes be done during the small hours after people had gone to bed and all lights were out ashore, their only aid to navigation being an old spirit compass. Between hires, acting as steamer agents, fishing, repairing boats and building houses, that family was kept busy. The money they were getting from the mails, although regular, would never have kept them going.

Another kind of chore people were doing was getting up at the break of dawn and searching the shore for loot. There used to be plenty of timber coming onto the shore at one time as there was a big timber trade from Canada to west coast ports like Greenock. These timber droghers, all wooden

built, would be sailing the great circle route from Canada on the same latitude as these Western Isles, so they would be sailing across half-submerged
with only the timber cargo keeping them afloat, until sometimes, the elements turning too much against them, they would lose their deck cargo and
sometimes even ships and lives. This is where most of the timber used in
these islands came from. Sometimes other things that would float, like cattle which were carried alive in the cattle boats, would be washed ashore,
the sea having preserved them. All of this coming in the hungry months of
winter and spring it is more likely people were inclined to get a taste for it.
With barrels of molasses, lard, flour etc., some sort of duff (dough) could be
made. There was one fellow who found a chest with gold bars in it. This
chest, which must have belonged to somebody who made his pile in some
foreign country, was made of wood and so had floated from wherever the
ship he was in sank. The chest arriving in a small place like Eriskay would
create quite a stir with some conflicting reports as to its contents. I heard of
its finder going to somebody who was curing fish and being offered £60 for
one of the gold bars. When the fish curer was told it was worth more than
that he agreed, saying that his generation did not have the kind of money it
was worth. I also heard of some fellow who was not too bright being given
a watch that was in the chest in payment for doing some menial job like a
day's peat cutting or a day herding the bull. This fellow could not read the
time but was going around showing off the watch saying, 'You wouldn't
think it was that time', and some person would reply telling him the time.
Anyway people got tired of him and would just mumble anything. But one
night a knock came to this fellow's door and when he answered there was
some smart Alex standing saying he was the ghost of the dead owner and
that he wanted the watch back. So the watch was handed over to the so-
called ghost.

To my knowledge that is the only expensive thing that came our way,
but there were plenty of wrecks where everybody had a good feed. The
first wreck landed 130 years ago on a small island called Orosay near the
village of Boisdale in South Uist. Being a wooden sailing ship she would
not have lasted long, her cargo of smoked ham, cheese, butter etc. spewing
out of her onto the beach. The second one was a tramp steamer and she
went ashore on Monach Island. What they managed to salvage of her cargo
was sold off. Being a total wreck, Lloyd's Insurance would have an agent
handy who was selling 140-pound bags of flour for a couple of old pennies.
The salt water would only have penetrated about half an inch into the flour
so it was good enough to buy. Also the large cheeses weighing fifty pounds
which shopkeepers used to cut with a wire were sold off for a few pence
each.

There was a ship once went ashore at the Rhu Dubh at the entrance to
the Sound of Eriskay and all of the cargo in the hole nearest the bow had to
be dumped in order to get her off, the cargo being bran for feeding cattle,

something nobody in Eriskay had ever heard of. The Eriskay folks were giving them a hand with this dumping until some panhandler from the Uist side who used to work for mainland farmers told them what it was for. Then they began to load their boats with it.

The best childhood memories I have of Eriskay are of wakening up on a lovely summer's morning with ones rowing small boats used for lobsters, or line fishing with a small breeze blowing and ones setting sails with the sound of blocks and halliards running through them. There is an old saying that people should never go back anywhere they have happy memories of and I believe it is true. Monday morning was another morning of activity with maybe three or four boat crews putting their nets out to dry after being barked in Castlebay on Saturday, sometimes at a steam drifter or the coal hulk. I have seen up to two hundred herring nets on the brae between my grandfather's house and the shore. After drying all day it used to be great fun with children joining in picking them up, the younger children not being quick enough, lifting up the cotton netting and falling flat on their faces and being left behind. The older hands would be in their stocking soles, all the children being barefoot.

My father's house in Eriskay was built well away from where crops were sown, crops being sown only on machair near the shore, within easy reach of the off-shore rocks. These rocks were shared out among the crofts for cutting seaweed, which was used for fertilizer. Some of these off-shore rocks could be reached on foot with horses, but for others further off-shore, boats had to be used. Sharing these off-shore rocks was not done in a fair way by the maor or factor's troubleshooter, in our place being a relative of my father, as I was to find out once from the Thearach, so-called because his grandfather, Panny, was a native of Harris. It was one Sunday about the time the seaweed was being cut when the Thearach, with his wife, Mary, who was also a cousin of my father, called at our house after church service and we asked them if we could cut their share of seaweed on Oigh Sgeir, one of the largest off-shore rocks, thirty crofts having a share of it. That was enough to get Mary and the Thearach started, with the Thearach standing in the middle of the floor pointing to the bit of Oig Sgeir showing above high water mark telling us that was his share of it. Then, turning on father, he started to give him what for about the evil ancestors of his who gave poor Panny a bit that nothing would grow on but *fumain cearain* because he was a protestant from Harris. Then it would be Mary's turn. Money would be her topic, ones robbing the country getting school bursaries, family allowances and the like, and mother crying out what a pity there was no family allowance when she had the whole squad of us growing up. So it must have been a favourite game all along with ones sharing out the cream of things for themselves and their relatives, leaving the underdogs with practically nothing.

So, according to the Thearach, that is what happened when Oigh Sgeir was shared out and Panny was given a bit where only *fumain cearain* would grow. This *fumain cearain* was no good for fertilizing. The only use I have seen it being put to was being boiled in a big pot on the stove to give to cattle.

I remember one day the Thearach and Driver John were arguing while aboard the boat called the *Virgin*. Driver John was saying about all the seaweed he cut for fertilizing, the Thearach replying that he saw more in a pot of *fumain cearain* in Tigh Ian Barrach in the small village of Smercialate one day he was there cadging seed for sowing.

With people staying on Eriskay for sixty years the place was becoming too overcrowded, and so the tacks they had been cleared from were being broken up as their leases had expired in 1908. Kilbride in South Uist was one of them where I had an aunt staying, and where there was always a bed for me whenever I was on the other side of the Sound. Other tacks broken up in 1908 were North Bay, Vatersay, Peninerine and Gerernish. I also had two uncles at South Glendale, which was crofted together with Bhaigh Hartabhaigh after the First World War, the three communities of North and South Glendale and Bhaigh Hartabhaigh being served by one school in the middle of nowhere. Bhaigh Hartabhaigh was crofted without success as it was too isolated, those living there having to walk a few miles to South Glendale, then ferrying across the Sound to Eriskay to get to church. About half an hour's walk from South Glendale lies North Glendale, both communities crofted by relatives of ours.

Chapter 2

Peat gathering—Childrens' chores—The stramash with Shonnag and Mari—The three trees—Schooling—Diet: cormorants, eels, cudegin, dogfish etc.—Trapping sea otters for pelts—Fanging the sheep—Radio—Religion—Haun Bay: a hive of activity—Grandpa, the surgeon—Different kinds of devilment—The Compulsory Education officer—Schoolmasters—The fighting priest—The post—The Gotha's wake—Bootsie's coffin—My troublesome relations fighting and drinking

During the school holidays in Eriskay in my young days the children carried peat with a horse for winter fuel. This was the only mode of transport, the alternative being to carry it on your back. We might get away for a short time, maybe a week, in the family boat *Ocean Star*, if that could be called a holiday, living accommodation aboard being very primitive and myself dying with sea sickness and waking up out of a drugged sleep with the smelly socks of older cousins who crewed the boat, Shonnie Bheag and Domnal Dubh, in my mouth.

At times it was all work and no play on Eriskay then for children, the gathering of peat in itself being hard work, as most of it had to be ferried in small boats from the Uist side, the island being so rocky that not even carts could be used there. The only cart that was ever used on Eriskay was brought over from Barra by a man the name of Belford, who owned a shop on Eriskay. I had a hand myself in ferrying, while aboard the *Lady of Fatima*, the cart and an old mare which Belford had bought from Mhuraidh Maltby, who lived on Eoligarry. The mare was over twenty years old and she gave us the biggest shock of our lives since there was hardly a bit of rope left aboard to tie up the boat when we reached Eriskay as most of it had been used to tie up the mare because she had been trying to jump out of the boat on the way across.

The first machine I ever saw on Eriskay was an old motorbike which had been acquired from some scrap heap somewhere by an orphanage home boy by the name of Flynn. This old bike was a bit of a local attraction with the children as they would gather round to give it a needful push in order to get it started. After being pushed for a few feet it would jump start for about fifty feet then give out a few puffs like a brewery horse and stop again. So much for Eriskay's road transport, Belford's mare and cart and Flynn's motorbike, neither of which could be called successful, and so it

Angus McIsaac and wife Mary Theresa taking peats out of the creels, with a view of Ben Stack and the Minch in the background

was back to the old way of the horse with a creel on each side for carrying something, the same as was seen used by the toffs for carrying grouse after the Glorious Twelfth.

With the lack of any kind of transport other than horses with creels, children had so much to do, as all the grown-up male members of the community were either away fishing or in the Merchant Navy, while the women were doing the herring gutting or in domestic service. The only adults left were the older ones or the married women who were pregnant or caring for the new-born. Of course the children did not ever think of their chores as being work, as it was all in the lifestyle of the island. They thought nothing of carrying groceries on their backs for a couple of miles. Boys over the age of fourteen would carry 140-pound bags of flour on their backs easily, also the 200-pound bags of sugar, which were never too heavy for them. Rolling fifty-gallon barrels of paraffin to shops was all done by schoolboys as there was no one else around to do it. The shopkeeper would pay the boys four pennies for one 40-pound bag of flour and six pennies for a 200-pound bag of sugar. Every article went strictly by weight, not a penny more was paid out.

Every schoolboy on Eriskay knew the day when the small coastal traders would arrive from Glasgow with foodstuffs on the *Challenger* and the *Ardachy*. Also any exports had to be ready for shipment, things like eggs, winkles and salt fish etc. If there were no girls left in the house to work the horse, the peat carrying had to wait as the boys dropped everything in hand in these days in order to earn a few pennies by lifting and carrying.

Another way they would earn a penny was to herd the bull. The sum of half a crown could be earned for this bull herding, hard money to earn when you had a couple of cross hands waiting for you for being absent from school, if before the summer holidays. This bull herding only started after the seeds were planted and lasted until the crops were harvested. The girls could get away with being off school by giving the excuse that they had to look after the baby, as the mother had to have someone to look after the baby while she had the work of a day at the loch to wash sheets, blankets and things which needed plenty of water. All of the washing would be loaded onto a horse on a fine day in summer and taken to the loch, where a fire would be kindled. It was a common occurence to see half a dozen families trampling away barefoot on blankets during a fine day. Fortunately this does not happen now as the water is piped to the houses, but from the same loch as before.

Getting cross hands for these days absent from school was a bitter pill to swallow, especially when you had to share the packet of Woodbines costing two pennies with your pals. Failing anything to smoke, John McKelvie would bring a pipe with him to school and we would smoke *milerach*, which was fine seaweed that was found on the shore. People would gather and dry it to put inside bed mattresses. When dried and put in the pipe it would light up, causing a lot of smoke, and tasting awful. How we managed to escape catching some dreadful disease is a miracle, as I was told long ago that badly-cured tobacco leaves could cause mouth cancer.

Playing football near the school would cause another stramash as the croft neighbouring the school building was owned by a couple of terrors, Shonnag and Mari Cumming. I remember one time things got so bad that they got a hold of the football, took it home with them, cut it up, then put it on the fire. They were telling some of their cronies that the football made a lovely fire and that it boiled the kettle in no time. Of course the ones who had owned the football retaliated by shifting all of the corn owned by Shonnag and Mari to the adjoining croft, which belonged to my uncle Eoin. That started a bigger stramash, with all sorts of law being threatened, when uncle Eoin, whom they called 'Kruger', told them he was quite happy about it. Their only way of telling one sheaf of corn from the other was the way Shonnag and Mari economised by using only three strands to tie the sheaves.

Apart from football, not many games were played by children except rounders, a game baseball originated from. The game of shinty was at one time played in the Uists and Barra but they seemed to have stopped playing that before my time. I used to hear the older generation say that as children, around the New Year, they would make for the highest hill to see if there were any signs of the herring boats coming home from the Skye lochs, a camain for playing shinty being the usual present for everyone. With trees growing in Skye any amount of camains could be had, but Eriskay was without trees except for the three small trees which were a big attraction, as children used to come from both ends of the island to have a look at them. So the boats arriving from the Skye lochs was a big day in Eriskay, with everyone from the cradle to the grave showing off their Christmas present of a camain from Skye.

But shinty seems to have died out altogether in the south islands while the Skye men have kept it up to this day. They were always making fun of the boys from the Uists who used to do their training along with them in the army reserve camps, saying that the Uist boys always took a back seat at shinty because they were afraid. It is a wild game—I used to hear Skye men talking and saying that whoever played fair was no use to them. The Portree High School, so they said, were the best shinty players on the west coast of Scotland at one time.

There was so much children could do in Eriskay apart from the endless tasks of carrying water from the wells and carrying peat for the houses. Winkles could be gathered, for which a fair price would be given if they reached Billingsgate alive. Also, at low tides, cockles and razor-fish and sometimes at low spring tides, a lobster. Depending what time of the year, seaweed for fertilizing crofts was cut and the children would lead the horses back and forth between the off-shore rocks and above high water mark.

In my young days in Eriskay schooling was never very popular with the children. There was a bursary given out once a year to whoever felt like sitting the exam for it. Some girls took advantage of it but boys were not so interested. Some years no one was interested enough to sit for the bursary and so it got wasted. With things so bad the world over in my young days, there seemed no sense then in becoming educated. You would hear sad tales from sailors coming home after being paid off, leaving ships in some lonely Clyde loch like the Gairloch in charge of a watchman. Another sailor would return with the tale of being the only one on deck without an officer's certificate and ones would come home considering themselves lucky they had a home to go to and a job fishing, since the worst thing that could happen to anyone was being unable to do the job one was trained for.

I do not know why but everywhere else those who had brains seemed to have the ambition to become educated, but in our part of the world whether they had brains or not, they were not happy unless they were given a bit of rope for working with. It would only be after a few years as deck hands that those who went in for certificates got any notion to study. I think being brought up in an atmosphere of hearing old timers spouting and arguing about seamanship, and what great guys they were when they could show anyone anything from a needle to an anchor, killed off any ambition young ones had other than being good seamen. You might get one in a thousand like our next-door neighbour, Donald MacDonald, who went through University and gained his M.A. degree with Honours. It is a mystery to me how that man managed to study with all the buzz going on around him, as there must have been about thirty school children in and out of the house shouting, screaming and carrying on between their own crowd and those of their neighbours. The grown-ups too, could shout and argue, especially the MacMillans next door, Ian, Fairy and Peggy, who were past masters at arguing, and there would be Donald in the middle of the melee with his nose in a book. How he managed to concentrate is beyond me.

With the limited amount of money which was available through bursaries, schoolmasters were rated as high as anyone in our islands could reach. Having one in the family would be someone for relations to boast about as everything connected with a schoolmaster was held sacred.

It was a hard struggle for some schoolchildren living up to two miles away from the school, especially for the very young who had to start schooling at five years of age. We were not so badly off in Eriskay, as the furthest anyone lived away from the school was only two miles, and all were within easy reach of their homes. But for some, who had to travel over isolated hills and moors like cousins of ours who lived in South Glendale on the other side of the Sound, it was a hard struggle. Their school at the back of the beyond serving three communities lasted only a space of ten years, until the ones in South Glendale demanded to have a school of their own, which they got, but only after refusing to send their children to this isolated school. They were taken to court at Lochmaddy at first and were ordered to pay a fine. It was a near thing they were not sent to prison.

Children going to school in winter would leave home in darkness in the morning after breakfast, usually of porridge with milk, when the milk was available, as the cows would dry up at this time of the year just when people needed some nourishment most. Hens would also be laying less in the winter time, after the glut of eggs lasting for a few months before the winter set in. I would see five-year-old children tramping to school in the depth of winter having had just some bread and butter with a cup of tea for breakfast.

Dinner time between one and two was for those unable to get home for some bread and treacle but there was nothing to drink, except in the house next to the school, as there was no piped water to the school. The council eventually laid on piped water but the only ones benefitting were the school and the house where the nurse and the teacher lived, then after some time and a bit of begging the church house which was beside the nurse's house. A couple of miles of pipe were laid on from a well up the hill. The loch where the island's water supply comes from today is only a quarter of a mile past this well. This pipeline served these three houses for twenty-three years, when another pipeline was laid on to serve all the houses, the original three houses getting their supply from the same source, the first pipe being left to rust.

This pointless spending of money during the war years was a bitter pill to swallow. People wondered what on earth they were fighting for, with children having to carry water from a well situated a good distance from their houses where it was needed most to wash and clean them and their clothes. All these years this original pipe was passing a few yards from my father's house, and the first thing the school-going members of the family did after coming home from school, where there was water in abundance, was to start arguing about whose turn it was to go to the well.

For the ones who were unable to get home for dinner at midday it would be a late dinner at night, one thing for sure being on the menu, the old 'murphies' (potatoes), which have been the best means of survival for the poor of the country for years. It mattered not if all you received was one murphy with salt, you could not say you did not have a dinner. At one time MacDonald of Clanranald, who owned South Uist, had to bully his tenants into growing the potatoes, but after growing them the people took the whole lot to him and left them in a heap outside his house, telling him to eat them himself. I bet MacDonald, looking at that pile left to rot outside his door, did not realise that one day they would be the staple diet.

It was usual when coming near dinner time for ones to say '*Dhol dachaidh gune buntata*', meaning, 'Going home to the potato'. There would always be the potato even if all you had to take with it was salt, which was the lot of inland small holdings. For ones living near the sea, fish could always be caught, even in the most severe weather conditions, when a meal of saith or cuddies could be had with rod and line from shore rocks.

I have often wondered what people ate before the potato was introduced to the country by Sir Walter Raleigh. Men on long voyages in sailing ships whose vegetable supply had run out or rotted would break out in scurvy, some crew members being so weak and unable to swallow that potatoes had to be broken up for them and the juice from the raw potatoes forced down their throats. It was a common occurrence for sailing ships to be becalmed for weeks with no wind near the equator with a 'Short of Provisions' flag flying.

Children being away all day without a square meal were ready to eat anything after tramping home over poor roads in the bad weather that you usually meet with in these islands. There would always be some kind of fish swimming in the seas in season at all times of the year, which was included in the all-day diet of our island. Mutton you would see only on Sundays, as shopkeepers did their butchering only at the weekend in summer. In winter the mutton would keep better and could be got home from Dingwall along with other perishable goods such as sausages, which were also a Sunday breakfast dish, along with a bit of ham. Everything had to be weighed out, the cheese cut with a wire and ham cut with a knife. How often have I heard in shops ones plaguing the shopkeeper to cut the ham thin, as there were probably ten in the family and everyone wanted a slice out of the pound of ham. The shopkeeper would have to be as good as the wizard of the north to attend to all of their demands. I was not too badly off, staying as I was in gran's house where visitors came to stay in summer and even in winter when teachers and nurses would come 'relieving'. All were usually put up in the house, and so I used to get the pans to scrape off the remainder of puddings etc. And whenever I would go to my father's house he would greet me with asking had I finished scraping the pans already. Everyone there in my father's house would be tucking into potatoes cooked with their jackets on, and the younger ones, being too small, would have to stand on a chair to see over the pile of peelings should they want to give another at the opposite end of the table a telling off.

People living on crofts butchered only twice a year, once in autumn and again at Christmas. There was always the 'Caoridh Nollaig', the sheep for Christmas, on the menu, none of it being touched until Christmas Day even if ones were starving. None of it would be eaten on Christmas Eve as everyone in our place maintained that not even a raven would touch a carcass in the hills the day before Christmas Day. The only place beef was sold would be in Castlebay when an army of strangers would be working during the herring season, and also if an old cow had been slaughtered or any other animal which had been injured in a fall, like the time the Eoligarry folks had something wrong with an animal they had in their club stock in Fuday during the time the country was on rations. They had this beast on their hands which they reckoned was unable to reach Oban sales alive, and so Coddie, after some haggling, gave them a price for it.

There was a crew of older hands from Eriskay, who knew the Coddie from his sea-going days, in his shop one day. The Coddie, as usual, was all business, with the carcass of the Fuday beast on the counter being sold. There was also a box of apples, which were a rare commodity at this time. The Coddie was asked by the Eriskay men what 'poison' he was selling today, to which he replied, 'Tha caraid fual urr Fuday agus ubhlan America'—'Fresh beef from Fuday and apples from America.'

In Eriskay at one time cormorants were eaten with relish. I do not know why but some people on other islands were self-conscious about admitting to eating cormorants, but like everyone else on Eriskay I loved them, and why some people seemed to scorn cormorant-eaters is something I could never understand. I believe that when people went to live on Eriskay at first they had to eat anything in order to survive, and it could be that when people get the taste for something they never seem to lose it. Also in Eriskay we considered it a delicacy to drink the first milk cows produced after calving. You would always be treated to a dish of it if visiting a house after the cow had calved. But the best delicacy of the lot was the homemade duff, or clootie dumpling, as it is called on the mainland. It would just melt in your mouth. I have never anywhere else tasted duff like they made at home, and the city-bred folks who would come on holiday went crazy for it. I remember once being home when the moving pictures were being shown in the schoolhouse, an annual event in these days, and my mother had just made the duff and left it to boil away while everyone, including herself, went to see the film, along with my young cousin, Peggy Stewart, who had come from the city on holiday. Everyone was enjoying the film and laughing away at the goings-on of Charlie Chaplin when my cousin, thinking my mother had forgotten all about the duff, nudged her, saying, 'Auntie Flora, what about the duff?', no doubt wishing that it would be ready for eating.

Another delicacy they had on the island at the spring of the year was liver scones. It had to be the spring of the year when cod and ling were in season. It started about the beginning of February and continued until the end of March. All of the islands would go daft for cod and ling at this time, not so much for the fish itself as for the roe and the liver. The liver was cut into small portions, then mixed with baking soda and cream of tartar and put into the pot along with the fish to boil. Once the pot came off the fire and the contents dried, everyone would crowd around like vultures to get a share of the liver scones, which were more precious than the fish itself. I believe the reason for this was that in the old days only the innards of the fish could be eaten, as the fish itself was salted and cured, mostly for Southern Russia, Italy and Spain. So once a population gets a taste of something it follows them through the years.

Every island seems to have its own delicacy, as in the northend of Lewis where the young gugas or gannets are exported to island exiles all over the world. Other Lewis islanders are again self-conscious about eating them, saying that it is the Neishach (those from the Ness area of Lewis) who are the culprits. One fellow I knew who was staying in lodgings in Glasgow, while serving his time in an engineering trade, went home one day with the house smelling like a bluenose schooner on the Newfoundland banks. Asked where the smell was coming from, the Lewis boys, who were also serving their time, pointed to the Neishach who had received the delicacy of the cooked salted guga by post, the other lads being quite mortified about it all. The guga seem to taste and smell like salt mackerel, which is cured for the winter in all of the islands.

Travelling south from Lewis to Harris, salted eels are the delicacy. I have only tasted them once, aboard a ship with a deck crew from our own islands. I was going aboard after working hours, and as soon as I went up the gangway I knew there was some Highland cooking on the cards because of the smell. On asking somebody at the gangway where all the island boys were, a look of disgust was my answer, then a pointing to the mess room. When I reached there I was treated to something you would see in a black house one hundred years ago, with all hands delving into this pile of food on a tray on the table, along with potatoes cooked with their jackets on. I knew it was some kind of salt fish by the smell, but was flabbergasted on finding out it was eels. On asking where on earth did they come from everyone pointed to the Harris man who had received them by post that day.

There is one delicacy which is enjoyed by all of the islands and that is cudegin, which are small fish that grow into saith. In winter time they come in shoals around the shores of all the islands and are very tasty when fried. These cudegin, remind me of when I was young and started sailing away from home, and I met a couple of hardies from our own islands in a pub in one of these Ayrshire coal ports. These two were on some coaster which had gone into dry dock. We were talking away when one of them mentioned the good feed they had had for dinner, it being buy and cook your own on the coasters these days. On enquiring about the feed I was told it was cudegin and on asking where on earth did they get them they said they had got them in the dry dock. Seemingly when the dry dock was emptied out they had found the cudegin at the bottom. Not so long ago I was asking after the health of one of these two geezers, who is still alive, hale and hearty, at ninety years of age. So it would seem that the cudegin he ate from the dry dock did not do him any harm.

I think any fish in the seas is edible, it is just easier for some who have boats and sheltered harbours to be able to moor them and catch the better type of fish. I knew some old-timers on the west side of Uist who would not give you a thank-you for a cod or a ling or haddock, but show them a dog fish and they would almost pull your hand off grabbing it. No other fish being available to them in the old days they would salt the dog fish and dry them in the sun for winter eating.

It is winter feeding the older people were more worried about. During the summer, cows were in milk and some things growing wild in the fields were edible, but in winter, in the days before fridges were in vogue, it took some figuring out to be able to survive. Even the cormorants were salted for the winter. There was one family living near Pollachar who used to catch them by the boat-load for salting. I heard my father say they were one night coming from Pollachar, which was where the road ended in these days, and they met this family with their boat filled with cormorants, taking them home to share among friends and neighbours to salt for the winter. Seemingly they were the only family who could climb the slippery rock at Fiary so silently in pitch darkness as not to disturb the birds while sleeping. Before the birds had a chance to wake up the family were there choking them. This family of McRaes were certainly admired by the crowd in our

Our family and relations' boat, Lady of Fatima, *after the war*

part of Eriskay, as even in broad daylight it would take them all their time to climb this slippery rock covered with cormorant droppings. There would not be any birds there during the daylight hours, as they all flew out to the fords to fish. It was during the night they would come back to their special rocks to sleep.

I remember when in our boat, the *Lady of Fatima*, we shone a searchlight onto the rocks where we knew the birds were sleeping, then fired a gun at the rock, the birds in fright would fly down into the boat. We were lucky they did not knock us out while we stood on deck. We were unable to eat all we were catching but we gave them to others who lived around. I also remember a cousin of my father, Ben Stack John, whose house was a bit isolated but in a good place for evening shooting when the cormorants would fly back to the Stack Rock for their night's sleep. Being one day in Lochboisdale he met some characters who started telling him what a nice crowd that was in the *Lady of Fatima* giving away as many cormorants as they wanted to eat. This tale put Ben Stack to high doh as he had not shot a cormorant for a fortnight.

You would never go hungry on the islands, as there was always something free for the taking, but it was a goat we shot at the north end of Canna was the toughest bit of meat we ever tasted. These wild goats were put there long ago to keep the sheep out of the high cliffs. We started to eat her while in Mallaig one day and I can tell you she was tough. We were wolfing into her when we noticed Robby Hepburn, the salesman, coming down the fo'c'sle ladder. My father got a hold of what he had on his plate, threw it onto my plate and had his pipe lit by the time the salesman showed his face. 'What on earth are you fellows eating?', he asked. Somebody mumbled, 'A goat', which made him shake his head, as all east coast men are very superstitious about having certain animals being mentioned aboard a fishing boat, goats being one of them.

There were many animals which could be killed and eaten, but never the sea otter. It was caught with traps just for its pelt. Some people were better than others at trapping them, Alasdair Currie being the best master trapper our way. I have never done any trapping myself but they tell me that the pelt of the dog otter eighty years ago would fetch a guinea for every bit of the pelt the size of a guinea. However a dog otter is very rarely caught, being seen only by ones that I know of who are dead long ago. The dog otter, or in Gaelic the *dhor cu*, has a harem of twenty-four female otters. I heard my father say that when he was a small boy an old man told him that he saw the *dhor cu* one day in Bagh Hartavagh with his harem of twenty-four females along with him.

The sheep is the most important animal for people to survive on, as almost anything inside a sheep can be used after her fleece is sheared off, that being the most important commodity of the sheep in the world in years gone by. Fanging or penning the sheep would be a big day in Eriskay, being done mostly by children and the very old, the rest nearly always being away.

Not many sheep were owned by ones on Eriskay, twenty at the most, and ten being the average. We had one sheep all through the years. I do not know how we managed not to run out altogether but ever since I can remember we seem to have had the one. I think she must have been the best looked-after sheep in all the world before lambing time, when the family, who were all young, would catch her to see if she had an udder. I remember when sister Bella was getting married to Angus over in Uist. Celebrations were to be in Eriskay and also in Uist. Bella and her future husband were telling us the number of sheep they had slaughtered for the Uist wedding when brother Raoghail Dubh, an unconscious comedian, piped up that we too were going to kill the *caoridh bheag*—the pet sheep—which had been like one of the family for years.

The first day of fanging the sheep would be in summer for shearing around the month of June. When the family were young half a dozen would leave our house to shear the one sheep. Numbers were always needed for fanging our way as we never trained dogs, we would just have one big circle of young and old around the sheep, shouting and throwing anything that was handy at them. Then a month after the shearing there was another fanging on for dipping them, with some of the strongest among us putting the sheep into the dipping trough. The head was to be kept above the dip but if the sheep started to struggle they would let her go and her head would be submerged. Then you would hear screams from some old body whose sheep it probably was. The ones catching the sheep would shout out the owner's name—identified by the ear markings—to the big noise who was doing the clerical work of marking down in a book three pennies for every sheep dipped.

Then you might get ones from other villages looking for strays who would start a stramash saying that it was two pennies in their fang for dipping and that the ones at Balla were a crowd of crooks. This would start off a proper row with children and old ones being the worst. For some there would be an old sheep or a two-year-old ram to take home to slaughter. The carcass would be sold to the shop for a bag of flour. The innards, head and feet would all be made use of, and would keep a family going for nearly a week. These white and black haggis sold today in butchers' shops were all croft house recipes which made the ones who were smart enough to produce them in quantity comfortable for the rest of their lives. The same goes for cottage cheese, which used to lie around uneaten in croft houses, as there was so much of it made.

There were radio sets in Eriskay during the early thirties. The first radio I ever heard was in the priest's house in 1933. I was sent there by some fishermen to get the fishing report that came on the radio twice a day, at one o'clock and at seven. I believe loudspeaker sets would have just been arriving on the scene then as the set I heard that day was a loudspeaker set. There must have been a dozen on the island by the time the war started, a few of them being for the blind. I still have to find out how blind you had to be to qualify for a wireless set, as I one day saw this geezer in the post office collecting his blind pension and telling his cronies about his wireless set and how by turning a few knobs he could hear ladies of easy virtue singing away like what they used to do in dockside taverns in his time at sea. He was inviting his cronies out to join him in this entertainment. If he were alive today he would have no need to go near a dockside tavern, he would only have to walk into any tavern in the country to see ladies from all walks of life drinking and enjoying themselves. It made you wonder about how blind this character was, especially when he had to walk a couple of miles over bad roads to get to the post office. Others drawing the blind pension when any officials were around would be jumping onto the backs of horses back to front, then giving them a good slap making the horse bolt while they would fly head-first into a heap of manure.

We acquired our radio in grandfather's house in 1936. Auntie Bella, who was a nurse on Barra, gave it to us when she got a more modern set. I remember there was a trawler band on it and my granny was for sending the radio back to Bella again, the rows she would give me for listening to the trawler band. It would be Fleetwood trawlers who would fish our west coast mostly, and if they spoke about Scotsmen it would be words like 'those burgoo scoffing b——s', burgoo being sailors' slang for porridge. If they fished well it would be 'happy as a pig in sheet' and my ears would be to the radio until granny crept up behind me from outside to give me a cuff.

We used to get religious services also over the radio on Sunday nights. One night we tuned in to the wrong service, either through mistake or devilment, but it was at the end of the service when it was announced that it came from some church of a different denomination from gran, who with grandfather and Neil from next door, had been down on their knees. Of course I got the blame. Neil, who had a protestant grandmother, was the worst. Nearly crying he was. He was related to the Gardiners who were protestants from Skye who had come over as gardeners at the time of Clanranald. These Gardiners by this time had married others from different denominations.

Barra folks like my granny did not seem to have the same tolerance towards other religions as the South Uist crowd who were more mixed, some of them living on Eriskay these days. One worthy named Saite told me the story of when his family had a herring boat called the *Lark*, and going into Lochboisdale pier one day his father, the Ruag, spied a man of the cloth standing on he pier. He told one of his sons to go and get ready a meal of herring for the holy priest. His son informing him that the holy priest, as he thought, was really '*Ministear Mhor na Fhergenaich*', the Ferguson's big minister, them owning most of Uist at the time, the Ruag had another look at him and bellowed out, '*Oh, nach e mart e*', meaning, 'Oh, what an animal he is.'

The strongest memory I have of Barra's religious outlook is of my granny with her rosary of fifteen decades, which according to her could be recited in half an hour, a long half hour as far as I was concerned. Her connections with the Barra Head islands no doubt made her more religiously aware, as I think during winter months there was nothing else they could do, as they were unable to launch boats on account of the terrible weather and seas you get there, the lighthouse boat being their only connection with civilisation. How often have I heard about '*Sgoath bhann Calumn Ach Calay thinn dh-fharr e Rhu Phabach*', meaning, 'Calum McCaulay's white boat coming off Pabby Point'. Having done some fishing off these Sounds I would think for a boat of its size this lighthouse boat experienced some of the worst seas around the coast of Britain in these days of sail. Granny used to say you could see her going up and down like a sea-gull.

When war came everyone was hungry for news, so by the time the war stopped nearly every family who had someone away from home had a radio. After the war every fishing boat over fifty foot had a set for receiving and transmitting. Their folks could not speak with the crews but they could plan out with the ones at home when to transmit and they would listen in. So almost every house got a new set again. I cannot help but think how the world has changed during my own lifetime, from being allowed out of school as children to see an airplane, one of the first to fly over our islands.

As soon as one person got a radio everyone else followed suit, even Lachlan who was living near us. With all the houses around the Haun Bay area with a set he decided to keep up with the Joneses and asked his daughter Mari, who was working in London, to bring one home. The set Mari Lachlan brought from London was some set. It must have been the one Marconi used for his first transatlantic message. Try as hard as we could we were unable to get a sound out of that radio, just unearthly screeching and loud puffs. The Spanish Civil War was on at this time and Lachlan's son Oisean was telling his father that all the noise we were hearing was being made by the big guns firing over in Spain. I do not know where Mari Lachlan obained that set. She probably had paid somebody a shilling for it at the barrows.

Getting accumulators charged for the radios was the biggest worry in Eriskay, as they had to be sent away to Kyle of Lochalsh, but when we got the *Lady of Fatima* boat we could charge them ourselves on a limited scale. Of course others got to know of this and would become very annoyed if we did not carry out the charging for them, especially when they could be charged for nothing.

Any work needing done outwith the islands was always very expensive, and isolated islands like Eriskay were even worse off. I know that paraffin was double the price there from what you would pay on the mainland, so we would have had an easier time of it if we had not been able to charge batteries or go to the mainland for paraffin. You wouldn't believe the things we were asked to do with that boat, with ones from other islands calling on the phone at all hours telling you that the plane did not land on account of fog and that they wanted ferried to the mainland, your only excuse being that the boat was high and dry on the beach, their reply being, 'well, get her out'.

The coming of electricity to the island was a blessing to us anyway, as with electricity and Calor Gas on the island no paraffin was needed any more, except by a few over-careful ones, who were forever forecasting that the electricity would blast the whole island to smithereens. I think that the electricity was the one thing which came to the island without ones screaming out for it before it came. A puffer arrived one day with the underwater cable, unknown to anyone. It was not long after that until the poles came and very soon every house on the island was supplied with electricity, even the older people who were afraid of it and said they did not want it, but who were happy with it once they became used to it. The electricity was on the island for ten years before the water came. Eriskay was always looking up to larger islands like Barra, and so long as the bigger islands did not get anything they were quite content with their lot. As it turned out, Eriskay had electricity for twelve years before Barra.

The Haun where I was brought up in these days was, and probably always will be, the hub of activity going on in the island, more so these

Head of Haun Bay, Eriskay

days when the Uist side of the Sound was not connected by road to anywhere, all their various necessities of life having to be purchased at the
Haun. It did not matter what time of day it was, there was always a twenty-
foot boat under sail or oars sailing in the Sound, there being one of this
kind of boat to every house. There would be twelve big herring boats anchored in the Bay in summer time, each crewed by six men, not counting
a couple on the Kilbride side and another few in the south harbour that
never saw Haun Bay. As well as this fleet there was what the McIsaacs
had floating to carry on their various duties as mail-carriers, steamer
agents, fishermen, as well as dealing with engine troubles and repairing
damage to other boats requiring their skills. It was unbelievable what that
family could do, especially as they had had no training. Mainland boatyard
workers just would not believe that the carpentry they had seen done to
one of the big herring boats was done in Eriskay with the little they had
available to them there.

Stephen, my godfather, was the oldest McIsaac next to Donald, who
was drowned through enemy action during the war. He was the best of all
of them at carpentry and when not working was happy enough to play
with the likes of me. One day in their house he and myself, together with
Aldag, the priest's sister, started the game of pitch and toss using one of the
legs of the table as a stake. I was about eight years old at the time and an
argument started between myself and Aldag about who had the rights to
the first toss. The argument became so heated that a fight broke out between myself and Aldag, who was a semi-cripple with bad legs, while

Stephen remained laughing his head off. It was Beinn Gillesbuig, Stephen's mother, who came home and managed to separate Aldag and me.

Shonnag and Mari, the two sisters who lived on the croft next to ours, although good fun, could turn into terrors just as quick. I remember the day their dog was caught with the *pangal* in his mouth. This *pangal* was what young boys put out to snare birds. It was a hook with a piece of fish on it, tied by a piece of string to a small stone. This day Shonnag's dog got the fish with the hook in its mouth and made for home trailing the *pangal* after him. It was not long until the two of them were at our door with the dog and the *pangal*. The services of old grandpa, father's father, were required and so he came to operate. Grandpa got the hold of an old jacket, put the dog's fore-legs in one sleeve and his hind legs in the other and so the surgery started with the help of a couple of boys, one holding each sleeve and the other holding a clamp on the dog's mouth, the dog yelping with pain and grandpa working at its mouth with a knife while some younger member of the family was crying and Shonnag and Mari were screaming blue murder, having hold of whom they thought were the culprits by the ears, the place sounding like a torture chamber.

Grandpa, although a crabbit old soul, was always on hand for surgeries on horses or cattle. The strongest memory of him I have is him with a bottle of paraffin throwing it on some wound a horse got while rolling himself in the grass. Every time the horse would get a dollop of the paraffin he would go berserk. Then it would be castrating lambs or calves. Grandpa would always have an audience of children while performing these operations, the calves being the most difficult where a hold had to be got of the testicles. This he did with his teeth.

Damming the river to sail small boats was another great amusement for the children. In our place every boy had a home-made boat carved by themselves out of a block of wood and an iron keel put on them with a couple of masts and sails. Away they would go to an island loch to sail them. Sometimes in summer the rivers in spate could be dammed off and also used for sailing small boats. This would start another row from Mari and Shonnag, their croft getting flooded. The two of them also had a cure for that as once they saw the boys damming the river they would creep up on them. Then there would be screams of, 'Mari and Shonnag coming', with everyone running away and leaving spades behind. Mari and Shonnag would then take the spades home with them for the rest of the year until they were needed next spring.

I remember one spring the two of them were down with the 'flu so bad that they could not get out to turn the ground they had for growing potatoes. Everyone else had their potatoes planted when we all started to turn their ground for them. We had forgotten all about this incident when one day Mari came to the house with a bottle of whisky they had received from their nephew, Ian Watson, who was at the time carpenter in Donaldson of Glasgow's paper boat, the *Geraldine Mary*. They must have told him in the letter about the boys who had planted their potatoes and so they wanted us to have a drink of the whisky first before 'Kruger', as they called uncle Eoin, got to it, as last time Ian was home Eoin had got more than his share out of the bottle, to their reckoning.

Then Neil next door would come to our house to ceilidh. He would have met various cronies while away fishing with his boat, the *Immaculate Mary*, and something would always have happened to him. He would start his story about coming into the harbour late at night, when a couple of his crew living handy to the harbour would go home along with a boy who was brought up in their house, James Daly, and another neighbour who used to crew the boat, Shonnie Ruadh. Shonnie Ruadh was always playing pranks on another crew member, Hector, a relative of ours from Bunivulin, who was scared of ghosts, so Neil would have to stay in the boat along with Hector as his house was a long way past Neil's home. Hector did not like to walk that isolated patch at dead of night, as in these days there was not a corner or brae where somebody had not seen a ghost. In the morning Neil got up and started to build a fire with sticks, but try as hard as he could he could not find the axe to cut the peat. Neil was going round in circles, getting excited looking for the axe when Hector, who was still in bed, asked him what he was looking for. 'The axe, the axe', says Neil.

'Oh, the axe', replies Hector, who there and then put his hand under the pillow, brought out the axe and handed it to Neil. Neil, flabbergasted, asked Hector why on earth he was keeping the axe under the pillow. 'Oh', says Hector, 'I was thinking that madman Shonnie Ruadh might come back while I was asleep and start carrying on.'

Hector had a long memory of Shonnie Ruadh. One day Hector was coming from the Sound of Barra with his small boat, fishing for flounders with small line. As he was rounding the point at Rhubhain, he spotted Shonnie Ruadh ashore with his gun out shooting birds. Hector made some signs to Shonnie Ruadh, daring him to do his worst, and then settled down nicely, steering the boat with his hand on the tiller, until he heard this noise behind him and saw a pellet going right into the rudder, which caused Hector to make one long jump, landing in the centre of the boat.

Neil himself was scared of ghosts, as one night Stephen, who had taught me the death lament on the chanter, the only tune I ever learned to play, says to me that I had better go to play it at Neil's window coming near bedtime. There was no one in the house, only Neil who was mending his net, and Mary, his sister, who was knitting. They both looked at each other when they heard '*Post Na Marbh*', the death lament. 'Well', says Neil, getting excited, 'ghost or no ghost that's the only tune that devil over there can play', meaning me.

∾

The Compulsory Education Act, when it came into force, was a bit of a stumbling block for all, as no earthly reason could be seen for keeping children locked up in schools for almost ten years of their lives when they could be doing something useful around the crofts. When this Act was passed, all localities had a Compulsory Education Officer, somebody appointed who in all probability was not very well-liked in the first place and who probably did not care much whether any more ill-feeling was stacked against him or not. This unenviable job of reporting children who were absent from school without reasonable excuse must have carried a lot of resentment with it, all of which was stored up until a day of reckoning came round. This would coincide with the business of paying croft rents, which in these days in Eriskay were paid at Pollachar, where people would take their fill of the golden liquid, resulting in all the pent-up feelings being loosed. On one such expedition our next door neighbour, Neil, was as a young boy walking back to Ludag with my great-grandfather Johnston, and on the way they called at the Kilbride house which was a tack house at this time. The two of them must have been at the tail end of the mob, with this call holding them up, when on approaching Ludag they saw this army of joggers running hell for leather towards them, with the Compulsory Officer out in front and the other bloodthirsty mob after him. This poor geezer must have been trained from youth to run away from mobs or else he must have been wearing sand shoes, for Neil and my great-grandfather were not long out at Ludag when the mob came back, having had to give up the chase as a bad job.

Maybe not much was learned in school by some but some discipline was taught with the 'cat', which was at that time used pretty freely by some schoolmasters, there being no European Court of Human Rights then to complain to. These schoolmasters, who in our island these days were mostly over from Ireland, and whose tempers left much to be desired, were also a wild lot. They had to be to get any discipline in these days at the turn of the century.

One master whom I used to hear the older ones talking about when they would be coming up to retiral age was one by the name of Riley, whom they nearly drowned one day in Rhu Caol. It was at singing class one afternoon when he nearly slaughtered them because they were misbehaving during the singing, making farting noises with their mouths. They bided their time to retaliate, knowing he was going swimming after school hours. They stalked him until he got into the water, then they showed themselves and started to throw stones at him. He had to dive every time a shower of stones was let loose at him. However he managed to get ashore alive, but the first thing he did on returning to the schoolhouse was to send in his resignation.

I myself in my own time saw a boy who was sitting next to me in the seat, John McKelvie, getting twenty cross hands of the cat for clapping his backside with his hand after giving the customary salute on passing the schoolmaster's desk. He was a hell of a boy, John, always up to some mischief. He would bide his time until the schoolmaster was giving dictation, when he had the habit of going up and down the rows between the seats. On passing our seat, John, with the nib of his pen well-filled with ink, would let the backside of the master's flannels have a dollop of it. Also, during the bit of dictation, John used to hold a copy in his hand, closing and opening it to coincide with the master having his back or front to him.

These long hikes to attend the school courts in Lochmaddy must have been a bit maddening. No wonder the Eriskay mob took the law into their own hands on that rent pay day when they were chasing the Compulsory Officer who must have been a bit of an Olympic runner to have got away from them. Taking the law into their own hands is something people are inclined to do when they are forgotten by their country—except in its hour of need when people are wanted for cannon fodder—and any semblance of law coming their way is inclined to be scoffed at.

It was something like this that happened in Eriskay at one time when they had a big herring fleet, the island being well-populated during this period. The trouble started when the baker's business in Lochboisdale during the herring season went into bankruptcy, a common occurrence in these days, with some herring seasons worse than others. This baker must have been strange to the ways of these islands, as it is the only time I have ever heard of ones being served with a summons for not paying their debts. Anyone going bankrupt in the islands during this time would just bow out gracefully, knowing it was impossible to get anything from people when they did not have it. Anyway the policeman who was staying in Lochboisdale came over to Eriskay with the summons and spent all day there trying to have them accept it, but without success, as debts were in boats' names, many having shares in them but with nobody owning up. He was always being given a bum steer in his travels and the few he would catch who had no boat shares said their story was that they were working at the gas works in Maryhill, Glasgow or at the railway line at Tyndrum—they were all navvies in Eriskay that day. He was walking between the two ends of Eriskay until he had to give it up as a bad job, since half of those living there were called by the name of John MacInnes. After going back to Lochboisdale he was all worried about serving the summons as the court had to be attended at a certain date not far away. He was trying to get hold of someone around Lochboisdale who knew Eriskay and who would be willing to go over there to deliver the summons, but he had no luck. Every individual he would approach would give the same refusal, with words like, 'Over there to serve a summons to that wild lot, you must be joking', and, 'anybody going to Eriskay with those summonses will probably leave his bones there'. This was the situation when the policeman was informed by somebody that there was a certain individual living in at the Strom, at the head of Loch Boisdale, whose wife came from Eriskay and it might be in his interest to ask him. So off the policeman went to the Strom to see this man, Gillesbuig Gotha, who was married to the woman from Eriskay but he also wanted no part of it as he had an idea what kind of reception he would get. However on being threatened and bullied to help the law, poor Gillesbuig had no option but to go over to Eriskay to serve the summons.

The day he arrived there was known for a long time afterwards as *'Lath Gillesbuig Gotha'*. The children had taken a half-day from school and they with all the dogs on the island, chased poor Gillesbuig until he manged to reach his relations, who gave him the only support and shelter on the island.

A relative of ours who lived in Bunivulin, Iagan Mhor, was married to a woman from Stoneybridge in Uist, and after settling down in Eriskay started up cloth weaving. She got all of our cousins in Bunivulin drilled for this cloth weaving and they were forever having these *luaths*, or gatherings for making the cloth, which were always a bit of an attraction for visitors and locals alike. In the old days to have the cloth soft for weaving it had to be steeped in urine, which was always contributed by the many, as it had to be stored in a tub for the *luath*. I remember in my childhood days going out to Bunivulin, old auntie Caordith being alive then. The relieving was just done in the fields as there were no inside toilets. Father would be telling us we had better hold on as it might be needed for the tub, a *luath* coming up soon.

People had to make their own entertainment in these days before television and the two villages of Bunivulin and Rosinish, which is the furthest away and today deserted, were in their heyday the star villages for trouble, with land courts always drawing boundaries etc. A relative of ours, a priest, first cousin of my gran, who hailed from the isle of Canna, was one day giving a sermon from the altar about them to his parishoners, saying that was where the devil was going to stop if ever he got loose—Clach Mhor (Big Rock), Rosinish. This priest, whose name was Father Samuel McIsaac, was not past enjoying being in the midst of trouble himself, and was always battling with the local council about getting roads and piers built to help the population. He left Eriskay when he moved to Borve in Barra, where he kept up his fighting, until the Bishop, getting fed up with complaints about him, warned him to mend his ways. This he found impossible to do and so he resigned. The Glasgow Archbishop, however, accepted him and sent him to serve in the mental home in Carstairs, where he must have found plenty of outlet for his energy, as he was there until he retired. He then went to Rothesay to a retiral home which was looked after by nuns. It was in Rothesay he died and is buried. Anybody in trouble because of the higher-ups acting it would go to Father Samuel who would give them a riling.

One individual in our place who thought he was the 'bees knees' and who was running the Post Office came a cropper when Father Samuel got to him a few times, threatening one day to kick the daylights out of him.

This Doughal was a crabbit old soul. If he did not like the way your hair was combed or if he had fallen out with any of your relations he would not even sell you a stamp. I saw this happen one morning when going to school. Our next door neighbour, Ian Mhac Mhuraidh, had joined me on the walk as the post office was in the same direction as the school from our houses. Knowing he was in the habit of playing cards with Doughal I enquired innocently enough why he had not got a stamp last night at the card playing for the letter that was in his hand, as that would have saved him a walk in the morning. It was then I had to listen to a mouthful of oaths from Ian, who informed me that as Doughal had lost out on the cards the night before, he refused to give him the stamp as it was not post office hours, hence Ian's morning walk.

I think Doughal hated almost everybody, especially ones who were worse than others for sending away for articles c.o.d., and any other things like free-paying postage companies who used dockets to attract business. One morning on arriving at the post office I was treated to a display of something like you would see on a rugby field, with Doughal and this boy tossing a sack of wool between them through the hole in the wall from where Doughal's business was transacted. The sending of wool to Pringle was common in these days, but by this time some dockets must have arrived on the scene to pay the postage, the likes of which Doughal had not seen before, and so this was what the battle was all about. After a while of this point-blank slugging of the bag of wool the young fellow gave it one good throw which landed it under the bed which was in view, so Doughal, being crippled, had to do a bit of excavating to retrieve it, which enabled the young fellow to run away to school. After some time Doughal, having recovered the wool, gave it to the postman as there were no signs of the owner. The poor postman now had an extra weight to carry, along with the many other things which he had to deliver all over the island.

This postman's job was the biggest slave job I ever came across. On the three days he was on duty the loads he had to carry on his back were almost unbelievable and all for twelve shillings a week. In these days every bit of the island was well populated and with mainland companies sending catalogues, almost every house had to be visited. He was receiving this twelve shillings a week until one time the island was served by a relieving priest, Father Calum McKinnon, a native of Barra. He was very good at writing on behalf of people and, on seeing this slavery of the postman, fought to get another twelve shillings for him. The resident priest at the time, Father Gillies, would not write for anyone and between him and his two sisters, apart from a few cronies, would scarcely even speak to anyone, one day telling somebody who went to complain that if the window was nearer to him than the door to jump through it.

Mainland folks had a tendency to look down on island folks, and that trio had a good share of it the day they were moved to go somewhere else, with the sisters hoping a few bombs would fall on the island. The people were glad to see the last of them. However it was not long after their brother died that these two were back to live out their retirement on the island. This nobody liked very much. I think that was the first time I saw nearly the whole of the island, except for a few of their former cronies, united in dislike against anybody. I think they must have mellowed a bit by this time, for I remember one of them used to visit granny. I was home at the fishing at the time when she was in granny's house, saying how much she would enjoy a glass of shandy, something granny had never heard of before. Every Monday as I would be going away to fish granny used to remind me about the screwtop for Aldag, as she was going to mix it with lemonade to give to Aldag. And so this particular Saturday in Mallaig, I don't know how but I had the price of a screwtop left or else I got it on credit from Donald in the Centre Bar, my name going into the black book, so I took the plunge and got the screwtop. In these days it was all walking to and from the harbour, coming home on Saturday carrying something on your back like kippers etc., which were not available on the island. Donnal Cimanach, who was ceilidhing in the house when I reached home, spied the screwtop and I had to tell him that it was to make a shandy for Aldag. To cut a long story short, the screwtop was made short work of there and then, Donnal saying that Aldag had plenty water in the well to drink.

We had only one cow between the two houses and I, staying in granny's house, was treated to a sermon about my character addressed by my granny to my mother when she came for the milk, concerning how Aldag's screwtop was drunk by Donnal Cimanach. Granny was also showing my mother what she had found stuck on some article of clothing I was wearing, telling her that it was the *'gouraig'*, the name Barra folks had for people who had joined the freemasons. She was holding this emblem in her hand when my mother burst out laughing, seeing that it was a flag for some charity they were collecting for in Mallaig, the place becoming modern by this time and having flag days.

Eriskay being settled through clearances became home to many different surnames. Just mention any Highland tribe and at one time there were sure to be some members domiciled there, and I must say it did not do the population any harm. In my young days, when the island was well populated, this mixture brought some fine-looking specimens of manhood. Some who had relations from other different denominations perhaps had a more tolerant outlook. Even when being prepared to meet their Maker some of them still had a bit of devilment left in them, as was seen with a relative of mine, the Gotha. He had been given the last rites and in his will had left his croft to Allan, his second son, who was incapacitated, having only the fingers on one hand, the other fingers had been blown off in a blast. Father William Gillies mentioned that perhaps he should have left the croft to the older son who was married, and who had the use of both hands. The Gotha replied in his dying gasp, *'Dual a hi-ifriun plochd'*, meaning, 'Devil in hell a sod'. After he died he was kept in the house for a night, this being the custom in these islands, for something resembling an Irish wake. This wake was in progress with people coming in and out to say their prayers, and drams and food being offered. This certain character, Neuka, was seated, having said his prayers, when another old crony, Shonnie Ian Rosinish, who must have been a bit short-sighted, came into the house to say some prayers. The house being a small thatched one and poorly lit with paraffin lamps in these days, Shonnie started to look around to see where the Gotha was laid out. Neuka pointed over to a corner where there was a bag of flour, a commodity kept in every island house at this time, with a sheet over it. Shonnie went over to the bag of flour and knelt down in front of it to say his prayers. It was only when he heard giggling at his back and he lifted the sheet and saw the bag with 'King's own Flour' written on it that he saw the joke.

Another day the Eriskay boats were in Lochboisdale when a funeral was taking place. A man by the name of Bootsie had died, so everyone went to his funeral to pay their respects. This Bootsie was a small, fat man and as the coffin was carried out it was noticed how high and short the coffin was. My uncle Alasdair was there and he could not help but remark 'I think he must be sitting in his coffin'. There was not any harm in what they said, they just could not help coming out with something.

I guess people had to make their own entertainment then, some comedians being better than others. It did not matter what form it took. Often it would be fighting between families, which was common enough these days with people intruding on what they called their territory, or stock going over one another's boundaries to graze, or herring boats drifting into another's fleet of driftnets. It was more than likely squabbles like that would be settled by the ones involved coming to blows. This entertainment was free to all. On clearing-up days at the end of herring seasons, especially for isolated islands like Eriskay where there was no pub, it was more than likely that scores would be settled. I heard an old Barra man say that in his young days it was an Eriskay girl, again a relation of mine, he saw giving the best wallop in a fight on the pier at Castlebay, which place had, at one time, seen more fighting than Madison Square Garden in New York. It was at the end of the herriing season and some Eriskay folks were around squaring up, drink as usual being involved. The children could scent some exciting entertainment was afoot when the cry went around that the Eriskay folks were at it again. Gutting girls who would be finishing off for the season were around to take passage home on the boats and were also in the centre of the melee when this girl, Catriona Mhor, seeing her brother Donald not getting fair play, let this cousin Dreever, one of the McIsaac brothers who were forever in fights, have a wallop that flattened him out on the pier, all of them being troublesome relations of mine.

All down the generations some families were worse than others for trouble-making after having a few drinks. Some would be drinking happily in a pub while others after only one drink would be squaring up to somebody. It would not seem to have anything to do with any place in particular, it would just be in some people's make-up, this troublesome way of life running in certain families who could be living anywhere. You would be telling old people at home of squabbles by islanders you had seen away from home, and on being informed who were involved it is more than likely the old ones would shake their heads knowingly, saying, '_Chan ne ceannac erein aid_',—'They did not buy that carry on from anybody'. Perhaps some families were spoiled and had taken to drinking after some money had come their way. An old acquaintance told me when I asked after a certain family who would go on the booze and challenge people to fight that it was money they had been left in a will by someone who had owned a bar which must have been cursed. I always used to hear old people at home say that money made through selling drink had some curse attached to it, and this was why a grandson never sold drink from the same pub as the grandfather.

Chapter 3

Stories of the second sight—Hector and the papish cross—The woman of the ruins—The roaming of Alastair MhacMhaightear—'The Eriskay Love Lilt'—The mad bull—The big winter herring fishing of 1931—The curse of the crofts—Death of old grandpa—Shemus Lachlan's unlucky boat—The mischievous seer of Eriskay—The Gili Gili man meets his match—Eating Ian MacLaughlan—The fight over the stolen pants—Shonnie the merchant

There were plenty of second-sighted people who could see and hear things in the islands in my young days. I experienced something myself when I was only eight years old. I was walking with my grandmother from my father's house to my grandfather's house. It was during the summer and just beginning to get dark when we were passing the schoolhouse. We heard crying coming from the west direction. Thinking someone must be hurt, we went into the MacLellan's by the school house and got the old woman and grandaughter who lived there outside. The crying was still going on after we came out, then it began to fade away, until at last we could not hear anything. What was puzzling us was the fact that no one was staying near where the crying came from, the next house being about half a mile away from where we were standing. Between us and the Balla in those days were only fields of corn and potatoes. We knew that an old woman was poorly at the Balla, but on enquiring about her the following morning we were told that she was all right. Even if she had died the crying we heard was not like that when someone dies, it was more like a crowd of people going in and out of houses. That happened sixty-odd years ago, and as far as I know nothing to cause crying like that ever happened around there. The only thing I know is the way we were looking across the fields of corn and potatoes there are today twelve council houses, a hall, a co-operative shop and lately a pub. It is up to anybody whether to believe it or not.

Some people are inclined to laugh at things like that but I know of another case of a couple of brothers from our island who were on some business over in Barra with a small twenty-foot, engineless boat. It was very late when they left Barra, and by the time they got out into the Sound of Barra and were heading for Eriskay it was well past midnight. About half way across the Sound they noticed a light ahead of them. This made them wonder who would be out at this time of night in the Sound. As it was close time for herring fishing all the big boats were hauled up on the beach getting painted. Small twenty-foot boats out in the Sound never carried lights, as small-line fishing was usually done during daylight hours, and so they wondered about this light ahead of them, since it never seemed to go further away or come nearer to them. As they approached Eriskay they saw that everyone had gone to bed, since no lights were showing in any of the houses. They were coming to a tricky channel called Caolis Oigh Sgeir, with this light still keeping the same distance from them, when all of a sudden they noticed the light veering to the right. It kept on going into a rock called Sgeir e Chase, and as soon as the light reached the rock it went out and the windows of the church and two of the houses in Eriskay lit up. They then realised that this light was not of this world. They told people about it, mentioning the church getting lit up, but whose the other two houses were they would not say. It was ten years after this that a boat from East Kilbride was fishing in the Sound for flounders, when one of the crew collapsed while hauling in the small lines. As these places on the Uist side of the Sound of Eriskay were linked together for church, medical care etc., it was decided to cut away the gear and make for help in Eriskay. The man collapsed and the gear was cut at exactly the same place where the light was first sighted ten years before, and the boat landed at exactly the same place where the light went out. I remember this well as I was at school at the time, the school being out for the dinner hour. There was nothing surer to attract the attention of the school children than a boat being sighted in view of the school. She was recognised right away as a boat from East Kilbride while she was approaching Caolis Oigh Sgeir but why she was turning in towards the Balla set us wondering. It was when she touched the rock and two men jumped out that we knew there was something wrong. The man who was running to the right was making for his brother's house at the Balla, the other man was making for the nurse's house and the church, but sorry to say there was nothing anyone could do, as the man died, I believe long before they reached the shore.

The two brothers who saw the light admitted then that it was these two houses they saw lit up along with the church, the nurse's house being occupied then by a family who later sold it to the county council for the nurse and teachers to stay in. The man from East Kilbride who died was a cousin of my father's family, Ruaridh Taramoid.

There was another first cousin of my father staying at the Balla, Iagan Donnall Mhor, who fished all his days along with my father's family. He was building a house and the stone mason who was helping him was another man who had the second sight. The house was next to the graveyard, and another house belonging to my uncle Eoin through marriage was about thirty feet away from it, and also in line with the graveyard. This day Iagan and the stonemason, whose name was Eoghain MacDhoughail, were walking from the shore over to the house, the stone masonry part of it being nearly finished. Before they got to the house Eoghain said, 'you had better stand here for a while and let this funeral pass'.

Iagan said to him, 'I'm afraid you're off your mark this time Eoghain, no funeral ever came this way between the two houses on its way to the grave-yard. You have seen yourself every funeral since you started building the house, and that they all went past at the back of the house.'

'Well', says Eoghain, 'this one is going to go between the two houses, but I can't see any signs of you among the rest.'

Iagan thought that Eoghain was just putting fear into him because this was happening in broad daylight during working hours. However time went on, the house was finished, and Iagan spent the first New Year in it. Then during the last winter when the herring was inside the gut in Loch Eyenort and they were on their way to Mallaig with the last shot out of there, Iagan collapsed and died. His brother Hector did not keep too well because of some sickness he got while in the navy during the war. He would be all right one day then suddenly he would go sick, and this was the case when Iagan died. Hector was sick in bed when the boat came home with Iagan's body, and so was unable to attend the funeral. It was decided that the funeral should go between the two houses, and so pass in front of the house where Hector was and could see the coffin through the window. It would seem that Eoghain's second sight had come true.

Hector was a bit of a comic. He was once coming home during the war when he was in the navy, along with a commercial traveller from Benbecula named Sundachan. At this time everybody who stepped onto the pier at Tobermory had to pay a penny to get off and another penny to get on again. The mailboat would lie at Tobermory for a while discharging cargo, so Sundachan and Hector decided to go for a drink. They were collared going off to pay the penny, got to the pub and had their drink, then were collared again to pay the other penny on their way back. Sundachan pays his penny and Hector is about to walk on after him without paying, when the fellow starts demanding a penny from him. So Hector asks him, 'Can anybody take luggage through without paying for it?'

'Oh yes, all the luggage you want', replies the fellow.

So Hector there and then says, 'Well, I am luggage', and jumps on to Sundachan's back.

Sundachan then walked up the gangway with Hector on his back, while the fellow collecting the money stood speechless.

Another time in Western Ross-shire Hector was with a crowd from Eriskay buying a boat. They were known as 'the men from Uist', north and south Uist being two different islands, with the island of Benbecula in be-tween, the north being protestant and the south mostly catholic, but the old woman who was in the house where they were invited to a meal did not know that. All she knew about Uist was that they had a minister in their parish who had come from their part of the world. She pointed out to them a picture of him that was hanging on the wall. The Eriskay crowd were telling the old woman that they were all acquainted with the minister, his people and so on, but they had never really met him as he belonged to North Uist. When the meal was over and Hector had eaten his fill and had nothing to lose, he decided to shock everybody by making the sign of the cross. 'The papish cross!', says the old woman. She had been away at service in her young days and had seen people doing this. Anyway she was calmed down by telling her that Hector was the only papist among them.

I think Eoghain MacDhougal built more than half the houses in Eriskay, along with his brother Neil. With building houses and seeing ghosts there was never a dull moment around Eoghain, or the Soldier, as the Eriskay crowd called him, because he had served in the Boer War in South Africa. He stayed there for a while afterwards in the fire brigade in Cape Town. One day he was going across in the mailboat to Eriskay. He says to one of the MacIsaac boys, 'There's a boat capsizing over there'.

'Rubbish', MacIsaac says.

'All right', says Eoghain, 'I'll show you', and he stood on MacIsaac's feet. When anyone who has the gift of seeing stands on another person's feet that person will also see the same thing. This is what happened to the MacIsaac fellow who also saw the boat capsizing, an event which took place sometime afterwards. Luckily, no lives were lost.

There is another sign and that is if you are leading a horse along the road and he suddenly stops, do not look between his ears, for if he is seeing anything you will see it also and the gift might stay with you.

Eoghain the stonemason was once building a house, and as they were laying the stance out he started to argue with the man as to where the best place to build was. Eoghain wanted the house in a different place. The other man won anyway, but wondered why Eoghain did not want the house in that particular spot. However the house was built and a family was brought up there, going their own way until it was left to one son, the father being dead by this time. This son died young and the night he died he began to haemorrhage, the blood lying on the spot where Eoghain had seen it thirty years before, which was his reason for not wishing to build the house there.

There are ruins in our place, and a woman has been seen there for the last eighty years. She is always standing on the road looking as though she wants to speak to someone. I knew a man and she even stuck out her foot for him to stop, but he broke off the road. My own auntie Morag saw her one night before she died. The cow had not come home this night, and so auntie Morag and uncle Angus went searching for this cow. That was when auntie Morag saw the woman. Luckily uncle Angus was not far away, or Morag would have fainted on the spot. Eoghain saw her one night, and, on telling some folks about this, he was informed in turn that other people were seeing her also, but that no one had the courage to speak to her. 'Well', Eoghain said, 'next time I see her I'll speak to her', but he never did see her after that.

The harbour at south end, Eriskay

There was another man who saw someone from the other world who had been dead for thirty-five years. This man was good-living and never told a lie in his entire life. I was only young at the time, but I have it on good authority, and I am sure every word of it is true. There was a man staying in my grandparents' house and he was very keen to hear about anything of this sort. So my grandfather took him to see this man, as there was a rumour going around about him seeing something. Eriskay being a small island, something like that causes quite a stir. The man, Ruaridh bheag MacLeod, was staying in his mother's house at the time, about half a mile away from the harbour at the south end of the island. This time, during the small hours of the morning, the wind started blowing, and he was worried about his small twenty-foot boat which was moored on to the shore. So he got up and went to the harbour. He reached there, had a look at the boat, saw she was all right and started back for home. He passed the last house before his mother's house, turned the corner and there was a man standing about a hundred yards ahead of him. He had an idea that anyone standing around on his own at that time of the morning was not of this world, and so he broke off the road to avoid speaking to him, as you have to speak to the dead first before they speak to you. He managed to reach his own house after this detour and said to himself that he would never again travel on that road at that time of the morning without someone with him. Some other night after this he was visiting a crew member who was with him on the big herring boat. He left this house about eight o'clock, and when he reached near the spot where he had seen the man before he took a detour off the road and followed the same route as he had done the other night.

After walking for a while he came within line of his own home and that of his neighbour, and immediately made straight for his own house. He then saw a man approaching, and thinking it was his neighbour, he had no fear as Ian usually visited their house every night. Still thinking the man was his neighbour, he said, 'You are going home early tonight, Ian'. As he had spoken first, the man from the other world had him, but whatever passed between them he never told to anyone. But when he had finished telling the story he took the pipe from his mouth and said that he could put into the pipe once what it was worth the man from the other world coming back about after all these years.

There was another night a boat was fishing for cod and ling to the west of the islands at the time of the haaf, or deep-sea fishing. If the weather was fine they used to make hay while the sun shone, as the saying goes, by staying out all night, as it did not take much weather to make you stop fishing there. They stayed out this night anyway, and sometime during the night they saw something coming towards them. Thinking it was another boat they just waited until she was within hailing distance, but were horrified to see on approaching that it was a coach drawn by two horses. The coach was coming near to them, but they began to sprinkle holy water on their boat and so it passed by and went on out of sight to the north of them. They recognised the occupants of the coach as one who had just died that night and others that were dead years before.

I heard a near neighbour of ours, Lachlan, telling us that when he was young he and another two were fishing lobsters in a small, deserted island called Eilean Fudach. They had only a small boat with no accommodation so they were living in a bothy ashore. This night they heard noises outside and they knew it was something out of this world as they were the only ones on the island. It got so bad that at last they thought the bothy would cave in, and so one of them got a hold of this bottle in the dark, thinking that it was the bottle of holy water, and began to sprinkle it inside the bothy. The noise kept on and was getting worse, so one of the MacCaordith brothers says, 'I'm going to shoot it, ghost or no ghost'. So he gets a hold of his gun and starts to unlock it to get the cartridge in, but the lock was jammed. He then began shouting and asking where the oil for the gun was, but on getting the bottle that had the oil they found that it was empty, as they had sprinkled it on the bothy thinking it was the holy water. When they realised this, they then began to sprinkle the real holy water on the bothy, and on doing so the noise began to subside until it died away altogether.

Another time my godfather, Stephen MacIsaac, being newly married and staying in Glasgow, was on a ship that used to run up the west coast. The *Dunara Castle* she was called, and belonged to McCalumn Orms. This time they were working the islands from the north to the south, Castlebay being their last port of call. They called in at Lochboisdale this day about the beginning of summer, the time when all the herring boats were up on the beach for painting. The *Dunara Castle* carried passengers as there were always people on tour during the summer, and also islanders travelling between the islands and all the way to Glasgow these days. After leaving Lochboisdale, Stephen was approached by this man from Loch Carnan who had relatives in Eriskay, my own people being some of them, asking how people in Eriskay were. This man, Aoghais Mhor Seonaid, had married late in life. His wife was a Barra woman, Marie Cailen Domnall Roger, and so he was down seeing his people in Loch Carnan where he boarded the *Dunara Castle*. Before he finished conversing with Stephen he said, 'That was a terrible thing that Eriskay man getting drowned at the pier last night'. Stephen had not heard anything about this, but as he had been working down the hatch on cargo he took him at his word. On asking who the man was, he told him one of the *Virgin*'s crowd, one of the three brothers of Clann Aoghais Ian Mhor, but he did not know which one as the body was lying under cover on the deck. He knew it was not the one who was staying in East Kilbride, Iagan, as he had seen him coming out of Ruaridh Ian ach Ruaridh Mhor's car and going into the boat. Stephen could not say much but on arrival in Castlebay he phoned his father, Gillesbuig the ferryman, asking how everyone was, but not mentioning anything he had heard. He also asked if all of the boats were home. Yes, all the boats were on the beach getting painted, he was told. Stephen just thought that this story was imagined and put it down to Aoghais Mhor having had one too many at Lochboisdale or else getting doddery in his old age. But before the summer season was over everything happened just as he had seen it the day at the beginning of summer.

I was told by somebody who is dead now that when he was young he was sailing on a ship. There was an old man on her who was around pension age. They started talking this day about what they were going to do when the trip was over. He said to this old man, 'You'll be going home, anyway. It's time you showed your face there after being so long away'. 'Aye', said the old man, 'it's time I did, but the time is long past for that'. Then, with tears in his eyes, he added, 'I don't believe I ever will. I'll tell you the reason why. When I was a young man out on the hill at home I met this man who had been missing for a while. He began to tell me what had happened to him—that he had been murdered and his body buried somewhere. I went home and told my mother about this, but she began to cry and begged me not to tell anyone, as people would say I had done it. So I kept silent, but when I was out on the hill again I met this same man who said to me that I had not told the authorities, as he had asked, and that until I did I would always see him. This happened, as every time I went out on the hill I would see him. At last my mother and I decided that I should go away for a while. I stayed away for twenty years, but when I went back the same thing happened. So I decided to leave home the very next day.' He died a long time ago, having never gone home.

I heard from someone else who is also dead now, that when he was sailing on a ship after the First World War he saw a woman standing on the foredeck. After he came down from the crow's nest, where he had been on lookout, he mentioned it to one of the men, and so the word went round the ship about it. Being aboard a ship on a long voyage is like being in a small world, and so the tale of the sighting of the woman was getting bigger and bigger, until at last the men were becoming afraid to go on the foredeck at night, never mind climbing all the way to the crow's nest. This fellow was taken on the carpet about it and was told he had better tell the crew that his story was all lies or he would be put in irons. But at last he convinced the Master that he was telling the truth, and next time he would see her he would let the officer of the watch know. The vessel having a short well deck on the foredeck, it was difficult for anyone to see her unless you were looking down from the crow's nest, as she was always standing at the foot of the ladder. This night on the 12-4 watch, about two in the morning, there she was, standing in her usual place. The fellow shouts to the second mate, 'You'd better get the Old Man'. The Old Man, mate and stand-by man all went on to the foredeck to investigate, and, on reaching the top of the ladder, they saw her there, standing at the bottom. The mate said, 'I'm going to make sure it's not one of the crew playing tricks on us'. So he started to descend the ladder, but as soon as she saw him she jumped over the high bulwark into the sea. All hands were called, a count was made, and it was found that no one was missing. She could not have been a stowaway because the ship had the usual tramp style of life and was nearly two months at sea by now and no food had gone missing from anywhere. Some investigation was made into the ship's history. As she was a German captive ship taken over as war prize it was not easy to find out much, but they did find out that before the war the German Master had his wife with him on a trip and that she disappeared one night at sea. Whether it was her or not it must have been someone from the other world anyway.

I have known people of the cloth seeing and hearing things not connected with this world. One night in my own island of Eriskay there was an old woman who had died and her remains were in the church, as this is the custom. Around the small hours of the morning the priest and his two sisters were awakened by some noise coming from the direction of the church, the church and the house being one building. For the rest of the morning until nearly daybreak, this moaning kept coming from the church. Did the woman wake up from some trance she had been in? She was an old woman and had been pronounced dead for two days, with people all around her all the time, as a dead person is never left unattended in these islands.

The priest and his sisters were not island people brought up on ghost stories, as island children in my young days were. How often have I seen some character telling ghost stories and everyone pulling their chairs nearer the fire? If someone behind them had shouted out, probably half of them wold have fainted. Like the time there was a crowd in this house having a ceilidh, the house belonging to an old tailor. Ghost stories were being told, until somebody mentioned there was no water left in the house. Everyone was scared to go outside to fetch the water, everyone, that is, except the tailor, but as he was unable to walk, somebody had to carry him. Lots were drawn as to who should carry him and the two buckets of water. Two of the lads must have drawn the short straws, so off they went, one carrying the tailor on his back, and the other the two buckets for the water. On this same night there were two crooks trying to steal a ram in the neighbourhood but were separated at the time the other three were on their way to the well. One of the thieves mistook the tailor who was being carried by this fellow as his partner in crime carrying the ram, and so he shouts, 'Is he fat?' 'Well', the fellow carrying the tailor shouts back in fright, 'fat or thin, he's yours'. So saying he threw the poor tailor in the ditch and made for home, followed by the lad who was carrying the buckets.

I remember one night being in the shop when I was about ten years old with one of these characters who I think was seeing more of the dead than of the living. He told a ghost story, and just as he was finishing the story everything was quiet until a sound was heard by everyone in the shop. It sounded like someone dropping wood outside. This man who was telling the story saw the ghost of someone drop the wood and come into the shop to pay for it, all of which was the usual procedure. The wood would be used for the coffin of the person who was to die in the future.

I remember one boat in our place which everyone was scared of. She never drowned anyone, good boat that she was, but people shied away from her because of all the rumours going around about her, and everyone who would repeat the rumours would add on more. At last, as she was getting a bit old, it was decided to put her to another use. The usual thing done with these boats is to saw them in half and use them for a hen house. She was sawn in half and one half was taken home, the other half left lying above high water mark. About this time, at the beginning of the war, there were plenty of ships being torpedoed in the Western Approaches. Bodies were coming ashore all over the islands. This one landed in Eriskay, and, as it was nearly dark before he was found, it was too late for burial, so it was decided to put the body in the half-sawn boat. This is what was seen all these years the rumours were going about, the boat broken in two and a dead man inside her.

This next story was told to me by my grandparents, concerning a half brother of my grandmother. This man, being a priest, served for a number of years in several parishes when he was young. He was also chaplain to the forces in France, where he was wounded during the First World War. Older men who served with him in Highland regiments will remember him, although not many of them are left now. There is a woman staying near me, Mrs Molly Toal, who remembers him, her only Highland connection being her uncle joining a Highland regiment while he was serving as schoolmaster in the Highlands before the war. She remembers well my great-uncle coming to the house while on leave to tell them how her uncle had died, and how he had given him the last rites on a battlefield in France. But the strange thing that happened to him was not on a battlefield, but in a remote Highland village. He was not long there serving as a priest when one night heavy snow began to fall in the evening, and lasted until about bedtime. Just as he was getting ready for bed he heard a knock at the door. He went to the door and on opening it there was a man asking him to go to an old woman's house as she was dying. My great uncle was strange to the place, but the man pointed out the light of the house in the distance. He told the man to go on ahead to the old woman's home and he would follow as soon as he got together everything he needed. He had his hat and coat on ready to leave, when another knock came to the door. This time a second man was there from the old woman's house, and said, 'You don't have to go over now, she is all right'. When my uncle asked who he was the man said he was her son, and gave his name. The person went away but my uncle felt dubious about the situation because of the worried state the first man had shown, and so he decided to have a look in on the old woman. It was a calm night now with a full moon, the snow having stopped falling a while before. He was not long walking when he noticed something peculiar. He saw the footprints of only one person in the snow coming and going from the church, but no sign could be seen of the other person's footprints. He just thought that perhaps one of them had taken another road. He arrived at the house, and as soon as he was inside everyone was in a panic and asking him what had kept him so long, as the old woman was at this very moment about to draw her last breath. He did not say anything but proceeded to give her the last rites before she died. He then asked those in the house why they had sent a second person telling him not to come, as she was alright. 'We didn't send anyone', they said.

'Did you not send her son?', he asked, mentioning the son's name.

Everyone stood petrified.

'What's wrong?', asked my uncle.

'We never sent him', they said, 'he is not here. She had a son by that name but he left here a long time ago and nothing has been heard of him since. '

After a few years serving in parishes around the west coast and then war service, he was sent to Morar. He served there for many years as Canon MacNeil and it was there that he died and is buried.

This next story I heard from somebody who was sailing on a ship with an open fo'c'sle under the fo'c'sle head at the bow of the ship. The beds were one above the other, right round the fo'c'sle, with a table in the centre for eating. The man who was in the bed below my companion was very poorly, next to death's door. There was not much that could be done with sick people at sea in these days if they died, but there was always canvas

62

and weights aboard to sink them. The man came off watch at midnight this night, did his best for the sick man in the bed under him by giving him a drink of tea, then turned in himself. He had a good idea that the man below him would not last long. He slept for a while, but before he was called to go on watch again, about two in the morning, he saw in his sleep the fo'c'sle door open and this awful-looking creature coming in. If there was anything human-looking about this creature it was the picture of the joker on a pack of cards. After this creature came inside it made straight for the bed under him and started pulling the sick man out of it and out of the fo'c'sle. As soon as it disappeared with the sick man through the fo'c'sle door he woke up with a start, looked down under him at the sick man, jumped out of bed and looked again at the sick man, who was now dead. I remember when we used to play cards and he would see the joker he would start about the man that looked like him and frightened him out of his wits.

Another time I was on a wee coastal ship and the Master belonged to one of the islands. We started talking this night about ghosts, some lads on board believing and some not. The Master, since he was older, was asked for his opinion. 'Well', he says, 'I don't know if I have seen anything or not, but I was home on leave once staying with my father and mother, and one night I was visiting a friend's house. On the way home I saw three lights, one after the other, making from the sea towards the island. They came from the west, carried on past the island and out to the Minch, then went around in circles and dropped right on top of a trawler which was fishing out in the Minch.' He then left home when his leave was up but he could not get these three lights out of his mind, wondering what they were all about. He must have been trading around the west coast of England at the time, when one day not long after this, he picked up a newspaper and read about three men being drowned off a trawler at anchor in the Isle of Man. He began to wonder of these three lights could have any connection with this trawler. He was thinking about it so much that he told somebody coming from the place where the trawler came from. This man made enquiries, but of course trawlers' personnel are very secretive. However he found out that she was a trawler which always fished that part of the Minch.

This next story is about an old man my folks knew who lived at the back of beyond. They would only see him at winter fishing. One winter his wife was alive, the next she was dead. They were offering their condolences, saying how sorry they were that his wife had died, but the old rascal seemed quite unperturbed about it. No need to be sorry for him, he said, he would soon have another one. They said to him, 'But surely at your age you're not thinking of getting married again'.

'Well', he said, 'I had no intention of getting married, but what can you do when you hear her snoring every night at your back?'

'You hear her what?' everyone exclaimed.

'I hear her snoring every night at my back in bed'.

The first person to find his voice said, 'It must be your dead wife you hear'.

'No', he said, 'I know the way she snored, this is a different kind of snoring'.

To cut a long story short, he did have a new wife the next winter.

I heard of another case, but it happened a long time ago, where people were seeing someone dressed in white at a certain cross-roads in the country. It got so bad that everybody in the area was scared to pass this place at night. But there was one tough guy who was not scared of anything. He would pass this way at any time of the day or night. This particular night one of his neighbours said, 'I'll scare the wits out of him', and he goes and gets a white sheet and takes it with him to the cross-roads. When he saw the fearless fellow coming, the neighbour put the white sheet over his head so that he was covered all over, except for two holes for his eyes. The tough guy sees what he thinks is the ghost and makes for it, and putting his strong hands around the neck of the fellow covered with the white sheet, he chokes him so hard that the fellow dies. So this was the ghost they had been seeing all these years.

Gillesbuig's son, John, who had the ferry after his father, saw a man at Ludag one night. John was waiting for a passenger and the man was standing to the west of where the car park is today. Gillesbuig himself was nearly thrown into the sea by a ghost one night in Bun Struth. He managed to get away from the ghost and into the boat. Fishing for trout they were in the loch. The two who were with him had gone on ahead of him but when they saw he was not following them they up and turned back to where Gillesbuig had shoved the boat away from the shore.

Godfay Freer or '*Caliach na Bochan*'(Woman of the Ghosts), as she was known, spent some time of her life in Eriskay. A bit of a terror she was, always on the prowl at all hours of the night looking for ghosts. Wherever she heard of one being seen, off she would go. She must have had some nerve to visit these places, especially during night-time hours, places I would not go to on my own, not even during the daytime. One place she was very interested in was at the back of the hill Glen-e-Bharr Mhor. Even passing this place in a boat at night would give you the shivers. Some boat crew saw a ghost there one night and it took them all their time to get away from him. He was throwing stones at them, the stones weighing a hundred weight each, and at the same time shouting after them. On his first shout he claimed that his son was in a rock, Greg Chuil e Brath, which stands on the border of Bunivulin and Roshinish, and on his second shout that his daughter was in Glen Na Goe on the Uist side, while on his third shout he was saying that somebody was in Ben Mhor. So these are the kinds of places Calaich na Bochan would visit at dead of night. I have been told that half of Eriskay were terrified of her. Only Father Allan would give her shelter.

Whether Father Allan himself would see anything he would not say, but

I heard Gillesbuig the ferryman say that he had to take the ferry for Father Allan to Ludag one night before the Kilbride tack was broken up, the place being very isolated at the time. It was after they left Ludag that Father Allan spoke, saying that they were now away from Alasdair MhacMhaighter Alasdair's roaming area at last. Alasdair MhacMaighter Alasdair always roams the length of South Uist and never seems to go further than Cachelie e Struthan, a burn between East and West Kilbride. He has been roaming from there to Clachan Loch Bee for the last two hundred years and has been seen by quite a number of folks at night and during the day, walking and holding conversation with them on their walk together. One man who met him was Domnall Uileam Alasdair Calumn from Bruernish in Barra, when he was on his way back from the court in Lochmaddy. Why the ghost walked the length of South Uist I do not know, but sometime during his life on earth he must have been domiciled there. He seems to have been a minister in Knapdale at one time and changed his religious views. The next I heard of him he was among the followers of Bonnie Prince Charlie during the '45 Rebellion, being their bard, as all skirmishes like that needed these kinds of people to help them on in the battles. It was during this time that he composed the song, 'Gabhaidh Sinn e Rathad Mhor'. After this when the Highlands settled down after Culloden, and with him being an educated man, he was a factor on the isle of Canna.

Canna at this time being one of the Clan Ranald estates islands, it is more than likely there would be some communications between Canna and South Uist, which he must have visited, for it was while sheltering in a rain storm under a boat which was lying on the beach in Loch Eyenort that he composed the Bardach, 'Sgioberach Clann Raoghail' (Clanranald skippering). It was also in Eriskay and staying in Mhaighster Ellen house that Marjory Kennedy Fraser got the song that she made world famous, namely 'The Eriskay Love Lilt'. She picked up the tune from the woman next door to the church, Mary MacInnes it must have been, an old tune that was not sung for years. It only takes people interested in these things to stir up memories, and with Eriskay being settled by almost every tribe from different denominations from wherever a clearance was made, people must have brought in their minds old tunes.

Bones used to be unearthed at Lag na Cnamh (the hollow of bones) in Eriskay. Another place called Port e Gunna Mhor (the big gun) must have had some bearing on a battle fought there, as the little artillery they had in these days must have been kept there.

A few battles must have been fought before the Vikings finally relinquished the whole of the west coast of Scotland, but one thing they left behind which is still with folks staying there to this day is the cursing, or Butchachin, as it is better known. Whenever ones domiciled there of any denomination meet with trouble or ill-luck they tend to think it has been caused through being cursed.

At one time when Eriskay was sparsely populated there was a family of Campbells, my great-grandmother being one of them, who had a part of the island rented, the space between the two rivers from Abhain e Mhuilean to another river, Abhain Mhac Coiain. How they landed in that part of the world can be anybody's guess, but being Campbells after Culloden and Glencoe and being the Crown's bully boys with all the rest looking on them with distaste, they were in a good position to scoop up any cream that was going. Along with that bit of land they had a smack which they used mainly for ferrying cattle to mainland markets. One night their smack was anchored in Haun Bay and they had to get up in the small hours in case she would start dragging her anchors, as there was a change of weather. They were on their way back passing Rhubhain when they saw this awful-looking dog. It was much smaller than either of their own two dogs, a male and a female which they had with them. They were trying to set their dogs onto this terrible-looking thing which was following them, but try as hard as they could the dogs refused, keeping around their feet for protection. They reached the safety of their own house, but this animal was raising hell outside so it was decided they would have to get rid of it some way. By this time they had come to the conclusion that it must be the devil himself, and this being the case, the thing to do was to cut the ears of their own dogs to make them bleed, this being the way to either kill or be killed. After the two dogs were let out the noise gradually abated until they could not hear it any more. But it was two days after this occurrence they found the body of their male dog on the hill at the back of the island without one bit of hair on the carcass. The female dog they never saw again.

Life in Eriskay carried on in the same way for many years, with those who had a croft digging with the spade to keep a cow and horse. Those who had no croft were obliged to go around asking for a bit of land. These people had to work hard just to keep themselves supplied with a drop of milk and a peat fire. The horse was kept for carrying the peats. By the way, I have sailed in Dutch ships and never yet saw a Dutch man take milk in his tea. I told them at home about this but they would not believe it. They could not understand how anyone could survive without milk in tea. But survive they did, and looked very healthy to me.

There were six months in the year when Eriskay had to do without milk and those were the winter months. When the summer came round the boasting would start about how much milk their cow had and if they made a pound of butter they would go to high doh. It took them from the time they were first cleared until the present generation to figure out that they could survive without a cow.

A new bull coming to the place was always a local attraction. The children, especially the boys, would take time off school to see the bull being swum across the Sound water. Once, about the early thirties, this young bull arrived and was met at the mail boat and taken to Ludag, walking all the way. As there was quite a breeze blowing, they decided against using the tow boat and put the bull on the engine boat, the *Yawla Mhor*. Those who went with the boats for the bull had one look at him and said, 'Oh he is only a calf', but those who were waiting at the mail boat for him were saying that he was a bit of a devil. Anyway the older hands in the boats won, and he was taken aboard. No sooner had the *Yawla Mhor* left Ludag when she started pitching and spraying, and the bull started to take charge. It was so bad that by the time they reached Eriskay there was not enough rope left to tie the boat up as it had been used to tie the bull. When at last the bull was taken ashore a large audience had gathered around him. He would never have seen so many people before, being reared on a tack. He had to be taken to his 'house' and locked up to see if he would calm down, but calm down he did not, for as soon as he was let out after mass on Sunday, another big audience having gathered again, he was off like a shot trailing two ropes behind him. He made for the shore at the Balla with all hands and the cook after him. He reached Balla, causing a bit of a stir there, until he cleared the place and followed the sands over to Rhubhain. When he saw he was being cornered there he jumped into the sea and started swimming away with what was left of the ebb until he reached a rock off shore. Boats were then hauled up to high water mark, as it was the weekend, and so the job of launching them had to be undertaken until they were in the water. Three boats went after the bull who remained standing on the rock, defying anybody to come near him. Some of the braver ones managed to get on the rock and catch hold of his ropes which were taken aboard one of the boats, while the other two boats began rowing, and in this way they managed to get him ashore and back to his 'house'. What to do with him was the next question as the Department was not too clear about the situation. Telegrams were sent back and fore. Tiree wanted a bull but it was a shorthorn they were looking for. The other islands got to know about the mad bull in Eriskay and so somebody sent a telegram saying, 'SHIP BULL BY CHALLENGER, CUT HORNS FOR TIREE', the *Challenger* being the small coaster owned by the Jacks of Hopeman who were trading with her up the west coast. They were a bit green in Eriskay concerning cattle, but I think that is one thing they knew—how not to change a Highland bull into an Ayrshire shorthorn by cutting his horns.

Anyway it so happened that he was sent away with the next mail boat. This happened in 1931 during the spring, following the big winter fishing in the Sound of Barra.

It was some fishing that, the nets full with herring during the day. One night they were failing to catch any herring in the Sound, and everyone thought that it had cleared away to the deep water of the Minch. About four o'clock in the morning, after shooting and hauling all night with nothing to show for it but half their nets torn, our family's boats, the *Ocean Star* and the *Virgin*, decided to have another look in the Sound. After passing Weaver's Castle they came on a shoal and shot all the nets that were not torn. Our boat shot fourteen nets, the *Virgin* the same. After a cup of tea they started hauling but in our boat they were unable to haul because the nets were too full of herring. They realised they would have to get help and after a couple of hours the *Virgin*, having hauled fifty crans, came alongside, but as they had been working all night both crews were all in. So it was decided that the *Virgin* should proceed to the herring carrier *Loch Alsh* and on the way try to get hold of a fresh crew. They had not gone very far when they met the *St Patrick*, who was informed of the situation. The *St Patrick* reached the *Ocean Star* and both crews then began hauling the herring nets. They were still hauling when the *Virgin* came back after discharging at the *Loch Alsh*, but when the three crews started hauling, three of the nets just fell out of the ropes with the weight of the herring. At last the *Ocean Star* was full up and was anchored off with the gulls eating their fill from her decks.

The three crews went aboard the *St Patrick* and at last managed to finish hauling. The *Ocean Star* discharged one hundred and five crans besides what the gulls had eaten from her decks, the *St Patrick* had sixty-eight, a total of one hundred and seventy three crans out of eleven nets. This heavy catch was hauled in eight fathoms of water inside Weaver's Castle. If it had been deep water they would never have managed it. The strangest thing was that the winter before hardly a scale was caught at our end of the Minch, until it came in shoals early around September, when everybody thought it was saith. It was only when the winter fishing started that they discovered it had been around in shoals a month before.

It was a ship owner who had the most ambitious plan ever to be undertaken in the islands, Lord Leverhulme, owner of the Palm Line and builder of Port Sunlight on the Manchester Canal. He also had many other interests in Africa. He had great plans to develop the fishing industry when he bought the islands of Lewis and Harris in 1918. He bought them at a bad time, as the war was about to come to an end and returning servicemen were clamouring for big farms to be broken up for crofting. Except for his croft, the Highlander was always a man without security. The croft, providing he could pay the rent, was always his to be handed down to his heir or whoever he wished. To be without a croft was to be considered poor, as there was a certain stigma attached to it. So this was the situation when Leverhulme started with his plans in Stornoway. Land-hungry soldiers and sailors were returning from the trenches and the navy, while Leverhulme wanted to hold on to the farms near the town. So he left Stornoway to start building a town in the Sound of Harris which is named after him to this day, Leverborough. From 1921 until his death in 1925 I would say that he was the saviour of the Outer Isles. It is not for me to judge whether the work he did there was of any lasting benefit to the place or not, but I know that for some people in the islands it was the only time in their lives that they got what other people in other parts of the world take for granted: a wage packet.

I heard my folks saying that they were once in Leverborough with their boat after Lord Lever died and workmen were finishing off any work that was left on hand. There was also some building material being sold locally, things like bricks which they were after, as Alasdair in Glendale was build-ing a house at the time. There was a fellow there, Ian Mhac Fionghall, who was by nature an unconscious comedian and who was married to a cousin of our family working on the site, along with many others from the islands. They got talking to Ian anyway, who had the unenviable job of holding the thumper for a fellow who had done time working on the breakwater in Peterhead, having been convicted on a murder charge. The prisoners on this breakwater must have had a hell of a life, for this fellow would keep up this slogging pace all day until some boss would tell him to stop, coming with the hammer from the back of his heels and telling Ian if he didn't keep the thumper steady he was going to get it on the knuckles, a breakwater trick on the city toughs. But it did not matter which angle Ian held the thumper—the 'murderer', as Ian called him, would hit it.

On my folks enquiring about his health and well-being Ian would screw up his face remembering about the hammer coming into contact with the thumper and telling about how he was bullied into holding it for this—as he called him—the only murderer who was ever in the Western Isles. If it was his good fortune ever to reach Eriskay alive, he said, it would take some upheaval to shift him from there forever more.

I used to hear some of them talking in my young days, men and women, of sending money home or receiving money at home that was sent from Leverborough. There seemed to be work there for everybody as no one ever seemed to be turned back. The only place I ever heard of to equal it was a yard Everatt had near Greenwich on the Thames. There they used to do their own ship repairing, had their own houses and also had a big hostel for single men. No one was turned away from there either.

This ambitious scheme came to the islands when things were looking very grim. Herring fishing and markets were at a very low ebb. The winter lochs fishing was finished in the Skye and mainland lochs by 1923. Big emigration schemes were on with C.P.R. (Canadian Pacific Railway) boats making calls in the islands on their way to Canada. After Lord Leverhulme died at the beginning of the summer of 1925 things looked very bleak, as all that was left to do then was to tidy and finish off any work in existence. There was an emigration scheme in the spring of 1925 and another for the late summer. It was the day in late summer when the emigrants were being seen off by their relatives from the pier that the first herring of the season

Father, cousin Nonnie and Donald MacDonald, the Eriskay schoolmaster and Crown Bard

was landed in Castlebay. It must have been a heartbreak for those leaving to see herring shots coming in from the Lochmaddy bank. Those going to the bell with the samples for auction could hardly get through the crowd that had gathered on the pier. It was because Castlebay had been so long without a decent fishing that they were forced to emigrate.

If this poverty and want had carried on for another year I guess all of them would have had to emigrate, especially ones with young families. There was nothing else left in the islanEds with Leverhulme's scheme finished. His idea of getting trawlers to fish out of Leverborough and fish carriers to take the fish to the English markets all came to nothing with his death. So things looked very grim at the beginning of winter, 1925. Another bad season and it would have been the bald-headed prairie for what was left of them. But something like a miracle was going to happen this winter and the one following. A miracle, because nothing like it had ever happened in the history of the place, and it has not happened since. It lasted until February 1927.

The place where the herring was caught during those two winters was Loch Eyenort in South Uist. How the herring managed to go through that narrow gut, with a rock right in the middle and a tide strong enough going against it to stop a two-engined boat, is one of the mysteries of the sea. There was just enough room between the rock and the shore for a boat to squeeze through. The inland loch was so shallow that only half the net was fishing, the rest was lying on the bottom. The herring was packed so tight that it would not go into the nets until the herring drifters started steaming to get it moving. Prices fell and you were lucky to get a pound a cran if you went to Mallaig or Oban. Drifters were buying it on the spot for five shillings a cran. True, the herring went into the Skye lochs wherever the salt water was, but there was width at the mouth of the lochs. And where the herring went these two winters in succession remains a mystery to baffle the people. This was going to be the turning point of the herring fishing, as it did not get any worse after this, and the summer fishing began to pick up. However it was too late for some businesses that went bankrupt, with drifters being sold for a song.

One summer night in 1927 at the Heisker Light there was not a boat under forty crans. Our folks with the *Handy* lost thirty-five nets that night. It was not because of the amount of herring that was in them, fifty crans they got out of the ones they hauled, but they went to the bottom at fifty fathoms so it was a straight up and down job for them. With no help available, as all other boats had enough to do to haul their own heavy catches, they had to cut them away. If it had been shallow water and another boat had been there to help they would have managed. This was going to be the second fleet of nets the *Handy* lost during the eighteen years they had her. She lost another fleet the year the First World War started. My father was not in her at the time, he was in a Buckie drifter, the *William Riach*, and a poor fishing they had in her, just a read of the accounts. When he arrived home the brothers there had lost the summer fleet. So herring fishing was not all a bed of roses. The nets in 1927 would cost £6 each new, so with spring, stoppers, and buoy ropes they lost well over £200 worth in one night.

The *Handy*, as she was getting old for our part of the Minch, had to be sold to Scalpay the following year and another tarpaulin muster had to be made to buy a new boat, the *Ocean Star*, which cost £900, what they got for the *Handy* only covering a third of it.

My old grandpa lived until he was ninety-four and he was a pest around the shore guarding the wee twenty-foot boat. It did not matter where he was, if you went near the boat he was on top of you. He suffered plenty of abuse over that boat. Luckily there were half of us over on the other side of the Sound at South Glendale, so he did not have to police that lot. I was at home the night he died, the war being on. There were not many of us home at the time, just my uncle Iagan and auntie Morag. Just before he died he wanted to know which way the wind was blowing. Iagan replied that it was from the south west and added, 'You'll have it fair going over'.

My uncle Iagan was one day aboard the *Dunara Castle* at Carbost in Skye during the Skye lochs fishing. They were after having a bad spell after a heavy haul so they went alongside the *Dunara* for a bottle of whisky. This was before the First World War, so people did not go away from home so much as the herring fishing was good. There was a big mirror on the *Dunara* in which you could see yourself full-length, and it was near the place where the steward was giving my uncle the whisky. The steward handed him the bottle and Iagan was lifting his oilskin frock to put it into his pocket when he happened to look the way of the mirror. What he saw caused him to come out with a mouthful, thinking it was his brother Angus who had also come aboard to buy a bottle. He heard the steward whispering to somebody that the fellow from that fishing boat must be well away, as he heard him shouting to himself in the mirror.

After these bad years following the First World War the herring fishing picked up. There was plenty of buying and selling of boats for a number of years. The most unlucky buy was a boat they got in North Bay in Barra from Appin. She was bought by Shemus Lachlan and he spent every penny he had on her. He called her the *Margaret Sinclair* and they gave him a number CY13, why that number I do not know, there must have been plenty of figures to choose from. One evening he was leaving the pier at Lochboisdale with her, with his nephew Iagan down working the engine. After getting the engine going he came up on deck to give them a hand as they were hoisting the sail, the boat being underpowered at this time. Before the sail was on her, flames were coming from the engine room. All they could do then was to run ashore on Gasay where she burned out. This disaster ruined the poor man. He never did any more fishing and died shortly afterwards. He was a good seaman. My auntie Bella, who was sixteen years nursing in North Bay, told me that one Saturday, the first year she was there, there was a bad case of appendicitis. There were no aeroplanes these days, but they had to do something or the woman would certainly die. So my aunt and the woman patient were taken aboard Shemus Lachlan's boat, the *Stella Martina*, and set sail for Oban. They managed to make Oban and have the woman operated on, saving her life. This might not seem such a great thing to people today, but it was quite a feat in these days in a zulu-built boat depending on sail with a nurse and a woman patient at death's door aboard.

Shemus had been well warned not to buy the boat by an Eriskay man, Eogh Calum Mhor, who had gone to see her first of all. Eogh could see things that were about to happen in the future and he had met the Barra crowd in Oban on their way to buy the boat. Eogh pleaded with them not to have anything to do with her and to go back home. He told them that the boat would only bring them bad luck.

When fishing was bad people went to the local seer for help. One in Eriskay they called the Gotha (blacksmith), why this name I do not know, for I do not believe he could have shoed a pony, but he got the name anyway and it stuck like glue. He was a wee dwarf fellow with a beard and staring eyes and it was to him that those in desperation went for the 'snalenian'. This was made with wool, black wool it had to be, and you took it with you and tied it to some part of the boat or gear. He used to go sick after these rituals, the period of sickness depending on how badly the boat, or sometimes crews, were cursed. I do not remember that he ever did any kind of work except to cause mischief. I remember him once filling a well up with stones, the well being on his croft, and this action brought the police to Bunmhullin. Angus Nichoson, the shopkeeper from Staffin in Skye, was told to draft a telegram to the police which read, 'BUNMHULLIN WATER SUPPLY CUT OFF BY JOHN JOHNSTON', this being his proper name. The big policeman, Jimmy, nicknamed the yes-man, was in Lochboisdale. He travelled to Bunmhullin and made the Gotha take every stone out of the well, standing in front of him until he had finished the job. He was a relation of my folks and I sometimes wonder if I have some of his devilment myself, for I sometimes think what a stramash I would cause if I cut off the town's water supply.

People always say when they hear of these *snalenian* that it is a lot of rubbish but I do not think so. All this was left from the old Norsemen days and no amount of religion of any kind could put a stop to it. It does not matter what anybody says, some families in the islands had some power handed down to them.

There was a ship going through the Suez canal once with the usual crowd that came aboard there selling their wares and so on. Among this crowd was the Gili Gili man with his usual bag of tricks. To young, first-time voyagers it was a great sensation with the Gili Gili man putting money into their hands, then making it disappear with words like 'Gili Gili come, money come and money go'. The Bosun who looks after the crowd is usually an old-timer picked for his experience and age. This Bosun was an old-timer from one of our own islands of the Outer Hebrides. He was standing looking at the crowd around the Gili Gili man when somebody said, 'Come on bosun, let's see him take the coin out of your hand'.

'He won't take it out of my hand', says the Bosun.

'Oh yes he will', said somebody else, 'he's taken it away from all of us already.'

So the Bosun got into the act with the Gili Gili man putting the money into his hand from the usual distance of about twenty feet. Then the Gili Gili man said, 'Money go', but the Bosun still had the coin. The Gili Gili man tried again with the same result, until at last he was rolling on the deck with his hands up in the air shouting until eventually he called a halt when he saw that he was beaten. The Bosun still had the coin in his hand but when he opened his hand to show he had it, the silver coin had turned black.

No policeman being on Eriskay it was always the priest who was called in for diplomacy when trouble was afoot. This time it was my granny's half brother, Canon MacNeil, who was there.He finished his days in Morar and is buried there. He was young at this time, this being one of his first parishes, and he was a bit hampered with language difficulties, as every island has its own dialect. Even Barra and Eriskay, although beside each other, had their differences in speaking. For instance at this time they did all of their own baking, and sometimes Indian meal was mixed with white flour, baking soda and cream of tartar, the combined ingredients being known in Eriskay as Ian MacLaughlan, why is anybody's guess. Well Bunmhullin where the Gotha lived was the star village for trouble, people coming to the priest complaining and the Gotha being in the centre of it all. The Gotha had an old auntie staying with him, Mhor, who was bedridden. This day the priest was in the shop with a crowd, and who came into the shop but the Gotha with his usual bitch in heat and every dog in Bunmhullin following them. I remember as yougsters always getting a kick out of asking the Gotha whose dog that was and whose dog this one was etc., as he had a nickname for everyone in Bunmhullin. To get back to the story: this day anyway the priest asked after auntie Mhor and the Gotha replied, 'Oh she is very well today Father, very well indeed, because when I left she was sitting up in bed drinking a cup of tea and eating a big piece of Ian MacLaughlan'.

The priest was taken aback and started looking around the shop to see what reaction there was from the crowd, but everybody in the shop just looked as though eating Ian MacLaughlan was an everyday occurence. So he says to himself, 'I had better keep quiet before they think I am another fool from Barra'. It was only after he reached his interpreter, granny, and asked if she had heard of any cannibalism going on in Bunmhullin that he was told of the ingredients that were in the bread Mhor was eating.

This troublesome family kept their feuding going right up to the end. I remember the son Allan travelling with me in the ferry over to Eriskay. I said that I was glad that he and his brother and sister were now on good terms.

'No, we aren't', says Allan.

He was coming back from Pollachar where they sold the drink and he was loaded for trouble. 'When I get out there I'm going to get a hold of a pinch and put it under the corner of his house and knock it down', he said, referring to his brother's house. Allan had fingers on only one hand. He lost the fingers of his other hand when a blast did not go off and he had been sent by his brother to dig around it too soon.

Strangers travelling between the small islands at these times used to have a hard time of it climbing over rocks at low water, Pollochar being the worst. I think you had to be born in these islands, where you had to jump over rocks with creels of seaweed or bags of peat on your back, before you were able to survive.

At this time doctors were always mainland folks, and they never seemed to get the hang of this kangarooing amongst the rocks and so they had to be carried on peoples' backs. Doctor Reardon, who used to have Eriskay in his practice, had to be carried in this way sometimes. I remember seeing him coming off the boat, always wearing the same rig-out no matter what the weather. Whether the raven was hanging out his tongue with thirst or the ferrymen were hitting their arms against their bodies to keep warm, Doctor Reardon would have the same grey, heavy coat on and wellies or spats, they were black in colour anyway. After visiting the patient, somebody would have to go with him for a bottle of some concoction, and then walk back from Dalibrog to Ludag. People tell me Doctor Reardon was more active than the one before him. His surname I never seem to have heard mentioned, only the *Dotair Cloimhe*, the Woolly Doctor. I suppose he got this name because of all the woollen clothes he would wear, as carrying him with all these clothes was like carrying a bag of guts.

One of our near neighbours at the Haun was Ian MacMurchaidh, a hardy loon who these days while Gillesbuig the ferryman's family were young, would take turns with his neighbours if at home from the fishing to go across the Sound for the mails. This day Ian was over, and who was coming back across the Sound but the Woolly Doctor and his wife. Gillesbuig would be getting enough of the Woolly, so it was left to Ian to carry him. It was not hard to get Ian riled up but by the time he arrived at the boat at low water he was fuming. So he throws the Woolly onto the rail and shouts, 'Get aboard, Doctor Sheet'. The Woolly's wife, who was kangarooing among the rocks, starts on at Ian saying how her husband was a member of the medical profession with letters after his name. Ian says to her, 'Shut up you old wreck'.

Another neighbour who was nearly always in our house was Dunache Mhac Domhnall Cailen, another hardy whose biggest interest in life, being retired, was reading the *News of the World*. How he got hold of this sailors' bible I do not know, it must have been some newsagent in Glasgow who was sending it to him. But Duncan was always causing a stramash over it. The priest Father Gillies would say to him, 'You'll never see there what the pope did last week'. Duncan did not want to see or hear what the pope did last week. I heard granny getting on to him a few times when he used to tell her what he saw in the *News of the World*. He joined the navy in the First World War and he was then well into his fifties, a good age at that time when, with all the hard work they were doing, they were old men at fifty.

But I think his best yarn of the lot was the time he was up in court in Fraserburgh for fighting over a pair of pants. He had two pairs of pants, one pair for working, the other for the Sabbath. One of the girls from our place who was at the gutting washed his working pants on Saturday and left them out to dry on the rope. A tramp comes around and steals the pants, then sells them to a wild fellow from south Lochboisdale, Eoghain Mhac Ailean, who was also at the fishing. Duncan was told by the girls that his working pants had been stolen and was also told by one of the boys that Eoghain had bought a pair of pants at bargain price. Duncan went to investigate and saw that the pants were his own all right, but being Saturday night and having a few drinks inside them it was no time to mediate, Eoghain being known as a wild man and Duncan being the have-a-go type. With no T.V. in these days fighting between Heilan' loons would be a local attraction in these east coast herring ports, so by the time the fight was on for a while a crowd had gathered. The police came and arrested the two fighters, the reason for the fight being told to them. The two fighters were charged and told to appear in court on the Monday morning early before the boats put to sea.

Monday morning came and the boys were sober but the question as to who owned the pants still had not been settled. The court house was crowded with girls and boys from our own part, and by the time Eoghain went into the witness box he was getting worried. Buying stolen property was an offence and he must have had an idea the pants were hot stuff, having bought them from the tramp for a shilling. Now one of the nicest things you could do for anyone at these times was to give him a smoke of your pipe after having a smoke yourself, and so as soon as Eoghain went into the witness box he takes out his pipe, lights it, and before the sheriff knew where he was, Eoghain was over at his chair giving him a blast of his pipe. After Eoghain had been given a scolding by the sheriff for contempt of court, the two fighters were let off with a reprimand: 'Any more of this and it will be the breakwater at Peterhead for you two'.

Other neighbours of ours were the McDiarmaid brothers, Roderick and Neil. They were God-fearing, peaceful men who hardly ever took a drink. They had a nice zulu boat called the *Immaculate*. It was built for themselves in Banff. There was only a 13/15 engine in her all the time they had her. They kept to the old barrel nets, never changing over to spring, and they would get herring when others did not at the beginning of summer when herring was close inshore at the back of our own island on the hard ground. Neil once joined the *Lily Riach* of Buckie in April 1912 until the end of September and received £72 in his hand at square up, plus £8 in subs. They left Buckie at the beginning of April for the Irish fishing grounds, as all Scotch herring ports were closed until 10 May. On arrival they shot off the Old Head of Kinsale, started hauling about one o'clock in the morning, and finished about noon. About one hundred and eighty crans they hauled, but it was very mixed with mackerel. After they had finished hauling they made for Kinsale, but on arrival, what a welcome! I have seen Union Castle boats on the Cape run going into St Helena being met by the whole island when passengers were run ashore, but the crowd who welcomed the *Lily Riach* into Kinsale that day, so our neighbour Neil informed me, was nothing compared to it, only this crowd were mad Irishmen with murder in their hearts, out for blood for breaking their herring close time. As there had been no close time the year before, the *Lily Riach* went alongside to see what all the shouting was about. Somebody threw a rope ashore. One of the Irish got a hold of it, walked with it near to the wheel house, where the Riach was looking through the window, and let him have the end of the rope in his face, giving him a bloody nose and a black eye. The mate dived into the wheelhouse and backed her away from the pier. The Fishing Protection took the Riach ashore with his black eye and bloody nose and fined him on the spot. They then had to go to sea and dump the lot of herring, then make for the south west corner of Ireland as the south was getting a bit unhealthy for them. They had to keep away from all of the fishing ports as their name was mud.

They went into Bere Haven, which was at that time a British naval base. It was here that the fleet which defeated the Germans at the Battle of Falkland Island sailed from. As the *Lily Riach* crew were strange to Bere Haven they accidentally moored her to a place where they were blocking some steps which were used by naval personnel going ashore. Luck was still against them, as it was Sunday morning and a naval sloop was making for the steps, taking some personnel to church. On approaching they saw the *Lily Riach* after taking the bottom at the steps. The officer started shouting in good old naval fashion at the Riach for blocking the steps and was told that he could walk through the drifter to the steps. 'Do you think,' he says to the Riach, 'that I would walk through your dirty boat? You'll be hearing more of this.' So saying, they went right about and turned back to the battleship, and before an hour had passed the police were aboard with a summons to appear in court the following morning. So they had to wait there until the Monday morning. The poor Riach had to appear in court again still sporting the black eye and bloody nose he got from the rope end in Kinsale.

I think they were glad to get away from that part of Ireland and make for the north ports, as nearly all of the Donegal ports were in the herring trade then, namely Downings, Buncrana and Killybegs, as well as Portrush in Antrim. Riach, although from Buckie, made most of his money out of Castlebay, working Tiree and Heisker grounds. He had a lovely house in Buckie called 'Heisker Holm' where all his hired hands were welcomed while in Buckie. He lost a few of his drifters at the Dardanelles during the war, where they were used for landing troops on the beaches.

After the war he started an oil and coal business in Oban but, sorry to say, with the depressed state of the fishing he died a poor man. Neil spent most of his life fishing except for the First World War years in the navy. Perhaps there are a few in Eriskay who would not agree with me but I would say Neill caught more herring than anyone there. He was well on in years, about forty, before he and his brother Roderick got the *Immaculate*, which he was in for the remainder of his fishing life. But it was on the east coast boats that he served most of his young days. He was for years on the *Hero* of Brughead, both the sail boat and the drifter. It was along with the man whom he called Cailan that he spent many years.

Balta Sound in north Shetland was the klondyke place when the big steam-hauling zulus were on the go. A common practice in these days after hauling a hundred crans with no wind was to start dumping it. Balta Sound, with just one farm house, must have been a sight then. All the various necessities of life had to be brought in there, even water. The bakery there alone employed about fifty girls, all about school-leaving age, but too young for handling herring. These girls would trample away all day in the dough, singing and dancing to fiddle music.

The merchants who had to feed the crews of these fishing boats were taking more risks than anybody. At least the fisherman had his boat at the end of the season. The curer had to take a risk and many of them went under when foreign markets collapsed, but the man who was taking more of a risk than anyone was the merchant who had to feed them. Crying and shouting after going bankrupt was not going to help anybody, as the risks were known before they started.

There were a few braver than others, starting out with only washers. I know one man who I do not think had a penny to his name the day he arrived in Eriskay from his home in Skye to mend shoes. This man's name was Shonnie Clarke. He was brought over from Skye by relations, the McLennan family, who in later years had the post office in Lochboisdale. At this time they were shop-keeping in Eriskay for Donald Ferguson, who owned another couple of shops and a fish-curing business in Lochboisdale. Well anyway, Shonnie came to Eriskay. They must have been wearing some kind of clogs in Eriskay for the McLennan family to see a bit of business there for Shonnie. To some of the older generation of Eriskay people he was always known as Ian Dubh na Broig. How long he stayed in Eriskay I do not know, but I next heard of Shonnie with a shop in Lochboisdale standing security for bank loans to purchase fishing boats, curing in the klondyke trade to Germany, a finger in every pie. He survived good and bad fishing all these years. I do not think bad fishing made much difference to him. When everyone else was down in the dumps over it Shonnie was going about on the prowl to see if he could get hold of some youngster around the boats to kid on about girls.

He never married himself but he was always matchmaking, always acting the goat, but behind all that he must have had a great business mind to keep the wholesale merchants in the city at bay. He must have been the right man in the right place at the right time for Lochboisdale at the beginning of the century, as Lochboisdale was being developed as a herring port.

I heard people domiciled in far-away places with a far-away look in their eyes telling about their first time leaving home, how their mother managed to give them a pound and Shonnie giving them another, maybe all of what they needed to take them away. I do not know if they were good to him in Eriskay when he was there but I have seen him with tears in his eyes praising the Eriskay people.

Some young fellow came into his shop one day asking for the loan of a pound to go for petrol up at the hotel and giving the name of our boat, this being a common practice among us, but there was no such fellow aboard. Three generations of Eriskay men he had seen coming into his shop but no one ever did this to him before. If we wanted anything we would ask him for it. I think he lost quite a bit of money over the German klondyking business. German currency not being very good between the wars I think he was leaving some over there, hoping for things to turn out better. He had a big stock of crockery in the back of his shop, so perhaps he was getting plates, cups and so on from the klondyke's bartering kind of business.

Chapter 4

The haaf fishing—Life on the Barra Head islands—Mixing of religions in the islands—Travelling to the east coast fishing—Boom-time for Eriskay—Drift net and ring net fishing—Stories of St Columba—I drink all my money, bar sixpence—Composing of songs—Ruairidh 'the Case' Campbell—Telling tales and playing pranks—Sea-sickness—Peter e Gillesbuig's heart transplant—The iron man and the big beast from Point——One-legged fishermen——Pelorus and the lobster

The only fishing done around our part of the world before herring fishing started was for cod and ling and this was known as the haaf fishing. For this haaf fishing they would go out as far as the sixty-fathom line, the only land they would see being the top of Bhen Mhor in South Uist. The fish was cured and dried locally, as nearly every cove with a population had a fishing station. For about twenty years this was their way of life, as was the case with the bigger neighbouring islands of Barra and Uist. Cargoes of dried, salted cod and ling were sent direct to southern Russia.

No one now wanted to move these people from Eriskay as the island was no use for large-scale cultivation, and so for once since their first clearance they were left in peace. I have often wondered if this way of life was best. The one thing certain was that, weather permitting, they were sure of catching enough to keep the wolf from the door. I have seen coves in isolated places in Newfoundland and maritime provinces of Canada with thriving communities living the same way as their forebears did for centuries before them using hook and line. By this method they could almost carry their catching power on their backs on one go. But what happened was strangers got to know of the herring in the haaf, the fish that caused more jealousy, despair, anxiety and bankruptcies than any other fish swimming in the sea.

These seas around the British Isles at that time, and for many years after were free for everybody. Towards the end of the 1860s the east coast herring fishing was well commercialised but the season was a short one, July and August being the only two months of the year when herring used to pass the Buchan shores on its migration south. The herring, as it has always done, was moving in an anti-clockwise direction around the North Sea, down the east coast of England in the autumn, around the French coast towards the end of the year and heading north up to Norway in the spring, then over to the Shetland ground in the early summer, until it struck the Buchan shores again at the beginning of July.

In the early days of sail, herring boats could not venture far as they had to land their herring fresh daily. With the flat calms that come in summer, a few miles from their base was far enough. Curers would at times get annoyed when the herring boats did not come in during calms and would send out tugs to tow them in. They were looking for virgin grounds and they found them where the haaf fishing was carried out on the west of the Outer Hebrides.

For the next thirty years, from the middle of May to the end of June, Castlebay and Stornoway were like wild west boom-towns. Every herring fisherman and shore herring worker from Wick to Berwick-on-Tweed gathered between Stornoway and Castlebay. Over a thousand boats would be fishing out of Castlebay alone at one time. In every available space between Castlebay and Vatersay a herring station was built. The population of Barra must have swollen to nine thousand during these two months. All the young men left the haaf fishing and went as hired hands on east coast boats with the result that the haaf line fishing died out altogether through time. Those who had shops on other islands also descended on Castlebay to join the boom and feed the army of fishermen, gutters, coopers, curers and foreign buyers, setting up temporary shacks and selling provisions. I have often heard my grandparents speak of these days, as it was in Castlebay that they first met.

My grandfather's folks had a shop on Eriskay, so it was over to the boom-town to set up some temporary shacks. My grandmother's folks, who were staying in Berneray, also sent two of their boys over, grandmother's father and his brother, Neil. It was not a temporary shack they built but the square house which stands on the street to this day. This house was built in 1870. My grandmother was born there but when she was only three years old her mother died and so she was sent to live with her mother's relatives in Boisdale, South Uist. Her father left his brother Neil in the house and went away sailing for a number of years, and it was while he was away that he met Michael Buchanan, who was at this time a customs officer in Liverpool. They must have gone on a drinking spree and before it was all over Michael Buchanan had lost his job. It was then that he composed the song in Gaelic telling of this event. Sad to say, this self-educated man, the best who ever left Barra, is buried in an unmarked grave in Hallin cemetery in South Uist. He died in Dalibrog hospital.

After a few years sailing, my grandmother's father came back home, married again and went to stay in Berneray. The place there was kept going by his parents all this time. My grandmother was then brought from Boisdale to Berneray to stay.

For about eight years the family resided in Berneray. Most of her step, brothers and sisters were born there, two of whom died and are buried

Granny, mother's mother, and Angus John MacKinnon, both from Barra, outside granny's house in Eriskay. Angus John was shopkeeping for his mother in Eriskay.

there. A wild place it was in the winter time, but in summer it was all activity, with fishing and curing cod and ling. All of the Barra Head islands at this time had a few families. It was Mingulay that had the biggest population, but as Berneray was the only suitable place for landing fish, this is where everyone gathered. Children who were big enough to handle the fish had to be fed and it was here that my grandmother began the task of making meals for people, something that would remain with her for the rest of her life, as nearly every stranger who came to visit Eriskay stayed in her house since it was nearest to the ferry. People were always in and out of the house, either waiting for or coming off the ferry. I have met some of these Barra Head islanders in later years, long after they had left there, coming to visit my grandmother in Eriskay. So I have a fairly good idea of their lifestyle in these remote islands. How they used to stearie the birds on top of Creag Mhor in Mingulay, using nets on the ends of poles, having been well warned by the priest that if any one of them should fall his name would be left out of the dead list on Sunday, as death from falling over Creag Mhor was classed as suicide. Fortunately no one ever fell, as each one was well roped before venturing over the cliff top with a pole used for the stearie. They also fished on the Sgriob Bhann with open boats, staying out all night if the weather was fine. The only other fishermen I heard being mentioned were Islay fishermen who used to fish there with luggers, curing and salting aboard. This fishing must have died out in Islay long ago, as this is the only time I heard Islay being mentioned doing any fishing. There was, however, an old zulu clinker-built boat in Eriskay called the *Rival* which the old-timers said was built for the Islay herring fishing.

There was one regular contact with the outside world and that was the lighthouse boat. The lighthouse keepers had their wives and families with them there. The coming of the lighthouse boat must have been a welcome sight for them every time she arrived.

Getting the winter over was the most trying time, as no boats could be launched in these awful seas you get there. So families began to drift away, until by 1908, when the island of Vatersay was broken up and crofted, those who were left went also. My granny's family moved over to Castlebay in 1888 and built the bank house which they used for living in as well as for selling provisions. So that is two houses in the street, the square house and the bank house, both built with money made in Berneray. As is usual with these remote islands, any money made there would be put to use. Only when over in Castlebay would they be able to buy any drink, and that would not be very often. I think most of their time, especially during the winter, would be spent praying. I know that up to the end of her life my granny had a rosary of fifteen decades. An ordinary rosary usually has five decades. I maintain that it was her strict upbringing in Berneray that made her so devout.

Castlebay catholic church was not built until 1890. Before this the whole island had to walk to Borve on a Sunday. It was just an open-air service for all religions, and people, especially those over from Eriskay and Uist who were a bit mixed in their religion, were inclined to get a bit upset. Nearly all in Barra were catholic, but they were having some fun egging on the mixed ones who were giving their relations a mouthful for practising a religion different from their own.

There was an old woman, Bellag Taramoid, who was living near our house and she was forever visiting us. I remember she took snuff and I think that was the start of my being a slave to anything, as I always looked out for Bellag coming just to see if I would get a pinch of snuff. Bellag was one of the Gardeners, who were originally protestants from Skye, and she and granny would talk about the events in Castlebay at the time of the west side haaf fishing as both of them had been there then. There must have been a turncoat to the catholic crowd on Bellag's side as the man she always gave the telling off to at the open-air services on Sunday was a very near relation of hers. Cailan was his name and he was an elder in the church, and would attend the minister dressed in a long, black gown, so Bellag said. Anyway it was becoming a local attraction for the Barra crowd on a Sunday to go and hear Cailan getting his desserts from Bellag. She could not see any side of it other than her own, because it was the catholic side of the mob who were the turncoats.

I remember years later being on a ship in some foreign port and meeting another crowd from our own part of the world. We started swapping stories about who we had seen since the start of the voyage, and we were informed by them that they had spoken to a crowd from a City boat in the last port of call. They were rattling off the names of the ones who were in her until they came to this MacIntyre from South Uist. He was, they said, some elderly man. It hit me like a rock who this man was. By this time, of course, Bellag was dead, but I could still picture her up on her soap box getting on to Cailan and the daughter of that family coming down to the hut they were in, begging her and asking her nicely to stop her Sunday carry-on. 'Did you stop then?' someone had asked her. 'Did I stop?', she replied, 'that's when I really got started'.

Anyone looking at Castlebay today would wonder how the bay could accommodate over a thousand boats, but at that time curers were working on a bounty system. The curers hired the boats at the beginning of the season, and that was the crew with the same curer for the rest of the season. Like everything else which has been abused on this planet, this way of working was to come to an end, and it was therefore towards the end of the century that the fishing started to deteriorate, until by the early 1900s there was no herring left in the haaf. I have never heard of anyone getting more than a few baskets from the haaf since I can remember. Old timers were forever trying to encourage the younger generation to try the haaf, but time after time it has been tried with always the same result. It is hard for anyone to believe that a sea which was once so prosperous would become so poverty-stricken without picking up through the years. There was one bad disaster during this fishing out west in the haaf, but fortunately with no loss of life. This disaster overtook the fleet one morning while out west. The wind had started blowing from the south east. The fleet was big and space in the Sounds was small. Anyone knowing the geography of the place can picture what was happening. There were over a thousand boats concentrating and tacking in a small area, with the wind dead against them. The majority of the fleet was making for the Sound of Sandray and it was while going through that Sound that the biggest disaster happened. With so little room to manoeuvre, boats were colliding with one another and one crew had to rescue the other while boats were sinking. After a count was made in Castlebay, when all surviving boats and men reached there, it was found that thirty-seven boats had gone down, but not one soul had been drowned. It must have been a record for life-saving, as there were nearly three hundred lives saved.

By this time men in Barra had acquired bigger boats. Barra had a population of two thousand people, while Eriskay had only four hundred, as they were more or less getting over being cleared from one place to another. I would say about the turn of the century was going to be the finest hour in Barra's history. They had acquired thirty years of expert herring fishing and a fleet of fine, big, steam-handling boats. The buying of these boats meant many debts were accumulated. The Castlebay season being short, it was the Barra men's turn to look for virgin grounds for survival and this they did.

The Shetland Islands up to this time were untapped for commercial herring fishing. The herring they needed was for bait for the line fishing, which was done with boats fishing out west as far as Rockall. Continental merchants had some hold on the place by keeping the fishermen always a year in debt, so that it was more or less impossible for them to turn their hand to any other kind of fishing except cod or ling. Men from Barra managed to get in there anyway, and it was they who caught and cured some of the first herring that came out of the Shetlands for continental markets.

Herring boats sailed from Castlebay with tugs in attendance for the Shetland fishing before many others went there. It was in Lerwick that they started curing, but I do not believe they had it too long for themselves, as soon enough other fishermen moved in, and it is only reasonable that locals seeing the bonanza going on around them managed to break away from those who were keeping them line fishing.

The Skye lochs fishing was also on at this time, as I heard my granny say they had a station for curing herring in Soay. As Mallaig was not opened up by rail then, the herring had to be cured on the spot. There was one disaster towards the end of the century and that was the Pabach boats which were lost on 3 May 1897, just off their own island, with five men drowned. I don't think there were many more than themselves staying on Pabbay at the time. Those of the family remaining afterwards—Aoghais Pabach, who had his two brothers lost, and his brother Ronald's wife and son—lived in Oban for a good number of years after the drowning.

There was also a disaster which hit the Eriskay crowd one night during the Skye lochs fishing. The night was bad and they were at anchor at a place called Ullart between Seavaig and Soay Sound. The wind must have shifted onto the shore during the night. With it blowing a hurricane, they were unable to set canvas to get out of there, so the ones who did not hold their anchors were driven ashore. The crews managed to get out of their boats, only to spend the rest of the night marooned in the hills above the shore. It was only when the wind eased off the following day that the ones who were ashore were taken off by what was left of the fleet. It was a poor home-coming, boats arriving home with two crews in them. It must have been Eriskay's darkest hour since they went to live there forty years before. This happened to them when they were just getting on a bit in the world after all the agonies they had endured being cleared from one place to another. It was going to be ten years before an Eriskay boat would go near the Skye lochs again.

The Skye lochs where they used to fish in these days were, and still are, very isolated. Before the Mallaig line was open, their only way of getting provisions and other necessities was by walking to the nearest village. If a storm struck around the Loch Eyenort or Loch Brittle area the only means of getting stores was walking to Carbost. Loch Slapin and Loch Eishort were just as bad, as they had to walk across the island to Broadford. A fellow was telling me he once carried an anchor from Broadford to the head of Loch Slapin while his mate carried a bag of provisions.

Castlebay was never the same again after the west side fishing finished. All the herring landed in Castlebay came from the south and east of the Minch. The coming of the steam drifter on the scene meant that the east coast fishing could last from the time it struck Shetland waters at the beginning of summer till they had finished in Yarmouth at the end of November. These drifters had the speed to travel fifty or sixty miles and still land every day.

Those who went to the east coast fishing before the railway came to the sea on the west coast had a hard struggle. One thing that could be said for them is that they were not lazy in travelling to where a pound was to be made, when you heard them talk of sailing small boats to Corpach, leaving them there and working their way up the canal side to Inverness. Another way they used to travel was by going to the Skye side of Kyle Rhea, hauling the small boats up on the beach, and crossing the Kyle Rhea by ferry. The only road out of Skye was then before them to Fort Augustus. They would get the boat there to Inverness at this time. The first easing they had was when the train came as far as Strome Ferry, to where the boats could be taken then. So this was the situation with Eriskay at the beginning of the century, elderly men fishing at the home fishing and younger men going to the east coast fishing. This fishing for ling and cod with lines, but on a small scale, by the very old and the very young, was to carry on until a few years after the First World War.

Getting to the east coast fishing was not the awful journey it used to be, as by 1901 the rail had arrived in Mallaig and Kyle. As soon as the Barra west side herring fishing stopped, Lochboisdale had a big winter herring fishing which was to last for a number of years. The reason for this is not known, but it was going to be Lochboisdale's heyday. The herring went up as far as the Strome, and was so plentiful that it was drying itself out on the

Grandfather on mother's side and myself aged seven

shore. The people who had crofts there never had to cut seaweed, as there was enough dead herring on the shores to do them. There was not one bit of land around the pier that was not used for curing. Anything that could float would have a few nets laid on, mostly small boats which were used only on the west side lobster fishing during the summer months.

After the disaster at Ullart in Skye it was the first pick up Eriskay had, as they began to aquire bigger zulu-type boats. These boats were up to thirty-five feet keel and up to fifty feet over all, which would work forty nets. Eriskay was a long time in shifting over to spring rope hauling, as the ground east of their own island was very shallow and rocky. Any boats using spring could catch the bottom and besides causing damage to their own gear, would have other boats drifting on top of their nets. By keeping to this smaller size of zulu, which cost in the region of £70 to £80, and as there was not much capital involved, everybody had a share of the boat and nets.

I would say during this time, up to the First World War, was Eriskay's finest hour. Houses were built at the rate of two and three a year—fine, two-storey houses which stand there to this day. Some folks had acquired the method of blasting stones out of rocks while working on the railway lines during the winter months. Even in my own young days this was the method. Stones had to be blasted at the first kick off. Concrete houses were to come later. The boring was done usually with children holding the thumper. This must have been my first terrifying experience. There was a man on either side swinging a heavy hammer, shouting and swearing and telling me to keep the thumper straight. The children on our island were exploited, when you come to think of it. Whatever about factory acts, the convicts on the breakwater at Peterhead had an easier time of it.

Houses built before the turn of the century were only put up with stones found around the seashore. The house where I was born at Haun, which is still standing today, would be one of the first thatched houses where no beasts were domiciled. I was looking at the stones which had been used to build it and found that they were small stones which could be picked up all over the place. Some of these thatched houses were so good that when two-storey houses started being built with upstairs accommodation, they needed only to add a felt covering to them. It was only when repairing schemes started after the First World War that slates were added, along with what was done inside them. The straight stairway was taken away and an L-shaped stairway put in its place, which gave more room upstairs. The ones who had a hand in building and repairing our house in Haun, it is their great-grandchildren who are there today. It was Domnall Mhac Ian Bhain from south Lochboisdale who built it first, then Aoghais Mhac Ian Mhor from Kilphedar altered it from a thatched to a two-storey house with felt. After the First World War in 1920 it was tackled again, the first in Uist to have an asbestos slate roof put on by Iagan Niall from Boisdale, with every-one forecasting disaster saying these asbestos slates would never last in the wild weather up there, and that anyway the sarking under the felt must be rotten and the nails would not hold. Domnall Na Bannach from Daliborg put the L-shaped stairway in it, without one nail to hold the steps. Again people foretold of more disasters—somebody was going to get killed as the stair was going to collapse. Well, the house is still standing, and there must have been a few up and down these stairs, and a few bad gales must have blown on top of the roof, but the house is still there intact, a monument to tradesmen who knew their job.

I remember well when my father and my uncle Angus through marriage built their houses. My grandfather's house, being the family house which they all had built long before this time, went to my uncle John, as he was the oldest. The other two brothers were over on the other side at Glendale so this was the scene when more houses had to be built. My father's house was not too bad, as there was a temporary thatched house up for a few years and so not many stones were needed for the new one. But uncle Angus had to blast the new house and byre all in one go. What a carry on! Being near the school the children would gather over at their playtime trying to do what they saw their elders doing, and so younger children were press-ganged, so to speak, into holding the thumper, whether they liked it or not, and the older boys would swing the hammer. How no one was injured or maimed for life through blasting that house remains a miracle. There would be cries and blood about, although it was nothing serious, nothing that a *steall* (a good drop) of paraffin would not cure. Their pay for all this carry-on was seeing a blast go off. There are not many living in these houses today who took part in this slavery, but the houses are still there, repaired with bits added on to them, and the blasted stones will always be there, monuments to the memory of a population gone who liked to have the most important thing in anyone's life, a nice new house.

The spring of the year, when herring was out of season, was usually the time for building. As soon as April came in the seaweed had to be cut to be used for fertiliser. This was carried out with the small, twenty-foot boats and with two or three men to every boat. They used to let the boats out at our part of the island, Balla, from Lon Na Leabaig in the morning after high water, and take them to another mooring place called Sgeir Bheag e Caise where they would not dry. Then they would go off home for a bite to eat, then back to the boats about half tide to sail for the off-shore rocks. Some of these off-shore rocks were shared out to whoever had a croft. The job of cutting the seaweed would start using sickles, until flood tide began. Then came the loading of the boats. This was done with a creel having a stout rope around the top, usually the sheet rope of the sail, a rope that was spliced and unspliced every day during the seaweed-cutting operation. At half flood the boat was usually loaded and sailed back to Sgeir Bheag e Caise. There the shore gang, that is, the children, would meet them and board the boats to let the men home for their meal, just like the big London ships when they were met at the locks by shore gangs before entering K.G.V. (King George V Docks), another carry on which is just history.

The children would start to bring the boats in with the tide, arguing and laughing at any boat that had her white beat forward showing, on account of not being fully loaded. At high water the job of discharging the seaweed would begin. Nearly everyone in the community, male and female, would be involved. Once the boats were empty, bags of sand had to be taken aboard for ballast. Sometimes small lines that were shot first thing in the morning had to be hauled, or else a load of peat had to be taken home. So it was non-stop as long as the daylight lasted.

This slavery carried on for about six weeks. All the seaweed had to be taken to the ground at low water, usually by the young and the old, the more able-bodied being away in the boats to cut more of the seaweed. As soon as the seaweed was on the ground the job of turning the ground with spades had to be done until all of the seed potatoes were sown. Then the ground for the corn had to be turned and this again done with spades. No ploughs could be used on Eriskay as the ground was too rocky and shallow.

When all of the ground was turned and the seeds sown, then came the task of cutting the peat and painting the boats. All land work had to be finished before 10 May, as the herring fishing would then begin. So this was the way of life up there until the Second World War, and with no seasonal herring fishing people began to drift away. The herring fishing before the First World War was very qood. Lochboisdale was built up at this time, and was going to be the centre of business for the whole of South Uist and Eriskay for ever more. A big fishing was carried on by local boats and boats from Western Ross-shire, Skye and Loch Fyne.

There was one boat lost during those winter fishings, the *Cheerful* from South Lochboisdale. She sank with all hands, six men, in Loch Eyenort while hauling in nets full of herring. The night was bad and as she was the only boat there, no help was available when she sank. There were no herring boats lost from Eriskay through bad weather during all the time they were herring fishing, from the time it was first settled up to the present day, although they had some boats lost through grounding and collisions, and a few drownings through small twenty-foot boats capsizing. Whether it was good luck or their seamanship instincts, they must have been good at figuring out when to go to sea and when not to go to sea. Either way it must have been a record for a seagoing community that no herring boats were lost through bad weather. They had the worst bit of the Minch to fish in, as I know through experience of being on every run MacBrayne had. I was on the *Loch Seaforth* the first time she ever went on the Barra run. There was a big steel hatch lying on the foredeck in the same place from the time she was built and put on the Stornoway run eighteen years before. This particular day between Tiree and Castlebay she rolled so much that the hatch was being thrown all over the place.

Fishing boats that were getting past their best were sold to the North Minch and lasted another thirty to forty years. I know one of them, the *Industry*, sold from Eriskay in 1911, as she was no use there, was fishing out of Scalpay until 1960.

The skiffs from the Loch Fyne area used to fish out of Lochboisdale around the beginning of summer and were the ones which were going to finish off herring curing in our place. These skiffs were registered in Ardrishaig (A.G.) as this was the main fishing port for that area. A fleet of driftnets would be carried by them for camouflage, but a ringnet would be carried and covered with an old sail while alongside piers. The locals were always amazed at the 'Drishaigs', as they were called, keeping their nets under cover, as this would rot them. It took them a long time to catch on to why the nets were covered. They had Gaelic pet names for their ringnets so people would not know what they were talking about. Even to this day if you did not speak Gaelic you would have a job trying to figure out just what they were talking about. Their fishermen from Tarbert, Loch Fyne, are forever talking about 'sarach', the Gaelic for 'tired', 'ceo': fog, 'steall': splash, 'sugan': bunch and 'suag': patch. They were the first fishermen to use the ringnet.

Campbeltown and Ayrshire fishermen were working driftnets up to the First World War and before that time there seems to have been enough fish for everyone. It was only when things began to get scarce through overfishing that people started to complain. Boats were left rotting on beaches and fishing communities which supported a population were cleared. The fishing port of Ardrishaig which once had four hundred fishermen in one hundred boats, has not had fishermen staying there for sixty years. Their registration, 'A.G.' , has disappeared forever from the register.

It might be wrong for me to say it was the Loch Fyne fishermen who were the first to start the ringnet, for I heard an old man at home telling me once that no herring ever meshed for folks living on Tory Island. The reason he gave me was that when St Columba was chased out of Ireland by the Druids, he tried to land on Tory Island but was stoned by its population from the shore, and so St Columba left them the legacy that no herring would ever mesh in a net for them, hence the reason why they always had to use small ringnets.

Another story you would hear about St Columba from the old people was that he cursed the flounder while he was wading over from Canna to Sanday Island. Seemingly the flounder called out to him, '*Calumn gille cam casain*', meaning, 'Bow-legged Columba', because he had accidentally stood on her. St Columba then shouted back , '*Mha tha mise cam casain bhe uise cam bheul dhe dha suil air taobh dhe ceann*', meaning 'If I am bow-legged you will be squinty-mouthed with your two eyes on the same side of your head'. So this is the way the flounder is today.

The island of Tiree, meaning Iona's isle, in Gaelic Thioree, was where some of Saint Columba's monks were living, as there was not enough land to keep them in food in Iona and they had to use Tiree for cultivation. These monks must have left some blessing on Tiree as it was the Granary of the Islands at one time. The seas around it were always teeming with fish, its only drawback was that it was not blessed with a safe harbour.

These four years before the First World War the herring was drying itself on the shore. It was so close inshore that the men had to use ten-foot dinghies to catch it, and at low water they would shoot the nets onto the beaches after having carried them on their backs from the boats. Loch Bracadale was the main loch for the boats from our end of the south island, herring being caught there wherever salt water went. It was one solid sea of herring from MacLeod's Maidens to the beach at Roag. From there up to the head of the loch at Drynoch was also a sea of herring, but it was one morning in Scavaig that there was the biggest fishing of the lot. Every boat had as much in the nets as it could carry, and more. Our boat, the *Handy*, had just finished hauling ninety cran, and was getting the mast up when there were shouts from Murachaidh Ruadh's boat *Boy Peter*, to come and give them a hand, as she was hauling ten cran a net. There were cousins of theirs aboard her, the Ghostigh boys, so they went aboard. The day being calm they left the *Handy* alongside her. The twelve men then started hauling the *Boy*'s net, until at last, with the weight of the herring and all the men on one side, the water started coming over the rail and up to the coaming before all of them went to the other side of the deck. Some of the herring had to be shovelled over the side but she still managed to sail round Sleat Point, reaching Mallaig with a wee breeze of north west wind and carrying one hundred and three crans, while half the fleet of nets was left unhauled. There will never again be a fishing like the Skye lochs fishing, especially with the market and rail head being so handy in Mallaig.

By 1910 they were going for a bigger class of boat in our place, Banff built boats, some of which were to last for the duration of the drift net herring fishing. All of these boats were self owned and cost in the region of £200. Every crew member used to have a share in them, and as there were no engines in them when new, this kept the price down. It was only in later years that engines were installed in them, so by the time I remember them some had two engines.

These years before the First World War were good years for Castlebay, the steam drifter having arrived on the scene by this time. It is a wonder the locals' boats managed to survive among the catching power that had descended on them, they with nothing but mast and sail. After the end of June the inshore herring fishing almost came to an end. This is the time the drifter scored as she had the speed to land every day from Coll and Tiree bank. Oban then began to develop as a herring port with curing being done on the rail pier. The locals' boats out of Castlebay were well behind, as no local boat had an engine.

If families did not look after their money and save a bit they had a poor chance of ever owning anything in our part of the world. People who were not careful with their money kept on paying boat shares year after year to shore owners, usually a merchant or fish salesman. They were lucky in Eriskay as there were no drinking dens to do away with their hard-earned money. The only drinking they would do was when they were away at the fishing or over in Uist for corn or seed. They sometimes made fools of themselves in Pollachar, falling over rocks.

The first resident priest who was ever in Eriskay and who lies buried there, Father Allan MacDonald, was very much against drink. He managed to stamp it out among the younger generation, but there were older members well on in years who were given up as hopeless cases. So in my young days this was the generation, the ones Father Allan had kept sober, who were the mainstay of the island. I can only speak for my father's folk and they were all in the same category. They had to buy their own boats and gear and build their own houses with help from some merchant. The generation who came after them were mostly away from home sailing and were back to their grandfathers' way of life.

Looking at small islands like Scalpay, Eriskay, and a few other isolated ones with no pubs, they were more advanced in housing when there was no loan or grant available than people living near pubs on the main islands. I know myself I couldn't build a hen house while I was drinking, and after twenty-five years work I had only sixpence to show for it. The last burst I had, I woke up in the morning with no money as usual, so I had to stagger to the post office for some. On producing my post office book I said to the fellow behind the counter, 'Give me the lot'. He started babbling about having to take the book from me and sending it to my home address. That got me thinking with the cunning of the alcoholic who did not want my parents to see any mess, so I left the insignificant sum of sixpence in it.

Whether this way of life, sailing away from home, was a breeding ground for drunkards or whether Father Allan had it arrested with their fathers' generation I do not know, but I can only speak for myself. I was a hopeless case by the time I finished drinking. If it was not for the higher power in A.A. and, I believe, a few prayers, I would have died in some motel or else have finished my days locked up in some asylum. So I am telling this for the benefit of any of the younger generation who might think it is manly to drink. Well, it is not. It is only an easy way to get over weakness when you are feeling low. And it is progressive, in that the quantity of alcohol you need today to get over the weakness will double in a year's time, until eventually the time will come when you begin to lose employment and money will get scarce. It is then stealing can begin or mixing concoctions, for example putting gas into milk, or shaving lotion into cheap wine.

One seaman I heard talking one night at A.A. was telling how he used to boil gramophone records, a record player being on board, and everyone wondering where all the records were going to.

Most of the Castlebay herring fishing, especially around the autumn, was done by the steam drifters as the Tiree, Coll and Barra Head grounds were nasty places to work in bad weather, with the remnants of the Atlantic swell running in there. It was during these years that a song was composed which I heard John MacPhee (the Pic) sing in Custom House Dock in London. I learned only one verse of it before all hands would start shouting 'Shut up MacPhee!', and with the juke box blaring out Irish songs and people arguing and maybe a fight going on, The Mason's pub was like a Wild West saloon. Poor John did not get much of an audience to appreciate his talents when he began to sing his Gaelic song. He would not get further than the first verse, and I have never come across anyone who knows the rest of it.

I was at one time of my life Master on the Western Ferry, *Sound of Islay*, which ran between Campbeltown and Red Bay in Ireland. I was not long in Campbeltown until I met people I knew from my days at the fishing. Being sober at this time I was not going near pubs, but I was told there was a fellow who owned a hotel there and was married to one of the Meenans who had had the boats *Stella Maris* and *Regina Maris*, and who also knew many folk from Barra and Eriskay. My nose was bothering me once I heard this so I went into the hotel, and there was Denis who used to own The Viceroy at the Paisley Road Toll, Glasgow. Although I knew him right away, I could see he was not too sure who I was, as he knew hundreds from my part of the world. I realised he wanted to ask me something but the bar was too busy at the time. Soon, however, he got his chance and came up to me, then whispered, 'You're not John MacPhee, the Pic, by any chance?'. He thought he was going to have a racket on his hands. Barra always had Bards who could compose songs and some of the loveliest songs going were composed by Barra men living in exile.

The MacPhersons in East Kilbride could compose songs. Iagan Bachd, so called because he belonged to that part of the west side of Barra, and his brother, Alasdair Bheag, were orphans brought over from Barra by their auntie Ealsaid, who married an Eriskay man at the Balla. Alasdair Bheag married an auntie of mine. Iagan never married. They moved over to East Kilbride when it was crofted. If you were in their house and asked how their song-making was going, auntie Peggy would say, 'Oh, they are waiting for someone to die'. Iagan composed a nice song once about how he would be out fishing with a small boat and he used to get a tow from the bigger boats to Castlebay.

Between Iagan Bachd and Michael Ruadh, his nephew, they must have composed a thousand songs. Alasdair Bheag was no bard, but if he was not he had a knack, if he was given a good telling-off, for doing the impossible. I am sure that had he been given one of these kits from Woolworths and bullied into making a bomb, he would have had a go at it. He was along with our crowd in the *Handy*, and many a bad day they were glad of having him aboard when things started going wrong. He always had something up his sleeve to solve their problem in any awkward situation.

My father was the last of his family to get married and so all the family being now in the boat there was no place left for Alasdair Bheag, as there were also two cousins of my father in the boat. It was then Alasdair Bheag, along with another two families in his own community, Iagan Bheag and Big Neil the ferryman, bought the *St Theresa*, which they had for a number of years. The *St Theresa* was an old boat when they got her. This was another case of people spending good money on something that had had its day. However they were doing all right with her until one night coming from Tiree, and that finished the *St Theresa*. It started to blow after they had shot the nets, and with the battering she got before she reached Castlebay she started spewing her caulking and taking in water. Her final run was between Castlebay and Ludag. She never fished again, as she had one bad leak. I heard Alasdair Bheag talking about it years later, telling how he had a knife in the leak to keep the water pressure out.

I was only young at the time this happened, but I was once in the Marine School in South Shields, when one day a designer was brought in to give the boys a lecture on what to do if wooden lifeboats were damaged in any way or were leaking badly. He was lecturing on with half the class dozing off when he came to talk of the knife and the pressure of water. I looked at him right away, saying to myself, that fellow must have been to East Kilbride on holiday and got some tutoring from Alasdair Bheag.

There were two herring boats from East Kilbride at this time and some of the folks had shares in the boats over in Eriskay. It was all Eriskay they were dealing with in these days. The other boat there, the *St Bride*, belonged to a cousin of our family on my father's side, Ruaridh Taramoid. He collapsed and died one day hauling small lines in the Sound of Barra. He was just in his prime of life, nothing near retiring age. I knew these good people better than I did the ones living over in Eriskay, as my grandparents' house was just above the landing place. On Sunday afternoons they used to crowd there and any other time they were waiting to be ferried over or waiting for someone coming off the ferry. I do not believe I know anyone there today under fifty years of age. In the old days you were home when you reached there, whether you got across the Sound or not.

Another community across the Sound from Eriskay was South Glendale. I had a couple of uncles living there. It was very hard to work the crofts there as the ground was very steep. The first croft was bordering the bay, the rest being inland from there. The further inland the harder it was to work the crofts, as seaweed had to be carried from the shore. The bay was as difficult as the crofts for as soon as there were a few feet of ebb the whole bay emptied out.

There was hill common grazing for a thousand sheep, and that was all right while they had unpaid shepherds when the families were growing up. Once the children started going away it was a different thing, as the parents were getting old themselves by this time. It was a very difficult place to live in as it was so isolated before the road was built. They did not even have a school at first—they had to fight for it. They were taken to court at Lochmaddy and fined for not sending their children to the school which was at the back of beyond, midway between three communities. There were two of my uncles there, along with the MacIntyres, Murphy, Calumn Dubh and their sister, who was married to Manson. This man Manson could tell you a story and this day a few of them were talking about dogs who could run faster than others. Manson started telling about the fastest dog he had ever seen.

It happened when he was sailing deep sea, and he was on a train journey between Liverpool and Glasgow. He went into this carriage where a lady was sitting with a dog. Manson was smoking a pipe and the lady started getting on to him about it. Manson kept on smoking until the lady managed to get hold of his pipe and threw it out the window. To get even with her Manson got hold of her dog and also threw it out the window. So that was them even, with the lady saying she was going to inform the police when the train reached Carlisle.

But the dog itself solved all their rows and threatenings for it was standing waiting for them on the platform with Manson's pipe in its mouth.

There was also another worthy, Donnall Michael. Donnall was another one who had missed his vocation. It is a wonder that in his sailing away from home days he was not ever given a union delegate's job, being good at speaking and letter writing. I remember once being in uncle Alasdair's house and he was wild at Donnall Michael. They were fighting for the road at that time. Alasdair was saying that Donnall Michael starts off with the letter all right but before the end the devil starts land leaguing. But after all was said and done both of them died before the road was made.

Another time when these two worthies were to the fore was the time when a home girl, Mary Hatton, was about to be sent to the poor-house in Lochmaddy as nobody wanted her. She had been a while staying in houses around Eriskay and Glendale and being kicked around from one place to another. Donnall Michael and Alasdair were talking about the situation, saying what a shame that she was being sent to the poor-house. Alasdair said, 'I can't do anything for her. I have a home girl already living with us but your family should take her'. Donnall Michael looked at Alasdair and replied, 'I would sooner take the smallpox home than her'. He said this because Mary Hatton was a bit of a trouble-maker herself.

One day a crowd of them were talking about the time in Castlebay after one of the boats had a bad time of it with bad weather, spewing her caulking coming from Tiree. All of a sudden Donnall Michael was spotted in the crowd but he was not saying anything, which was something unusual for him. At this time he was in a boat called the *Rival*, an old boat that started fishing in Islay forty years before. Somebody then asked him how had they battled through and did they have it bad, to which he replied, 'I looked down into the fo'c'sle and there was Donnall Alasdair cutting the nails off Gillesbuig Calum Bheag'. This was the usual done thing when anyone died, their nails were cut and trimmed.

Another day selling flounders over in Barra some old character came round asking after all of his old pals over in Eriskay. He was asking about a particular person and was informed by Donnall Michael that he was for the last ten years 'playing hide and seek around the river Jordan'. The last time I saw Donnall he was in hospital in Stornoway. He had had his foot amputated and did not live long after that. He was a great favourite with the nurses. I remember a young nurse going on duty and asking him how he was today. 'I feel so good', said Donnall, 'I could run all the way from here to Tarbert, Harris with every dog in Lewis chasing me and not catching me'. So Donnall died in his bed at the end after a few close shaves with death on the sea.

One day he and another three along with him were pretty near it. They were fishing herring with a small boat and this particular Saturday they were in Castlebay with the herring catch. A good breeze was blowing when Donnall left with his boat. Luckily, a bigger engined boat, the *St Winifred*, left shortly after them. The *St Winifred* took the short cut through the Sounds at the mouth of North Bay, but they were puzzled when coming into the Sound of Barra when there was no sign of Donnall's boat. At last somebody spotted her. What happened next was going to be a bit tricky, as on approaching her they found that she was lying on her beam ends, with her mast and sail still set lying to the lee of her and her crew holding on to her rail facing windward. By this time the sail had been taken off the *St Winifred*, with the result that the rescue had to be done by engine only. The *St Winifred* could not get to lee of her, and also she could not go too near her to windward in case anyone would drown, but they had to do something and do it fast, as the crew were holding on to the capsized boat for their lives. The *St Winifred* was manoeuvred to a place to windward off her, where they would be able to get hold of the ropes which were thrown to them, and the four of them were on her rail at the same time, still with their oilskins and seaboots on.

Over the hill from South Glendale lies North Glendale, or South Lochboisdale, which was home to about twenty families at one time. It was also where the fish was cured and handled at Ferguson's store pier. It was the hub of activity in the old days where schooners were loaded with salt fish for southern Russia. The garden at the Ferguson store house was made with soil from Russia, ballast from schooners which had to be discharged before loading the dried salt fish. A Russian schooner-master who married a local woman is buried in the graveyard in Boisdale.

The ones I knew best at North Glendale were our relatives the Campbells, Clan Dhougall, whom I used to hear talking, while visiting our own crowd, about their various exploits back and fore on the loch where a few of them were drowned. One time some of the young fellows came over with a boat which Ferguson had, called the *Champion*. This was used for ferrying stores to his shops which were scattered between Eriskay and their own loch. The *Champion* was loaded with the usual commodities exported these days, things like dried salt fish, wool, eggs, winkles etc. I think these days there was not a soul unemployed, as anything taken to Ferguson's was always marketable. Aoghais Ruadh Campbell was the leader of this mob who were entrusted with the *Champion*, and getting the stuff aboard the *Dunara Castle* which was calling this certain day. On arriving over at the north pier there was some delay before getting the stuff aboard the bigger boat, and where better to spend the waiting time than in the bar, where people are inclined to forget their responsibilities with the demon juice having its effect. The *Champion* being loaded and low in the water with a rising tide, her rail caught in one of the jetty's piles, and with only one plank showing above water line it was not long until she began to sink. The shouting started from those on the pier to get the *Champion*'s lads from the bar, but by this time it was too late. The *Champion* was now on the bottom, with only a bit of her mast showing. Aoghais Ruadh, being for the heavy end of the stick, did what was easy enough to do these days, as he was sailing mostly, and took his passage aboard the *Dunara*, staying away long enough anyway for Ferguson to cool off.

The Campbells' father, Dougall, was our only relative from that branch of the family, as both of the uncles and his father were drowned together, leaving only Dougall and my great grandmother to struggle on, a hard thing for people orphaned at this time. They must have survived somehow, as there are a few alive today who can claim relationship to the mob.

Dougall must have been a bit of a boy anyway, for it was to to him that the Fergusons entrusted their smack, which they used for carrying their commerce between Glasgow and the islands. They also owned the island of Rhum and the inn at Pollachar, along with tacks and shops in Uist and Eriskay at this time. It was on one of these trips coming round the Mull of Kintyre on a bad night, and nearing the end of their tether with the elements against them, that Doughall's father and two uncles came from the other world to help him and remained with him until he got safely round the Mull. Another night sheltering at anchor in Canna during a gale, the smack was driven ashore, bursting at the seams when the sea water got in among the lime cargo she was carrying. They arrived home bare, with Ferguson conducting his own enquiry, wanting to know what had happened and where. 'We left her in Canna swollen as large as Ellen Dulaisach', says Doughall. This man, Ellen Dulaisach, must have been a bit of a heavyweight nobody in Uist could equal. This was the Fergusons' only try at carrying their own commerce, it being carried by others from then on. I sometimes envy these people who worked in these conditions having their own enquiry, judge and insurance, when I think of the times when a dent on a ship's side had to involve all sorts of paperwork, and if you were found more of the percentage guilty in stranding or a collision your whole career was liable to be ruined.

Doughall was a bit of a boy in more ways than one, like the time he was travelling from North to South Glendale along with one of our mob, carrying some container holding whisky which was to be used at a wedding in Eriskay. With the day so cold and snow on the ground, it was decided to have a *steall* out of the container, some of the whisky spilling into the snow in the process, after which Doughall started to scoop up the snow saturated with the whisky and eat it. Another time it was one of his own boys who was being married, and on our crowd getting over there it was found that Doughall was not preparing for the wedding like everyone else. On being asked why, he explained that he had not been invited as he had been a bad boy at the last wedding he had attended, where on being asked to propose a toast he repeated exactly what his wife had been saying before leaving home, which was nothing complimentary to the couple getting married.

There were a few herring boats in this community of South Lochboisdale. The Campbells had three at one time and Big Peter had one. Big Peter, another hardy, thought everybody should be the same as himself, like the time he was building his house and the stonemason went away to do some work on his own croft with no word of his coming back. At last Peter got fed up waiting, so this morning at first light he was off for the mason who lived about ten miles away. He arrived at the stonemason's house before anyone was out of bed, and when they eventually opened the door Peter wanted to know why they were not all out working, taking in the corn. He was informed that the horse's foot was sore. Peter never said another word, but got hold of the stoutest rope he could find so that he himself would take the place of the horse. Away he went for a load of corn, took it back and shouted, 'Make stacks of that'. Peter carried on all day bringing in the corn. He got a bit of rest when darkness came, then at first light he was on the move again. He worked all that day also, but the following morning he had the stonemason up on the scaffold building his house. Whether he carried him there too I was never told, but I was told by my grandmother's cousin, Lachlan MacIntyre from Boisdale village, that one night when Peter came to their house his wife was having a baby. It being a dark night and miserable with rain, Peter put Lachlan's mother on his back and carried her, running all the way till he reached his own house at South Lochboisdale. What I could gather from granny and Lachlan was that their family used to be in demand for any difficult birth. It must have been in the days before doctors and nurses were sent to the island, and so people had to make the best of it.

If Lachlan's mother's family were bringing them into the world, his father's family were the opposite. They helped them out of it, fighting. Clan Eachan Ruadh, Lachlan's father's family, must have been a crowd of wild boys in their time, when Lochboisdale was in its heyday for herring fishermen. They had a herring boat and one day in Lochboisdale they were having a free-for-all with another wild family who used to reside there, the ones who once put the local policeman in an empty herring barrel and left him floating off the pier until some fishing boat heard his cries and rescued him. Clan Eachan Ruadh had their father, who was getting old by this time, out at the pier with them. The free-for-all was going on, and Eachan Ruadh did not want to be left out of the melee, so off he went as fast as his legs would carry him to the nearest shop, Archie MacLellan's, shouting he wanted to buy a walking stick. He says to Archie in Gaelic, 'Hurry up with the walking stick so I can give one good stroke of it'.

Lachlan Ian Mhor, to give him his Gaelic name, was at sea most of his life, so he was more at home in granny's house in Eriskay as he knew everybody there from his sea-going days. He was telling me the biggest fright he ever had in his life was one night coming home from Lochboisdale after sending lobsters away with the mail boat. He was on his own in the cart and it was well past midnight, when suddenly coming towards him he saw, of all things, a goat. Lachlan was still shaking when he next saw two men running towards him, and thinking his end had come he says to himself, 'This is it', until the two were near enough for him to recognise them as two tinkers who were residing at the camp at Ceann Carisival. Lachlan breathed a sigh of relief when the two of them asked if he had seen any signs of a goat. It turned out that the goat had been purchased by them from Neil Walker near the other end of the island, and was running back home. Lachlan finished off his working years doing joinery work residing along with my granny.

They also had a cousin who married one of the crowd from South Lochboisdale, Seumas Airaig. He went to stay in Loch Eyenort when the place was broken up for crofting, and it was his son who was married to a first cousin of mine who was drowned there just before the war. It was coming near Christmas 1937, and after a spell of bad weather a lull came on the Thursday. On this same Thursday night they went out in the small boat for herring but had hardly shot their nets when it came on the blow again. With the nets full of herring, and being only an open boat, she sank, drowning two of them from the same family. There was only one who was saved, a sixteen-year-old youth. The short December day was over by the time we got to know of it in Eriskay on the Saturday, as communications were bad and their place isolated at the time. It was after mass on Sunday when our boat left for Loch Eyenort to see what could be done, as the bodies had still to be retrieved, but darkness had fallen before our boat arrived and so they could do nothing until daybreak the next day, as the boat was still sunk.

For months before this tragedy my father was getting very little sleep in the boat because of the noise he kept hearing on deck, just above his sleeping quarters, a noise resembling boards being thrown on the deck. At first light on the Monday morning the operation began to get the sunken boat up. Once they got hooked on to her they managed to winch her to the surface. There were still the nets and dead herring aboard her and so she had to be emptied before they could bale her. It was the floorboards that were thrown out of her onto the deck of our boat that were making the noise that my father heard months before. As soon as the boat was taken out of the way, and as no bodies had been found around her or the nets, preparations had to be made to sweep for them. Great lines were shot and a sweep was made to the north. It was not very long until one body was caught in the sweep. It was a while afterwards, when the Campbells from South Lochboisdale went further inshore with their sweep, that the other one was found, minus his oilskin. He must have managed to take his oilskin off and swim a bit for the shore before he drowned.

Being so handy for the north side of Lochboisdale and the bar, ones from South Lochboisdale were inclined to be a bit fond of the 'water of life', but I do not think it ever interfered with their work. One of them was Ruaridh Campbell, or 'the Case', as he was known to the island seamen. This was because in his sailing days at bar closing time, when others were buying bottles of beer for carry-out, Ruaridh would order a case of beer. It was a Glasgow publican, Tony, in The Moy bar, Glasgow, who stayed in Uneag's who gave him the name. Sailing from Custom House Dock, London, where he was for a good part of his life, Ruaridh was once on the verge of sailing on a trip, after spending his hard-earned cash from the trip before, when he received a letter from his mother threatening him, saying that if he did not send her any money she was going to the poorhouse. Ruaridh wrote back saying she had better wait until he went home at the end of the next trip, and the two of them would go together. Arriving home after being away ten years and not having saved a penny for all his sailing the seven seas, he and his mother were sitting at home one day, when his mother said to him that he was an awful drinking man, drinking every penny he ever earned. 'Yes', Ruaridh said, agreeing with her, 'and a good share of what the rest earned too'.

Seamen and builders that family were, the father capable of building some of these hotels in Oban and also the catholic church in Castlebay. The house where I was born in Eriskay was built by the grandfather of the family. It is now well over one hundred years old and is still standing and habitable. But it was for their Bardach they were most famous. Ruaridh's father, uncle Shonnie, his brothers Aoghais Ian and Ian who died not so long ago out in New Zealand, were all talented in composing songs. But Ruaridh was the prince of them all as many ceilidhs broadcast include his two most famous songs, 'Peggie e Gradh' and the Aeroplane song, about his experience of flying from Brisbane to Townsville, Australia in the 1930s.

It was Ferguson being in the middle of it all that made this small community so outstanding, as nearly all business dealings were hatched there.

Ferguson's books for various transactions for the years before the First World War would have made interesting reading, as I know he was the one to approach for transaction dates concerning boats when old timers used to try to get the Lascar pension, which amounted to five shillings a week, but were paid it in a lump sum every three months. These funds, I think, ran out long ago, as new entrants were having difficulty obtaining the pension before the war. Genuine cases like Eriskay and South Lochboisdale always blamed this on panhandlers getting it, whose only sea-going experience was wading out to fiachs, or small tunnels under the rocks, for lobsters in summer time. I believe if you had some tub that would float and were paying the boat coin (insurance) you qualified for it. Being young at the time I was not very interested in these things, only hearing old-timers talking, but I think it must have been a half crown a year they were paying to the Shipwrecked Mariners Society that qualified them for benefit.

I remember once, anyway, uncle Eoin having his boat repaired and I saying to him, 'I believe you'll be looking for our share to foot the bill', as we had the use of the boat like himself. He replied that if we had any surplus money he would take it, but the boat did not cost him a penny to repair as the repair bill was given to Aoghais Clerich, who was running Ferguson's store, and who forwarded it to the right sources. However on being reminded that these yearly subscriptions were only for damaged boats, his reply was that he was quite happy about it. Whatever the Big Fellow on the other side had to say about it we have still to find out, as I believe we all have to do a bit of dilly-dallying when we get over there.

Hearing these old-timers complaining about these panhandlers over in Uist receiving this Lascar pension, I was inclined to agree with them, as the only ones I ever saw were on trips over to Pollochar in *Sgoath e Bags*, the bag boat, or mail carrier, with their carts and horses, wearing heavy woollen clothes and tackety boots. The MacIsaac boys warned me to keep away from them before they would feed me to their big Clydesdale horses. They certainly did not look like the Cape Horn breed to me who would qualify for a seagoing pension.

Nobody our way was like Alasdair Aoghais Mhor from Bul nam Bodoch, Barra, for tale-telling. Alasdair was past master at telling tales, and although being a generation older than the engines when they came around the fleet, Alasdair was not going to be left out of having the experience and his own way to drive them. Someone remarking to him one day on seeing an engine working that it was a pity they were not around in his day, Alasdair replied that they were around in his day and better than that, he had driven one of them. It happened when he was at the east coast fishing, and one of the engines had been installed in the boat he was on, and the fellow who was driving it went sick. With so few mechanically-minded men around, a replacement for him was hard to find. A flat calm was on, something the engine was put aboard for in the first place, and it looked as though it was going to be a night on the beach for them when Alasdair volunteered to do the job. He got the engine going and off they went for the fishing grounds, but on arriving there Alasdair had a job slowing down the engine, with the result that the old skipper started getting on to him for taking them out. Alasdair was not to be beaten. He told the skipper to put the wheel hard over and keep the boat going round in a circle until the engine got dizzy and then it would stop.

Playing pranks on characters around the community was a favourite pastime of Ruaridh e Phosto, who was well known among merchant seamen for his many years sailing as bosun, but on spending any time at home was always up to some mischief. This particular time he was home, some travelling folks were around, and so Ruaridh and his mate Anthony, who resided for many years in Oban, decided to pay Alasdair Aoghais Mhor a visit dressed as travelling ladies. They dressed themselves up with clothes borrowed from old women who lived around and set off with the usual baggage these folks carry around in some newly-bought pails. The two of them were in business, making for Alasdair's house first as they knew the travelling folks had not been that far yet.

Most of these travelling folks visiting our parts were from the Marybank area of Stornoway, all of them speaking the Lewis Gaelic, and the two of them would have acquired a smattering of this lingo having sailed with Lewis boys in ships away from home. On arriving at Alasdair's home they went inside, where some business was transacted with pails being bought, but Ruaridh decided to get Alasdair riled up by demanding a place to stay for the night, which Alasdair refused, and so Ruaridh said something about his religious views which he was sure would get Alasdair's temper up. There is nothing to get the folks from the outer isles more upset than religion, especially the older generation who were in the habit of always sticking together when going to the east coast fishings, which were the mainstay of the islands in Alasdair's young days. The north islands were protestant and the south islands catholic, with the dividing line in Benbecula. If these travelling people had any religion the people down our way did not know what it was. But this night on hearing a Lewis voice passing some remarks about religion, Alasdair, even in old age, was ready for a fight. The shouting started, with Alasdair getting them out of the house saying, '*Beanichaid Ruadh e dueil dh fhearr e dorus oirt*', meaning, 'You ginger-headed, gypsy she-devil—take the door'.

These travelling folks' religion could not have been practised by the man whom I heard someone from Lewis tell me was playing the bagpipes on a Sunday and the minister went to him to give him a telling-off for breaking

the Sabbath. The minister asked him did he not know the first command-
ment, which tells people to keep holy the Sabbath day. This started the
traveller thinking of any tunes related to that name. At last he gave up,
saying to the Minister in Gaelic, 'You whistle it and I'll play it'.

Alasdair Aoghais Mhor, if in company, was always on about his fighting prowess in his young days, and this was the case with him once while
visiting his nephew Michael Bhan who had hurt his foot, an injury which
had to be put in plaster of Paris by the doctor. So this was the state of affairs,
with Michael Bhan lying down and Alasdair giving a running commentary
on some skirmish he had been involved in during his young days, getting
so worked up, with his hands flying, that he hit the plaster of Paris which
started panic stations. The result was that they had to send once more for
the doctor, as the plaster had been broken.

There were some hard men our way one time who would not let anybody trample on them, as the curers who tried to bring the trawler there to
land herring found out, the trawler men being too happy to escape with
their hides intact. These trawlers bred a tough race of men, but there were
some tough breeds our way too, as was seen by my folks one day they were
going into Lochboisdale with the *Handy* while there was a trawler ashore
on the point below the hotel. This trawler was the *Lily Melon*, whose skipper was well known around the islands for fishing too near the shore. Getting local men aboard for pilotage duties was his way around this, and this
day it was Eoin Neil Michael he had for pilot. They were in the wheelhouse
together when she touched the point below the hotel on a falling tide, but
with only half an hour to go to low water it was decided to leave her on and
let the flood lift her off. With the skipper and Eoin Neil Michael having
taken more than what was good for them of the demon juice in the bar, a
wrestling match was started in the wheelhouse after she touched, one blaming the other, but with space limited it was decided to get into the pond on
the foredeck to get into a proper battle. So this was the situation aboard the
trawler when the *Handy* went alongside them to see if any help was needed,
the crowd in a circle cheering away, the skipper and Eoin Neil Michael in
the centre of it all, battering hell out of each other.

Travelling between Lochboisdale and Eriskay in the old days was a nightmare if you were not met at the pier by a boat, and none knew this better
than the poor women who used to go to the herring gutting, and had to
endure the long travelling home from the east Anglia fishing around the
end of November. More gutting at the Clyde herring ports or mainland
west coast ports was on the cards, but their biggest nightmare, as sure as
anything, was the fear of a Minch storm waiting for them. Candles would
be lit and prayers said the day the *boranich Sasun*, or the English herring
gutters, were coming home. But on reaching the pier at Lochboisdale their

Gutters in Yarmouth, my auntie Mary Kate eighth from right, the rest all from the Isle of Lewis

nightmare was just beginning, as they used to have to hike eight miles to East Kilbride carrying a chest loaded with all sorts of crockery bought at the barrows. After reaching East Kilbride they were among relatives and more or less at home until, weather conditions permitting, they would get the ferry across. No wonder there would be sighs on reaching Eriskay shore, sighs coming from the cockles of their hearts and murmurs of *'Meudal air e Dh fhearr nach gluas'*, meaning, 'Love to the one that won't move'.

If you got into a conversation with one of these old-timers, ones who never got married, about the travelling they used to do from Shetland to Land's End and right around the coast of Ireland from Buncrana to Kinsale, they would have some stories to tell you. Like our next door neighbour, Caorsdith Nighean Ian, who would talk about the Dutch herring fishermen trying to get off with them saying, 'Me like frau', and the Norwegian whaling men trying to pull one of them away with them, and the girls knocking spots off them to get her away. These girls were so innocent and young, thinking that the Norwegians from the whaling factory were going to melt her for margarine, somebody having informed them that is what they did with the whales they caught at the whaling station they had in the Shetland Islands.

Caorsdith Nighean Ian never married and was at the gutting all her life. She never got rid of her sea-sickness. I remember one day between Eriskay and Castlebay, being aboard the family boat *Ocean Star* with gutters taking their passage home, when Caorsdith and myself were the worst for sea-sickness. All the girls aboard needed some doctoring, but I heard uncle

Alasdair on coming down to the fo'c'sle say to Ben Stack John, 'Are those two devils still at it?', and Ben Stack replying that he did not think we had any more to spew except our guts.

I remember one day at the time of the *Politician* being in my father's house, and a couple of characters from Eoligarry, Barra, were over for some loot. Caorsdith was also there along with this pair, Peter e Gillesbuig and Domnall Ailean, who was for years on the mail boat running from Oban to our islands. This Oban run I would say would surpass any other run on the British coast for bad weather. Domnall Ailean must have doctored a great many suffering from sea-sickness, as all the women in Eriskay of his generation would greet him like a long-lost brother when he visited the island. This day anyway, with the whisky in abundance, the talk was about one bad crossing when Caorsdith was nearly dying. It being after the end of season square-ups, with these old mail boats loaded with herring gutters, as well as boys who used to go to the east coast fishing, it is more than likely that drink would be flowing freely. They had this tough guy, Spog e Tustan, aboard, who was throwing his weight around, saying he would take on everybody. He was not long challenging folks when Barran from East Kilbride took him on. This then was the set up aboard the mail—gutters seasick all over the place and Spog e Tustan and Barran having a fight in the centre of it all.

While Caorsdith and Domnall Ailean were telling this story, Peter e Gillesbuig was not getting a word in, but when Peter had his say there was no stopping him. He was a character. I remember one time he had the boat over and moored at the Haun. Peter had friends everywhere and it took him days before he had finished visiting the lot. Granny's house was where most of them from Barra had their headquarters, so I went along with Peter to visit a family he had known for a long time. The most exciting part of his life was the journey he made to Canada along with the emigrants. He would tell you about the ones he had for neighbours there, Eskimoes, Red Indians, you name them, Peter had them next door to him. He had been out in Canada and back since he had seen one old member of the family who was bedridden. I managed to work myself into a position where I could hear Peter telling the old one about his ills. He had been away in Edinburgh to undergo an operation. Seemingly he was saying they took out his heart, put it on the table in front of him, saw the parts that were damaged, and he then had to wait for a week until parts came back from London.

Peter would have a notebook and pencil for taking down items anyone needed, as he was saying that a member of his family was working in a big wholesale place in some city. There were many children around father's house, and their names would go into the book for some item of clothing. When it was the day for Santa Claus to come, somebody recognised Peter's boat coming over from Barra and everyone began to rub their hands with glee. Peter came minus the bag plus a tale of woe, the big shop had been bombed and he began to give numbers of all the people and van horses that had been killed.

I remember he was with Squirry in my father's house, and we had to go to the Haun for Peter's boat so that my father and Squirry could go to the Rhu Caol with the loot from the *Politician*. When we reached the Haun some children had gone away sailing with Peter's boat, and so he started on saying to granny how on earth did she manage to live amongst such a crowd of thieves and robbers since she originally came from Barra. Anyway we got a hold of Peter's boat and sailed her past all the rocks to Rhu Caol, where Squirry boarded her.

It did not matter how much seagoing men from the west side of Barra (called Borveachs) did, the others were still hard on them for not being up to their own standard of seamanship. I know Squirry was in the navy along with uncle Alisdair in the First World War, whatever else seagoing he did, but whenever a joke was about to be told it was always about the poor Borveach. Any Barra man I sailed with who saw a big lift to be carried would always wish he had Each a Tun to carry it, the Tun being a Boreach who had a Clydesdale horse for working his croft.

There were some hard men and women from our part of the world, they had to be to survive. Their way of life meant being able to hold their own aboard anything afloat and ashore. I think herring gutting must have been the hardest work for women, along with the travelling they had to do, as herring had a habit of boom years in certain places, its fishing being very unpredictable. They had to be up and away at a moment's notice to some other herring port where the herring was plentiful.

The only enemy action one of the MacBrayne's boats was engaged in during the two world wars happened on the Oban run one day in May 1918 when the *Plover*, which was doing the run, was attacked by a German submarine. Being attacked by a German sub aboard any ship can be a hellish experience, but it was worse aboard the *Plover* where space was limited with so many passengers aboard her, a lot of them services personnel travelling home on leave. I do not know how many men passengers there were but there were thirty-five women, one of them with a baby in arms. It seems the baby was separated from her mother in the abandoning after being passed aboard the life boat, the mother not having been allowed aboard as the boat was overcrowded. This shelling of the *Plover* while sailing between Gunna Sound and Castlebay with that crowd of passengers must have caused some panic, the *Plover* answering back with whatever armaments she had and eventually scaring off the sub. By this time the two crowded lifeboats had left her, and they in their turn were left to their fate with one of them landing up on the west side of Rhum, the other making Castlebay under oars. I do not believe there are many alive today who were through that day's excitment, but the baby who got separated from its mother, if alive, will today be in the seventies. What was left of passenger and crew aboard her once the submarine made off managed to sail her into Castlebay, no lives being lost in the shooting, abandoning, or sailing of lifeboats towards the land.

The only other exciting thing that ever happened on that run, apart from the terrible weather conditions, was one day in the early 'thirties when the *Loch Earn* sank the Rosehearty drifter, *Craig Earn*. This happened in broad daylight when it is a common occurrence among seagoing personnel to drive themselves beyond human endurance, a human's constitution being able to take so much and no more. It was a cold day and they were waiting on great lines shooting time. All hands were asleep, except the skipper aboard the *Craig Earn*, who was in the wheelhouse on his own. With the boat sailing round at dead slow speed he decided to go into the fiddly, which is at the top of the stockhold, to warm himself. Having been too long without sleep the warm air helped him to doze off, leaving the drifter to go around in circles, with the wheelhouse unmanned. The *Loch Earn*, which was sailing from Gunna Sound to Castlebay, saw the drifter in plenty of time, but took this going around in circles as the ordinary day to day work of the fishermen who are always plagued with gear fast on the bottom and so forth. Not until it was too late did the *Loch Earn* realise that the drifter was sailing around with the wheelhouse unmanned, and before a course of action could be taken, she had hit her. Fortunately no lives were lost, but it was a near thing for the drifter crew, as they were all asleep when she was hit in the fish hold. The water pouring into it sent her to the bottom in a matter of minutes, but not before the crew had clambered aboard the *Loch Earn*. Although no one was lost or hurt, these collisions always have a habit of hurting the ones responsible. The two involved in this event I know well from my seagoing time, and although only partly to blame, their owners had no qualms about emptying them out a hard pill to swallow, especially for the early thirties. However by the time I knew them, after a few lean years, they were at the top of their careers.

This happening in eighty fathoms of water everyone thought they had heard the last of the *Craig Earn*, until one day a trawler became entangled in her with her gear, and not knowing what it was, kept on hauling to see if she could retrieve her gear. On the entanglement breaking water they were shocked to see that it was the *Craig Earn*, and if they could have got help from another vessel to lash her between the two of them they reckoned they could have salvaged her. However, with no help being on hand, they had to let her go, but not before they managed to retrieve all the great lines which were stowed aboard her under-deck.

I was with a Lewis man aboard a deep-sea ship once and we were talking about fishing. He began to tell me that when he came home from the navy he went to Stornoway and saw a fish salesman to find out if there were any jobs going in drifters. He was out of luck, no jobs, but the sales-man told him there was a small boat from over the mainland area of Ross-shire looking for a couple of men. He went aboard her and got a job, himself and a fellow from Point. This man I sailed with was in east coast drifters all his time at the fishing, so these barrel nets were new to him. I asked him if he had an iron man, or hand winch, for hauling her. 'No', he replied in Gaelic, '*Bha bheist mhor dhe Rhuach again*', meaning, 'we had a big beast from Point to do the job'.

Other fishermen who used to fish in the Minch belonged to Avoch in the Black Isle. They used to come from 10 May to the end of August. Fish or no fish, they were there. They seemed to be a sober, inoffensive sort of people who would mind their own business and who spoke a dialect different from their neighbouring towns and villages. At one time they spoke something similar to English West Country folk, from whom some were descended, as Lord Lovat had taken some families up from there to fish his oyster beds in the Moray Firth. When I used to go out in the family boat as a boy the one I remember best was Eoghain Dubh MacLennan, as Eriskay folks called him. He was an old man then—he must have been about the seventy mark—as he could talk about the day of the disaster at the haaf fishing, having been there as a young boy. He was forever with this boat the *Maggie MacLennan* and his big dog, getting crans of herring at the Curachan even with a fish famine on.

How these Avoch folks were different from neighbouring Easter Ross fishing communities, who had at one time a big fishing fleet, was told to me by the older generation. If asked what their strongest memories of the west side haaf fishing were, the answer was the Ross-shire men scolding and arguing with one another in Gaelic. There were people in Castlebay from every fishing community in the east coast, over a thousand boats, but the Rossich must have been outstanding among the rest. They can shout plenty when they are arguing in Gaelic, for I remember when I was young going into a bar over in the United States. The States at that time, over fifty years ago, had plenty of people who could not speak English, as they were old before emigrating. Sitting on stools at the bar along with my mates we were hearing this loud talking coming from a crowd sitting further away at a table, and on catching a few Gaelic phrases I went over to enquire where on earth they hailed from, and found that they were from Easter Ross, Suther-land, Embo and Balintore. I was thinking back to what I was hearing about them when I was young. If half a dozen could cause a din like that, what was it like when a thousand of them were around?

To say that they were all from Easter Ross might be a bit unfair, as all villages up around that area with a Gaelic-speaking population were Rossich to the west side folks, even the ones in Caithness. How Caithness never had a Gaelic-speaking population is a bit of a mystery, when people around the Mull of Galloway area could speak it at one time. But there is one nice thing that can be said for Caithness folks, especially the people of Wick, and that is the way the catholic church built in their town over one hundred years ago was never interfered with in all that time. I was very surprised that having no catholic population a catholic church was built in that part of the world. Thinking it was only a temporary place built for tourists I found out it had been built in 1850. The story I was told was at that time the French fishing fleet from Normandy and Brittany fishing ports were bound for Iceland, but having just sailing smacks in these days, rather than face the rigours of the Atlantic they kept for shelter to the east side of the British Isles, Wick being their final port of call. On arrival there they were horrified to see that the place, due to poor sanitation and bad water, was in the grips of a cholera epidemic, with those who were alive too weak to bury the dead. Wick at this time was very isolated and the sea the only link with the outside world. These French fishermen must have had a lot of courage, as when others might have left the folks in Wick to their fate, they started to tend the sick and bury the dead and saw that everything was all right before they left. As a mark of gratitude the people of Wick gave them a bit of land and helped them to build a church, which stands there to this day. This is another story of people born to the sea giving each other help in their hour of need, regardless of creed or country.

To nearly all herring fishermen between Nairn and Buckie before the last war, Castlebay was their headquarters in the summer. It was thanks to them and their patience that the place was kept open, as there used to be bad patches there with blank days in succession. Their patience would always be rewarded as a couple of good shots of Tiree herring would fetch a big price, having once in the summer of 1936 gone for a few shillings over the seven pounds a cran. The Eriskay crowd would get fed up with no fish and go home to carry their peat. I have seen them a few times, the young, the old men and the women, having to sail small boats home from Bun Sruth, the herring boats having picked their crews there. It was always after they went away to the peat that the telegram would arrive from the fish salesman in Castlebay, 'BIG SHOTS FROM TIREE', then the round up would start with messengers running all over the place to get the boats out of the Haun before the tide dropped. With crews living as far apart as Ben Stack, Glendale, East Kilbride and Bun Struth at the peat, the round-up was no fun.

If things were slack during the winter fishing these days it was Allen Bheag in Loch Carnan who would set the ball rolling with his few crans. But these boats, mostly from Burghead and Hopeman, the *Hero*, *Ardent*, *Ben Mhor*, *Letitia* and Sandy and Donnachie Jack with the *Rose Valley* and *Energy*, were the mainstay of the Castlebay herring fishing in the slack years before the war. The *Hero* once went for five weeks without cranning, a long time for an old drifter whose expenses were very high, being coal-burning. The *Ardent*, being a nice diesel-driven boat, the expenses were negligible. They acquired her when they sold their drifter the *Gowanlea*. The *Letitia* got shots when others did not for the simple reason that others valued their lives more than Jock Dean, and these hardy loons who were aboard her. I don't know how she managed to weather the nights she was at sea with a sixty horse-power right in her nose—the pounding must have been terrific. Slater with his blow lamp would keep her going in any kind of weather, but weather it she did, and as these summer blows did not usually last long, by the time daylight came the wind would start taking off which enabled them to haul their shot. By the time they reached Castlebay it would probably be dead calm, which would send the rest running.

The Jacks were also there and they were a hardy breed, old Sandy and Donnachie, but I think the hardiest of the lot of them was their nephew, Willie. Badly wounded during the war when the coaster he was in, one of Henry McGregor's, was mined on the east coast, he was picked up more dead than alive. One of his legs was so badly injured that it had to be amputated. A man with such injuries could have lain back for the rest of his life, but not Willie. What he lost with his leg he must have gained in his body, for he was still fishing and that can be a strenuous job for the most able-bodied. In my time at sea I have only seen one other man fishing who had lost his whole leg and that was David Sinclair from Portree, who used to sail in the *Marshali*. I used to wonder how he managed, as ring netting needed somebody lively jumping in and out of boats, but he stayed in the one boat. It was one evening when passing the *Marshali* hauling the ringnet that I saw David at the cork ropes with the crutch jammed between his elbow and the boat's rail, hauling away.

There was another hardy boy with a wooden leg below his knee. His name was John McLellan, the Taylor, and he had shops in Lochboisdale, Kilpheer and Eriskay. In his young days he did a bit of deep-sea sailing, a job that needed the use of both your hands and feet. He carried a bit of weight even in his young days. The crew had been aboard a couple of months when one day the chief officer said to the man at the wheel, on seeing John climbing up the mast, that McLellan for all his weight was the liveliest man on board. 'Aye', said the man at the wheel, 'considering he has got a wooden leg'.

'He's got a what?', asked the chief officer.

'A wooden leg', said the man at the wheel.

'You're kidding', said the chief officer, 'the man is at the truck already.'

I remember being in a pub in Glasgow one day with the sailors around the Taylor, who was on business there, as he had the three shops, cars and lorries on the road by this time. I think the talk was about rigging the *Jumbo* when the Taylor said, 'What a boy the Taylor was climbing the masts on one leg'.

There was another Taylor in Stockinish in Harris fishing in the *Fair Morn*, which he had before he finished with the fishing. He was a lively lad too. I heard somebody saying he tried to get a boat when the Highland Development started but they considered him too old.

I had a cousin John who was also at the ring netting and who also had a wooden leg below the knee. This ring netting could be trying for the most of us, with jumping from one boat to the other in bad seas, but John did it for ten years. He was dogged with bad luck from the day he was born, being only a few weeks old when his mother died. On his first trip to sea at sixteen the boat in which he was serving, the *Port Hobart*, was sunk by a German raider and the next four and a half years he spent as a prisoner of war. He was considered too old to be repatriated along with the very young ones and the women and children who were passengers aboard some of the ships captured, and who were taken home through Switzerland by the Red Cross. After this ordeal, and eventually being set free by the army, he was home for a while then went back to sea. He was hardly a year at sea when his foot got caught in a wire and had to be amputated below the knee. As things were pretty strict with the Merchant Navy Pool he was finished with deep sea so he was a couple of years at home getting used to his wooden leg. It was only when we started ringnetting that he got a job along with Bill Ritchie in the *Blair Mhor* of Rosehearty. Poor Bill was himself plagued with bad luck, so bad that he died while still a young man after his health broke. It was Bill who was in that escapade between the *Craig Earn* and the *Loch Earn*. During the war he was a lieutenant in the navy, getting decorated when he managed to throw an unexploded bomb that landed aboard back into the sea where it exploded, nearly throwing the craft he was in out of the water. Things like that happened during the war with bombs and torpedoes.

A ship once came into port with an unexploded torpedo on her deck. She was rolling heavily in the Atlantic when, as the torpedo was about to hit her after travelling near the surface, she took a heavy roll which put her bulwark right under long enough for it to come aboard. It was only with the first sign of daylight, when the second mate was called about breakfast time, that he took the deadlight off the porthole to see what the weather was like for taking sights, when he saw the torpedo wedged outside his room. The weather was so bad no naval personnel could come aboard, and so it had to stay there, giving those aboard a few anxious moments until she reached the Tail of the Bank on the river Clyde where the torpedo was defused.

There were certain well-known houses in the islands where fishermen and gutting girls from Eriskay would stay. One of the houses was tigh Aoghais Bochd in Lochmaddy, during its herring curing day. I was too young at the time except to hear them talking, but this Aoghais Bochd must have been a well-known character, who, along with keeping an open house for almost everyone, did herring-hawking all over the North Uist crofts. People going to attend at the court room all stayed at his tigh. These days court rooms went on shires, so Lochmaddy was central for the bit of Inverness-shire the islands involved.

I remember before the war a Lochmaddy man staying in grandpa's house doing post office work. He and grandpa were talking about the court there and how little they had to do, the Lochmaddy man saying that if it was not for Barra they would just as well close it, not knowing granny came from there.

There were always squads from Barra going there, especially at Hallow-een, when they went wild. I remember when they were fighting for the road and they refused to pay the road tax of the day for their vehicles. They hired the *Reul na Maidne* for getting there. After the court was finished they started drinking, and when the bar closed they went to the gutting girls' huts and a fight started between the vehicle owners, the *Reul*'s crew and some Lochmaddy boys. The gutting girls called the police and they cleared them out of the huts, or so they thought. It was in the small hours that some of the girls, three of them to a bed, heard some movement under their bed and started screaming to know who was there. It was Alick Eoin Mhor, who for safety had rolled himself under the bed when the fight began and had fallen asleep. Anyway their trip to court was not in vain as they were fined. A new road started to be built the next year, work that was going to last for three years. The gutting crew of girls belonged to Eriskay.

Another house was tigh Calumn Stewart in Uig in Skye, also in its her-ring hey-day. Those were the days when there were fifteen herring boats in Eriskay employing over eighty men, and there must have been sixty gut-ting girls gutting the herring. The island population at the time, counting sailors and girls at domestic service, reached six hundred, with over one hundred at school.

I stayed in tigh Calumn Stewart, which is now a bed and breakfast. I said to Margaret I would not be the first from Eriskay to stay there. She remembered having Eriskay girls sleeping anywhere they could find a space when there was a heavy fishing on and more girls had to be taken on to handle it.

Calumn Stewart was pier master. He owned a cow which must have been living on salt herring, as there were always screams that *bo* Calumn Stewart was in one of the barrels. I think she had a way she could use one of her horns to lift the lid off the barrel. Anybody making a beast of himself eating herring in our island was compared to *bo* Calumn Stewart.

Another Skye man who will go down in history is Pelorus, who was nearly all his sea-going life employed by MacBrayne's on their west coast boats, sailing from junior mate to master. He never married, why not I don't know, for he had plenty of girlfriends. Once when Captain Cowan, the su-per, was telling him to go home, get his gear and join some ship, 'Oh', says he, 'I have got my gear in the left luggage'.

'Why don't you get yourself a wife?', says Captain Cowan.

'I couldn't leave her in the left luggage', he replied.

His best joke was when he went into a posh Glasgow hotel and saw lobster on the menu. After a while the lobster came on a plate along with some instruments for breaking it up. Instruments Pelorus did not have a clue how to work but he was not to be beaten. After a while gazing at what was in front of him he got it on the floor under the table when no one was looking and started breaking it up with his foot. Poor Pelorus is not with us any more.

A word must be said of a man who had more hate and stones thrown at him than anyone in the Western Isles. This man was Roddy MacLean, skipper of the *Maggie MacLean* from Berneray, whose only crime was using a ring net full time when nearly all others were using drifters. My folks knew him well, as they were using ring net themselves during the winter. Last time I saw him travelling in MacBrayne's he was getting old and had retired, but he still had a little fight left in him, Scalpay being the place he hated most. Bad and all as the Eriskay crowd were the day they were going to throw him over the pier in Lochboisdale, the Scalpay crowd were twice as bad. Then he goes on about a Scalpay-born minister, newly ordained, who was sent to Berneray, his first sermon being how to be kind, charitable etc. to one another, and the last time he saw him he was throwing stones at him from the pier in Scalpay. Looking around the bay in Mallaig and seeing Scalpay and Eriskay boats all with ring nets on their stern he could only shake his head.

I relieved one of the brothers in the *Lady of Fatima* one year and she was neighbouring a Harris boat the *Harmony*. There were another two ring net boats in Scalpay. They were to build a fleet of new boats in years to come, twelve in number, with Highland Development help, but I think the days of the ring net were over by the time the generation of young ones who knew no other kind of fishing had made a success of it.

All these ring net boats are a thing of the past. There are none of them left. I have not met any of the *Harmony* crowd since. The last person from the bay in Harris she came from was a woman I met in Vancouver who was a cousin of some of the crew. She wanted to know were there any Harris men aboard our ship. There were none but I was able to give her some news from her homeland.

Chapter 5

Jimmy Boyle, the van and the flock of hens—Paisley Road, Glasgow: home from home for the seamen from our islands—Work on the rigging gangs—Sly grogs, speakeasies and the Lochboisdale Hotel—'Shipwrecked eggs and a mug of mud!'— Mallaig and the coming of the railway—A fishing boat with a bad name—Staying sober at sea—The great lines—A poverty-stricken time—On the fish van in Glasgow—A Saturday night in Stornoway—'Seeing the world' on the merchant ships

A fellow came to Lochboisdale to buy shellfish and had a van but had no one to drive it around to collect lobsters etc. There were not many drivers in Uist at the time so Jimmy Boyle took the job after one of Calumn an Aoghais's boys had shown him how to work the gears. Off he went to Ard Mhule where the lobster fishermen were fishing, collected the lobsters and started back for Lochboisdale. The roads being bad at that time, just cart tracks around these crofting villages, Jimmy Boyle was driving as best he could being chased by dogs, until he came upon a flock of hens. He tried to brake, but being strange to the gears the van went faster, ploughing right through the whole flock. Poor Jimmy did not have any choice but to carry on with feathers flying all over the place and people screaming blue murder after him. He did not stop until he reached Lochboisdale, and had time to examine the van. Underneath he found feathers, dogs' hair, a couple of hens and a big cockerel in the mudguard.

A great scholar, Jimmy was. Many a letter and fishing discharge he wrote out for the boys in the Black Man pub at the south side of Clyde Street Ferry, Glasgow, this pub being right where you came off the ferry which the boys used when travelling over to the Broomielaw, where the shipping offices were. Tommy, who owned the pub, and Peter, who worked there, knew almost every seaman from the Uists and Barra area, and if you wanted to see anybody or find out what was going on around the docks or at home, that was your place. Peter could even tell you how many dogs and cats some characters up our way in the islands had. From the Black Man to Lorne School at one time I do not think there would be a close without some family connected with the sea in some way, either building, repairing, loading, discharging, sailing or rigging ships. If the majority of people living around that area today saw some craft on the river I do not believe they would know whether she was a tug or a trawler.

I came off the wrong slipway from the motorway one day and landed in that area. It was a while after I had stopped before emerging into the Paisley Road that I realised I was opposite the close where I had lived when sailing out of Glasgow for twenty-five years. The close, Uneag's, is at the foot of Seaward Street and the Paisley Road. Old Kate lived around our corner then. She used to go to the Paisley Road Toll any night she had a few scoops inside her, where she would give her usual talk about being related to the Lord Provost of Inverness. Speaking broad Scots and hailing from somewhere up north it is more than likely she would feel homesick for her homeland. The nearest she could get to her childhood atmosphere was the crowd who used to gather on the Paisley Road Toll. This crowd, mostly from the Uists and Barra, sailors and girls working in service in Pollokshields, were the ones Kate used to talk with.

According to Uneag, my landlady, Kate had seen better days but was at this time staying on her own and her only enjoyment in life was to make her way to the Toll, which was not far away, to join the crowd.

I was looking at the Toll that day I took the detour and realised that there would only be room for half a dozen people to stand there now, as the space was taken up with plant pots. Then I thought back to the days when all these drunken sailors would be holding one another up, with Kate right there in the middle of them and the police trying to chase them away to make room for passing traffic.

Sailing in merchant ships was all right when jobs were plentiful, but during depression years with ships lying in tiers laid up it was awful, especially for landladies who had to keep seamen for months on end when out of work. It was these fine women like Uneag from our islands that our seamen and families have to thank, for in my young days it was a remittance from their children in allotments that was keeping families going. Once the first allotment money came home, that was one bringing up the other.

Calumn Morrison, who was Uneag's nephew, was one night standing at the Toll when this fellow came along challenging people to a fight. He was not long throwing his weight around when Calumn took him on, battering him so hard that the police had to take him to hospital. The bully must have known that it was one of the Morrisons who gave him the hiding, for about two o'clock in the morning all hands were called in Uneag's house with the police looking for Calumn Morrison. They escorted him from the house and he was fined ten pounds, a lot of money these days but everyone around the Toll was glad the bully got his desserts.

Calumn was still around there when I came down with measles and Italy had declared war on us at the same time. I remember that night Calumn giving me whisky from his half bottle and somebody else giving me chocolates. As every cafe was smashed that night on the Paisley Road I do not think there were ever so many chocolates eaten in one night as there were then. People had to vent their anger on somebody for being stabbed in the back. It is just as well the Italians never went into the spirit trade, they would never have left their own pubs alive that night if people had started taking drink instead of eating chocolates.

I could not have taken measles in a worse place than in lodgings, but anyway I got over it. However Calumn Morrison's ship had just left the Clyde for New York when he himself went down with the measles. I do not know why he was so long before taking them, as he was away from home for a few years then. Maybe the reason was seamen would be spending most of their time in pubs where mostly grown ups were, city folks having had them as children.

I remember being sent by a couple of the boys, Calumn being one of them, to Rutland Crescent for a 'livener', as they were feeling bad that morning with the after-effects of the night before. Sheena Mhor from South Uist was staying there and she was well in with some of the off-licences who would give the required cure.

I remember her brother, Donnall E. Toff, a deep sea bosun, was staying with her, being unmarried at the time, and home from sea for a short rest. He must have left the change that was in his pockets somewhere while he was shaving and on coming back it was gone. Sheena Mhor had a young family just waiting for a chance to pounce on uncle Donnall's change, so he was on to Sheena Mhor about her children being robbers, and her telling him to keep his change in his pocket and then nobody would rob him, when on looking through the window he starts pointing to every kid in Rutland Crescent with a sweetie in his mouth and all out of uncle Donnall's change.

Then Sheena Mhor's husband, William Tell, would come home from the *Arranmore* looking and smelling like a farm hand after spending all night discharging cattle manure for a pound. The slavery the men in these Clyde shipping boats went through after discharging the cattle at Merkland quay was something else. They had to move up river and barrow all of the manure to the back of the sheds, wash down the boat, and lime the hold ready for dockers to take cargo on at eight o'clock, an all-night job.

The Limerick run the *Arranmore* was on was the most wicked run on the British coast, from the west side of Ireland to Glasgow. William Tell was years on that run. Perhaps he would get a couple of weeks off in the summer, but that was his lot. Glasgow was going to be the port of Britain from now until the end of the war. In fact it must have been the port that saved Britain. All the English and Welsh ports were being bombed that autumn. It was very easy to bomb them as space was small. With the Clyde there were so many lochs and inlets to hold the ships over a wide area, along with many that were docked up-river. They were so busy that the tugs and dockers had to be brought up from England. The area around Cowal and Bute was where disabled ships were brought to await repairs.

Arriving in Glasgow with very little money and in search of a job at sea, ones from isloated islands could not manage without these good women from our own place living in the Paisley Road. Good, hard-working women like Uneag, who I would say fed more lodgers at her house in 462 Paisley Road near the Toll than anyone, and did so for over forty years.

I was only fifteen years and two months when I started staying there myself, when I was seven months in wireless school. After the war when things started getting better and ones up in the islands could afford to send their children to serve their time, Uneag used to have a squad of them, together with sailors in and out from the sea. Uneag never had any children herself but she helped to get others' children launched on their careers and trades. It was quite a sight to see her with a troop of these apprentice boys tramping away to first mass on a Sunday morning before breakfast, and off to work after breakfast, as all shipyards were going full blast then.

There were characters like Aoghais Gilbride staying in her house, who used for devilment to collect leaflets from open-air communist meetings, put them under his pillow and when Uneag did the bed and discovered them a stramash would start about his wicked ways.

I do not know where she got all the energy from, keeping all these lodgers, having to stand in queues for almost everything and up at all hours to care for sailors both arriving and departing.

That mile of the Paisley Road, Glasgow, from Lorne School upwards to the city, was always home from home for the seamen from the Uists and Barra, and once they had their feet on it they were among all of their relations and friends living on the Road and its side streets.

People connected with the sea chose this area as it was only a few minutes' tram ride or walking distance from their work. All these sailors around the Toll would be living with relatives in the area crowded together in tenements and eating fish and eggs which their relatives in the islands would be sending out to them. That is what you had to put up with at one time on leaving home, half the island on top of you with eggs to take to their folks in Glasgow, also hardened salt fish.

With jobs hard to come by, it was no fun for either themselves or the relative or friend who had to keep them until they were fixed up with employment, and so these tit-bits from home would be more than welcome. These city exiles would be mostly working in the various rigging gangs who used to have their rigging lofts around the Plantation area, and it was on the corner of Plantation Street that the gaffers used to pick up the required number of men for their specific duties. Anybody who wanted work could stand there and be picked up, usually for dry dock tides, with the worst of the work going to the Johnny-come-lately.

The Govan Road corner was the one with the most rigging gangs, Clyde Rigging, Cork, and MacKenzie. On the Paisley Road corner there used to be old King shouting down from a couple of stairs up how many he wanted to do some job. Sometimes I have seen gaffers coming up to houses where they had an idea sailors were, and even to the Toll and the dance halls if men were wanted for an early morning tide when they were short of the required number.

There were also Highlanders in the police force at one time and if on hearing a crowd talk about any scrap or punch-up that involved the law it is more than likely the big Highland bobby's name was mentioned in the centre of it all.

At one time there were men from the islands on the horse vans who had big crofts at home and knew something about horses. All these large grocers in the city did most of the deliveries to their shops in outlying towns and villages by this method of transport. It was a common occurrence if travelling to join ships on the Ayrshire or east coast ports to catch a glimpse of them in the most outlandish places. Lachlan MacDonald, who was married to a relative of my folks, and whose home at Kinning Street at one time, when there were not so many Highland people in the city, gave shelter to more sailors than any home of its size, was on the road with his horse and van all of his working life.

Most of these Highland folks residing in the city had one thing in common, the hope that one day they might be able to go back home where they were born and brought up, but families being so big these days there was not a place for all of them, especially crofting families from big crofts depending on them for a living. The croft was only for the one person, the rest had to leave with no other land available to them, as all the big tacks got broken up before and after the First World War. With smaller islands and postage-stamp sized crofts, people were not depending for a living on the crofts. A few houses could be built on the same croft but with the depleted state of fishing before the war there was hardly anything left to fish for any more. After six years of war things looked very grim indeed for these seamen from the islands. The best they could look forward to for any kind of home married life was to get a job in a cattle boat, shovelling manure for the rest of their lives.

Ring net fishermen who were on a good footing at the beginning of the war, and whose fleets were small before returning service men started buying boats with loan and grant help, were the ones who scored after the war. For about four years after the war, with returning service men trying to pick up the threads of the only pre-war work they knew, and the country rationed, fish being the only commodity that there was to eat in abundance, fishermen could not go wrong. It was only in later years when rationing stopped and people were discontented with eating fish for years that fishermen started to feel the pinch.

Clyde ring net fishermen got a fleet of lovely boats built in these years after the war and it was around the Outer Isles they used to fish in late spring, early summer and winter. The rest of the year they were at the Isle of Man, Scarborough and Whitby in late summer and autumn and their own ground in the spring of the year. While around the islands, Lochboisdale was usually their base, some of them knowing it better than their own home ground. The Gemmels from Dunure in Ayrshire were conspicuous among them because they were the ones who shouted and argued the most, never caring who heard or understood them. Willie Gemmel was the prince of them all, and he knew everyone at the hotel in Lochboisdale from the proprietor to the boots, as we found out one night we arrived late at the pier after the bar closed. Myself and another off the boat were trying to enter through the back kitchen of the hotel. The door was locked and so we were trying to catch somebody's eye hoping to have a drink inside, when who came around the corner but Willie Gemmel, who had the same idea, but was told by us that it was no use as nobody was paying any attention to us. 'Just lift me up to that window', says Willie. We promptly obeyed, but with difficulty, as Willie was no lightweight, being so fat and heavy, but we managed somehow. With Willie's eyes and mouth going all out at the same time and hands flying to attract attention from inside, the two of us were gasping for breath, and so we shouted to him to hurry up before we let him fall with a clatter. At last we heard him shout, 'I can see Duncan now, he's coming over to unlock the door, better let me down'. This was something we did thankfully. I have been in sly grogs and speak-easies all over the world, but I think holding Willie Gemmel up to the window in Lochboisdale that night was the heaviest price I ever paid to get in anywhere.

At this time Lochboisdale pier was the hub of activity for the Uists, as more foot passengers travelled by the mail boat then, air travel and car ferries being still to come. On mail boat night the pier would be crowded with people as two mail boats were tied together, and for a while you could hardly get standing room inside the bar door, especially on bad nights when the fishing boats were not at sea. It was well up the pier beside the road that Uileam Dotty from Grimsay was holing up one winter after he had finished with his west side lobster fishing. He used to have two boats, one for living in and another, smaller one, for fishing the lobsters. Uileam always picked some place like that for the winter, fishing away on his own after the bar closed. Once the summer and the good weather came Uileam went out west again, always on his own, and if ever in need of a new boat or repair of an old one he would go ahead and do the job himself.

Lochboisdale was the place where almost everything in our area of the Outer Isles was happening, all business being carried out there. It was also the main shopping centre. It was here that Angus MacLellan from Mallaig, having spent a dozen years of his life over in the U.S.A., started a butcher's business, a name that was going to stick to him for the rest of this life. I believe the biggest excitement he had in Lochboisdale was the day Tommy Ralston from Campbeltown, who was fishing on one of the ring netters, drove Angus MacLellan's van over the pier, landing on top of one of the Meenan's boats which was tied alongside. Like all Campbeltown fishermen, Tommy Ruadh, as he was known to the Eriskay crowd, fished around

120

our area, but with the depleted state of the ring net fishing ended his days as Skipper of a puffer. I was home visiting my mother and father before they died and they were telling me of all the strange faces that paid them a visit since I saw them last. Tommy Ruadh was one of them, being in Eriskay with a load of coal in a puffer. I heard from someone a while afterwards that he was drowned aboard one of them. I believe Tommy would have had plenty of experiences, like all who followed his calling, but the day he drove the butcher's van over the pier in Lochboisdale would be one of his most hair-raising.

Angus MacLellan, 'the Butcher' as he was known in Uist, and 'the Yank' in Mallaig, was a bit of a boy, and during his lifetime tried to have a go at doing almost everything. I was one night in a house in New York visiting a relative when the talk was about ones who had gone back home. Angus's name was mentioned, and I was asked did I know him and what was he up to now. Well I started giving them a list of all I had seen him doing, namely butchering, grocering, making ice cream, rearing pigs, then back deep sea for a while, working with a small ring net catching saith at the pier at Lochboisdale, and fishing lobsters. There was no end to what he was doing. 'Oh', everyone said, 'do you remember when he had the restaurant down the water front?' He was living there like a hermit trying to run it on his own. Dockers would come in shouting their orders of scrambled eggs and coffee in Yankee slang—'Shipwrecked eggs and a mug of mud!'—and Angus would shout the orders through to the back, then go and cook it himself, pretending someone else was there. Someone went into a speak-easy one night up around Times Square, the United States being 'dry' at this time, and who was there serving behind the bar but Angus. He was kept busy with people wanting to be served and at the same time making conversation with this fellow. As he was mixing up some concoction this fellow asked what the drink was called. 'Highball', says Angus.

'Well', was the reply, 'whoever drinks that tonight will be jumping high all right'.

Angus knew the States well as he had travelled all over them. Just mention anywhere, from the hillbilly states to the rich oil states and he knew them all, as well as their populations. A mine of information he was. After the war he was back in Mallaig again, buying his share of a ring net boat along with the two Gillies brothers, Porter and Ronnie, but that game I think was too crowded for him for soon he was back on his own at the lobsters on the west side of Uist. But it was in his years in the States that he did most of his wandering, inland around Wyoming and Idaho, where with gangs of Japanese he went around shearing sheep with cut-throat razors, never tying up the sheeps' feet but holding them with only one hand and the razor in the other. He always made for our Eriskay crowd whenever we were in Mallaig as we could talk some of his language, having all of us seen a bit of the world.

Mallaig men from the east coast were all full-time fishermen. Apart from naval service during the two world wars, the fishing was their life. I remember Angus once coming aboard in Mallaig all dressed up to kill, and talking to my father who had sailed with him in the First World War. We were all wondering why he was so dressed up, as dress had always been the least of his concerns. I heard him telling my father that he was just back from the Mod in Oban and that he and his brother Archie had been talking with the Premier of Nova Scotia, who spoke Gaelic. After a while everybody aboard was in the conversation and on somebody mentioning that he was now a big shot travelling with Archie who had the West Highland Hotel, and being introduced to these famous people he replied, 'No, it was myself who introduced Archie to the Premier'.

I knew his brother, Sweeney, when I was over in the States . This family of MacLellans brought up in Mallaig Bheag would be one of the best known of the original families to have resided in Mallaig before the coming of the railway, all of them being Gaelic speakers. The ones born there after the coming of the railway were always English-speaking, as there was an influx of strangers, mostly fishermen from the east coast, who never looked upon Mallaig as home and were away to their birth place as soon as their working life was over. The village itself never came up to expectations, judging by the posters I have seen of it that were made eighty years ago. It was going to be the Blackpool of the North.

The site the railway started to build on was unsuitable for building a town, so nothing much was done to the harbour through the years until recently. Up to then it was a wild place, swept by the North wind. Everything around the harbour was owned by the railway, who were always sure of getting something out of it, as everything was landed there, since it was the only place handy to the fishing banks of the Outer Isles. It is true Oban and Kyle were railhead centres but they could not compete with Mallaig. You could fish herring until three in the morning, land and discharge in Mallaig and still be back to do another night's fishing.

In Oban, where lorries were allowed onto the pier to load the herring from the boats, a few more pounds a cran was paid, but you lost a night's fishing, with the result that Mallaig was more or less getting the lot. For a mere village, with never more than a thousand of a population, I would say more money has been earned there than in big towns in Scotland. But the place was always cursed with people earning a living there who took no interest in the welfare of the place, between the ones residing there never calling it home and the ones fishing out of there who even brought their stores from their own local grocer at home.

Because of these attitudes, the growth of Mallaig harbour was practically nil for about seventy years after the railway reached there. If the harbour had been developed I believe the car ferries to the islands would still be sailing from there, as that is really where they should be, the place being in a position where three quarters of sailing time was in sheltered waters.

People who own cars sometimes forget about those who do not have this form of transport and whose mode of travel has never altered through the years, rail travel being more agreeable to the old and infirm. Also, having served the public in sea transport for part of my seagoing life I have always found that the travelling public much prefers sailing in sheltered waters.

My uncle Angus through marriage, whose house was only a stone's throw away from my father's house, was always part of my life during the time I was growing up in Eriskay. In almost all the sea-going I did at home, like fishing with small lines in open boats, he was always in the crew. He was a nice, happy-go-lucky man who could hold his own aboard anything afloat, both fishing and sailing. It was from him I used to hear stories of things that happened to him during his lifetime at sea, which helped me after I left home.

He bought a boat along with his brothers once from Gardenstown on the east coast. The *Gift* she was called when they got her, the man who had her dying young or something like that, and this was the cause of her being sold. They changed her name to a gaelic one, *Reul e Chuan* (Ocean Star). She was a nice boat with plenty of power for her time, having two 26/30 engines. Everything a fishing boat of her day needed was in her. She would do everything, leaving every other boat in Eriskay standing, but catching herring was not one of her good points and so after three years they were forced to lie her up to await a buyer. This is something that is hard to sell, a fishing boat that gets a bad name, as she had two owners in a short while, and so after some time laid up she was lying in a small inlet where the great second-sighter Donnall Ian Mhac e Tailler's house was. Donnall Ian was was one of these who was seeing more of the dead than the living anyway, so nobody was paying much heed to anything he would see around her. A crowd from Nairn came at last to buy her and, according to Donnall, one of them was going to meet his destiny aboard her. They bought her, took her away, renamed her the *Venture* and started fishing with her. They had her five years when one bad day, while fishing in the Moray Firth, she sank, drowning one of her crew.

After I got sober I had a hard job to stay that way as I had to sail with people who drank, ones who could take it or leave it, so they said anyway, but more often they took it. I was home about Christmas and as a member of the family was getting married I was put in charge of the 'grog', before our own crowd would drink all of it. Everybody was feeling a bit sorry for me being an alcoholic who could not drink, while they could take it and leave it when the money ran out. My uncle Angus was the sorriest of the lot, it was he who told me the best way to keep sober was to get a job aboard an east coast fishing boat among sober men. He had been with them in the herring drifters and they used to get annoyed with him if they smelt drink from him. When I went back to my own job I was not very happy with people inviting me to drink with them, until one night with a band aboard they all went wild. So I said 'This is it. I am off to the east coast'.

Purse netting was in its infancy then, so I got a job in one of them, the Westies of *Gardenstown Prowess* and the *Havilah*. Angus was right, they were a sober crowd, the Westies, Andy and all the young boys who were sailing along with them. They were the right type for that kind of fishing, as most of them were just starting. The older ones were a bit dubious about me, but I did not drink and I always made sure that I was around and not wandering off somewhere as drinking people do. I guess nobody could blame them for eyeing me with suspicion after seeing our crowd from Eriskay homeward bound with a bottle sticking out from every pocket. I believe it is easier for these good people to keep to the straight and narrow paths, going away together and coming back home together, never having much to do with strangers. The older, retired ones would come up to me enquiring how the old ones in Eriskay were. 'How is your father doing?', one old fellow asked me.

'Oh', I replied, 'he is busy praying, going to church three times a day.'

'I see', he says. 'I gave you fellows in the *Lady of Fatima* some hooks once when you were working the great lines. I don't think I ever got any siller for them.'

'I'll tell him to say a few prayers for you', I said.

Then he asks, 'What's Driver John in the *Virgin* doing?'

'Driver John goes to church four times a day', I said.

'Ah weel', he replied, 'Ah ken once in Lochboisdale there was something wrong wi' oor navigation lights and we had tae use emergency anes tae tak' us tae Mallaig but when we tried them there wis nae paraffin in them. Ah saw Driver John knockin' aboot the pier an' Ah says tae him, "Ah ken you've got a deisel engine now but is there ony way Ah could hae some paraffin for ma emergency lights?" John just lifted his hauns meanin' you've as good as had it. But next time Ah looked there wis John wi' a bit o' hose tappin' ane o' the paraffin barrels on the pier.'

To this I replied, 'When you get to the other side you'll get, as the Loch Fyne men say, the first *steall* of that paraffin because you were the one who used it'.

'But', he says, 'it wis such a wee drappie.'

I replied, 'You had better save your breath until you get over there'. I think I had him worried.

The hooks he gave the *Lady of Fatima* for the great lines would be a poor investment, as everything else connected with the fishing was at that time.

There was not much of a fortune to be made at the great lines. It would take you away from home and help to keep the boat clear, as these boats that came after the war were going into debt lying at anchor with insurance, echo meter and phones on hire. But one of the loveliest sights I ever saw in my lifetime, and I have been to every corner of the world, was aboard the *Lady of Fatima* while hauling great lines in eighty fathoms when we came on a fast and they broke. We had to go to the other end and start hauling against the tide, a job that would take two men instead of one. We still had a couple of lines out when they broke away from the fast and surfaced with cod and ling.

Too many ring net boats were built in the space of a couple of years after the war. Everybody who had seen war service qualified for loan and grant. It was all right for the few fortunate ones who had boats fishing during the war and did not have to go for this loan and grant. Other families who had lost boats when they were taken over for war service were just given peacetime value for them, money that would not pay one sixth of the price of new ones after the war. So people were saddled with debts that would take them a long time to pay back, if they ever did.

Control was taken off herring and buyers had to pay their own transport, with the result that they could not buy the herring. The ring net herring was the last any buyer would purchase, what home market was available was for drift net herring only. This was because the ring net choked the herring and did not let the blood out of it, as the drift net did. After a couple of hundred crans of herring went for kippering in Mallaig, the rest was fish meal. It was the most poverty-stricken time I have ever seen, all this together with letters in red ink from the Herring Board wanting their loan and interest repayments. The price of these new ring net boats was enormous, all in the region of six to ten thousand pounds, the kind of money that was almost impossible to pay back at fish meal prices. True, there was a third grant, but by the time the interest on the loan was paid you would have paid the full amount of the buying price. It was a bad scheme in the first place, but what could people like my father do, whose only worldly possession was taken over for war service, and on losing it was given a mere pittance in return?

To get out of this sad state of affairs was harder than staying in it. Families who had wage earners in the house not depending on fishing, and thank God our family was in this situation, could survive, but you were forever plagued with these red ink letters from the Herring Board. The ones who had no one to keep them, like men who got married during and after the war with young families to feed, were the ones who were hit most. In desperation, as they were on the poverty line, they were forced to stop fishing, their property was sold for a song, and any mortgage money the selling price did not cover was still a millstone around their necks.

Our country has always been very kind in giving interest-free loans to poorer countries, but why were interest-free loans not given to the men who served their country in its hour of need? Certainly we had that hour of need when we had to stand on our own and fight for the free world for a whole year.

From left to right: Mother, myself as a baby, Father, cousin Angus Eddy Campbell, uncle Michael, brother, Charlotte McIsaac next door, and aunt Annie. Eriskay, 1925.

There was nothing wrong with the *Lady of Fatima*, £6,500 she was at eight een months old. The Mallaig company that built her and another three of them never had much success with them, and so they were sold off. With the first two to be sold, the *Lady of Fatima* and the *Mallaig Mhor*, the company got their money out of them, but the other two, the *Mallaig Cruach* and the *Sweet Home*, were sold after the deadline passed for the grant and loan for second-hand boats, so they lost out on them. But things were against the *Lady of Fatima* from the beginning when she landed in Eriskay amongst an ageing fishing fleet. The last new boat to come to Eriskay was our own *Ocean Star* in 1928. She was taken away for service at the beginning of the war. All the others were pre-First World War. A couple of them had diesel engines and were repaired, but plenty of the old wood was still in them. So we had to neighbour an old zulu, the *Virgin*, built in 1912, which was unable to cross the Minch with herring except in a calm. When they did get something to take the weight off her it was one of these wartime M.F.V.s (Marine Fishing Vessels) with the engine of the old one in her, but for the first eighteen months in Eriskay she was forever on the hop across with whatever was caught. She must have been the only thing that was keeping Eriskay from becoming extinct as a fishing community. Everything from road compressors, horses, paraffin barrels etc. went aboard her. She was held up as a sign of a flourishing community when roads and electricity were being fought for, the electricity being in Eriskay fourteen years before Barra. I believe they would take a dim view of the flourishing community if the red ink letters were shown to them.

126

The coming of electricity was a blessing, as it saved all that carrying of paraffin and people scrimping when paying you. They all got to know about paraffin being two pounds and fifteen shillings in Mallaig, and this is how mean and miserable they could be—instead of giving you three pounds for all your bother they would give you two pounds and ten shillings, then start scraping their pockets for the five shillings until you called a halt and then saw the look of relief on their faces.

All through the fifties were bad years for the ring net fishermen. You might make a living during the winter but come summer everything was being eaten away. Everything was tried by these boats: great lines, lobsters, drift nets, seine nets, shark fishing. The prawn fishing was in the future. By the end of the fifties most of them had thrown in the towel, with most Clyde ring net men landing up working in the steel mills of Corby. I believe for once in their lives they were glad to see what others take for granted, namely a wage packet, as some of their years fishing, along with the war years in service, were very lean. Ones without property ashore were all right as they had nothing to lose, but of course there were some sad cases of people losing their houses.

I know one good-living man who was paying so much every week out of his wages to pay back what he owed to the Herring Board. He, along with others, got this old boat with money from the Herring Board, and when things started getting bad at the fishing she had to be sold for a pittance to be broken up for fence posts. Every week without fail he was sending some money to the Herring Board to pay his share of the debt out of his hard-earned money. You worked hard there in Burns Laird Shipping Line. He used to get two rest periods together, which would enable him to travel home, giving him a couple of days there. There was no forcing him to do it, just his own conscience. I am sure there will be a special place in Heaven for the likes of him.

In later years when prawn fishing and purse netting started and other developments were set afoot, I think I must have been one of the few, if any, of the former crowd to apply for anything. Ones with no fishing tradition of any sort behind them were being more welcomed. I was chased right away. There was the Tailier in Stockinish and myself, both of us must have been their only refusal. There was no fortune to be made at the fishing for me anyway. After the year in the purse netter I went back to the Merchant Navy but decided after getting married to have another go at the fish business, this time selling it in a city scheme. A whole winter I was at it. If it is hard to catch fish it is just as hard to sell it. The man who had the run before me drank himself out of it, so he used to go around with me in the van to show me where all of his customers were. I believe there was a good enough living in it at one time, but luck was against me with prices going sky high and petrol getting dearer, while wages were more or less the same. It is all right for people who do not know any better to say that if you buy it dear sell it dear. But when people cannot afford it they cannot buy it.

The man who was with me in the van had no love for catholics at the best of times, but for some time before this catholics were given permission to eat meat on Fridays. I was the one to suffer for this, as he was always on at me about my man in Rome who caused all the want that befell the fishing industry. He knew the religion of all of our customers and would hum religious tunes to suit them all. There was one day I got mixed up with the tune-singing. It was only after pulling out of this cul-de-sac that he turned on me saying 'You stupid b——, do you know that you were singing the wrong tune there, all catholic customers at the van and you humming away at "The Billy Boys". We're lucky to get out of that place alive.' So this was the carry-on. I think I was learning more about religion there than in a Sunday School. However after spending some more time in the fish van I decided I was not cut out for that kind of life and made up my mind to go back to sea.

The most amusing thing that happened to me during that time was one day when I had to go up to a house to collect tick and the young woman there was breast-feeding a baby. He must have had his fill, as she said to him, 'If you don't want any more I'll give it to the fish man.'

It is an eye opener how much you get to know about people when you are in a van. Women well on in years telling you they would love to buy your fish if they knew how to cook it. Sales people desperate to sell something coming to the van wanting to know if so and so is a good payer. What could you say, one was desperate to sell, the other desperate to get a hold of it, regardless of whether they were able to pay for it or not. For a nation where not many of the population are further than a couple of hundred miles from the sea, it is surprising how little fish is eaten in this country. It was the First World War that put fish on the menu for most of the inland population of Britain, and soldiers and sailors away in the services getting a taste of it in the city fish and chip shops.

I remember the time a local worthy, Dallas, who had one of the first cars to come to Uist, got some herring from one of his relatives in Eriskay. Being a nice summer day, the herring was cut up into small portions and left to dry in the sun, before being eaten with the evening meal. Dallas came aboard just before the evening meal and all the herring they had, which was not much, was given to him, the catch being too small to go to Castlebay. Before arriving home that night, Dallas was on some business with his car in one of the island villages, when this panhandler approached his car, and, on seeing the herring cut into bits which Dallas had left in the back seat, began to gaze at it rather mystified. At last his curiosity got the better of him and he asked where Dallas had got the herring. On being told it was from the Eriskay men he asked, 'Is it with the scythe the Eriskay men are killing the herring this year?' It was at Balla that Dallas had all the Eriskay relations on his father's side. He was always visiting uncle Eoin when in Lochboisdale after his driving days were over. His mother belonged to Pabbay, one of the Barra Head islands.

Fish or mutton was sold in vans or shops in the islands without much dressing being put on it. Fish was sold just as it came out of the sea. Anybody selling mutton had to do the killing themselves, sometimes by methods that left much to be desired. The butchering that I recall best was done by schoolboys, grown men being nearly always away from home at sea, so somebody had to do the job. This so-called butchering happened when a man from Barra, the 'Lambman', was shopkeeper at the Haun. It was about autumn and people were bringing their lambs to be slaughtered, a job usually done by the people themselves so that they would get the innards for making haggis. Butchers not being home they were bringing them alive to the shop. The 'Lambman' wanted a ram killed, but being too busy in the shop, a volunteer was asked for. Donald was the son of the tailor who owned the shop, a lad of about twelve years of age. Being over from Uist for the day, he told the Lambman that he would do the job. Preparations were made for the killing. The ram was brought over from where it was tethered by Callum, the Lambman's grand-nephew. Callum, by the way, was drowned on his first trip to sea during the war. I also helped Callum get the ram. The boy Donald was busy sharpening knives etc. A box was brought from somewhere. The ram was laid on top of it with his feet tied with some granny knots and that was him nearly ready for the pot, or so we thought. The first plunge Donald did with the knife the ram jumped, working his feet loose from the knots, with all hands jumping on top of him and blood spewing from his throat. To cut a long story short, the head was cut from him and he was skinned, ready to be sold. The following day some woman came into the shop and saw the carcass on the counter and enquired as to when the ram was butchered. The Lambman said to her, 'that ram wasn't butchered, he was murdered'.

A cousin of the Lambman was also keeping shop in Eriskay for a while. Having the shop in Eriskay, another one in Castlebay, and a lorry on the road, the family was a bit scattered between the two places. The shop in Eriskay was looked after by Caileach MacKinnon's son, Angus John, who was about fifteen at the time when we had to do a bit of butchering. This time it was a huge ram brought over from Glendale, and whether we started cutting his throat at the right places or not I do not know, but try as hard as we could we were unable to get his head off. The family boat the *Ocean Star* was on the beach being painted, and I said to Angus John that I had better sneak aboard her for a saw which I knew was kept in the boat. As he did not want to admit defeat and so become a laughing-stock, he agreed with me. I brought the saw ashore hidden underneath my jersey, polished off the ram with it, took it back after washing it in salt water and nobody was any the wiser.

That saw on the *Ocean Star* was put to some queer uses. I remember once it was the beginning of summer when the gulls and ducks were laying their eggs and we were dying to get away to the uninhabited off-shore islands for eggs. The wee family boat had had the mast taken out of her and put in

Father, myself, the baby brother and cousin standing up

the MacIsaac's *Yawla Mhor*, uncle Angus being in her doing the herring fishing. We took the mast out of somebody else's boat and on trying it in our own wee boat we found that the mast shoe was too small. Right away we went to the big boat for the saw and the shoe was sawed until the mast fitted. It was only when old gran, the detective, spotted the sawn shoe next day that the ructions started. Old gran was all for sending the lot of us away to the training ship until our teeth turned black, as happened in the old days to prisoners who were locked up for a long time on a poor diet.

Another character who used to stay at the Balla, Eriskay, was Raoghall Mhac Alasdair Ruadh. I think he was the jolliest man I have ever met ashore. He was always whistling and singing tunes, but aboard the wee boats fishing with small lines in the Sound, Raoghall turned into a right Tartar. If he saw one hook that was not baited he would say to Aoghais Ian Mhor shooting the line, 'God, father, I think it's a hook without bait that went out there', and on enquiring who the basket belonged to they would turn on the culprit with Raoghail threatening to use the tail of the sheet rope on him. So that was what you were in for if you committed the unpardonable crime of leaving a hook unbaited—the sheet tail from one and a hammering with the tiller from the other.

I would say that in those days the Balla at Eriskay was one of the easiest of communities to survive in around our place, as it was handy for the Sound of Barra where you were nearly always sure of getting a meal of fish. It did not matter which way or how strong the wind blew, there was some part of the Sound where you could work, with boats being launched and hauled up again on the sands. With others it was a hard struggle in the days of sail, when you had to start tacking to or from the Sound. Thank God for the Sound of Barra. It was a blessed pool these days as you would never go hungry. There was always a meal and a pound to be earned there when everything else failed. The only curse was the market being so far away on the mainland. It was only during the cold weather that fish could be sent to Mallaig.

These days the fish were coming and going from the Sound, but today the fish are all being caught in the deep water. I have seen the fishermen coming home with creels with over a hundred flounders in them from one share, not counting skate, ducks etc. Today it is empty. I was asking a crew at home if they were trying the Sound with their trawl. They said yes, they had had the trawl out for two hours a few weeks before that but when they hauled, all that was in it was an old shoe. Trawling was done in the Sound by locals in these days during winter months, but when the spring came there was always a pound to be made at the lines. It is the same story all over, locals having to stop going out with their lines for a meal of fish because it is all being caught in the deep water.

Toltsa Sands on Lewis was the most famous fishing ground on the west coast but I do not think there is much there today. I used to see Allan Cameron travelling on the *Loch Seaforth* going to council meetings, and if he is still alive I do not think there is much left for him at the Sands now to shout about. It was during my time in MacBrayne's, when I used to meet the island trouble-shooters who would come up on to the bridge on the way across, that you heard it all. It was all go on the *Loch Seaforth* in these days from the time she would cast off from Stornoway pier at a couple of minutes past midnight on Sunday until eight o'clock Saturday night. If you were lucky you just had time for a few drinks before they closed.

I remember one Saturday night, the bars being closed, somebody mentioned some sly grog where there was drink, so we all piled into the car which belonged to the engineer by the name of Bonzo, who came from Stornoway. We were somewhere outside the town when the fellow who was driving took the wrong turning and landed in a garden. The crowd of us had to get out of the car and start to push it out of the garden. Before we had finished, the lady of the house came out and what a telling off we got for breaking the Sabbath, it must have been past midnight by this time. Bonzo said her name was Ballag Nuase. She went to the police when some trouble-maker told her that the boys of the *Loch Seaforth* were wanting money from her for ploughing her garden. The police never came near us. I believe they would have enough trouble on their hands knowing it was the only night we could get ashore.

We used to have our share of sorting out drunks aboard ourselves. I remember one night the police came aboard with this drunk fellow at the last minute. Once the police got him up the gangway and into our charge they stood on the pier to make sure he would not come off again. The *Loch Seaforth* then started moving off with the drunk shouting that the Stornoway police were lower than a snake's belly, half an inch off the grass. The police just stood there, happy to be rid of him.

I have found any Lewis people that I ever came in contact with to be happy-go-lucky, nice folk, whether on their own home ground or away from home. The last time I saw a relative of mine, Black Duncan, who is today dead but was once sailing out of Custom House Dock, London, we both agreed we would rather sail with Lewis men than with men from our own end of the islands. There were Lewis men for a long time sailing out of Custom House, London, by the time I knew them.

After the First World War the line fishing for cod and ling which the majority of men from Ness in Lewis were engaged in was about finished. A change over to the herring was out of the question, as the boats they had were unsuitable, and to buy herring boats with the herring getting scarcer was too much of a gamble. People had to look elsewhere for a living and the sea was the only way of life they knew.

Men from Ness would be the first from the islands sailing out of Custom House between the two world wars. Sandy Ian Bard from Ness was in his seventies and a Bosun on the *Mataroa* when I sailed with him. It was only want at the herring fishing that drove the rest of them from the Isles there, for I remember well my first going away from home before I left school, meeting boys from Toltsa, Point and the lochs crewing east coast drifters in Castlebay. Between them and the east coast men being friendly and trying to open a conversation in English with the Lewis boys speaking Gaelic, the drifter might as well have been crewed by Hindus speaking Hindustani as far as I was concerned. It was only after leaving home and sailing amongst them that I could understand their lingo. There was one thing they all agreed on and that was the seas at the southern entrance of the Minch were the worst seas they had experienced during their time in the drifters. Some of them made a living, others did not.

I remember one of them, the Laiety from Tolsta, telling me that he was once fourteen weeks fishing out of Castlebay without going near a herring station. After fourteen weeks hoping against hope that their luck would change they decided to try the west side, so they went north and shot at the Flannan islands. This proved to be another blank haul in the morning, so it was decided to make for the Minch by way of the Sound of Harris, where his boat, the *Succeed*, touched a rock. They reached the mouth of Loch Glendhu, shot the nets towards dusk, and hauled them in the small hours of the morning, but this was another blank haul. The drifter got underway for Stornoway. Those of the crew not needed on deck went below for a bite to eat and to turn in for a few hours, as there was no herring and the nets did not have to be lifted before arriving in Stornoway. Laiety had just taken his sea boots off and was in the act of taking off his long sea boot stockings, when there came shouting that the boat was sinking. Those below dived on deck, where the men were shouting for another drifter to come alongside and help them off. The other came alongside and managed to get all of them aboard before she sank to the bottom. They were taken to Stornoway with Laiety still in his stocking soles.

This drifter, the *Succeed* of Buckie, used to do some carrying of herring for ringers working the outer isles lochs. Manson from Mallaig had her during the Loch Eyenort inner loch fishing, then Roddy from Berneray and the MacDonalds from Stein had her for another while. Whether she was cursed for carrying ring net herring or not, she finished Laiety with the fishing. He was sailing as Bosun in Donaldson's *Gracia* when I sailed with him. It must have been when his boat touched in the Sound of Harris that did the damage, although they never thought much of it at the time.

Before the war it was ring net fishermen from the mainland that the drift net fishermen from the northern outer isles of the Minch had to deal with. The Clyde ring net fishermen could work away to their hearts' content at the south end, with the Castlebay-registered fleet almost extinct. It was around the lochs area of Lewis and Harris that the ring net was tried first up at the north end, causing a few ructions, but with the drift net fishing getting bad it is more than likely the ring net men were getting bolder, with the result that they had it to themselves towards the end. Many a tale the Beatons from Kyle could tell about the way they used to be threatened, from being scalped to being skinned alive. Thirty baskets of flounders Aoghais Mhor had with the *Mary Ann* one night in Broad Bay in one drag. This was before the Highland Development and the Stornoway crowd had gone in for light trawling. Once they started this light trawling themselves some of them were the worse culprits.

I remember once when I was along with the Westies of Gamrie in the *Prowess*, and Aoghais Mhor in the *Girl Norma* came aboard at Mallaig with a tale of woe of how he had escaped more or less being tarred and feathered out of Stornoway. He fished with the Westies at the drift nets, so he was looking for some information and charts that would take him down to the Clyde to fish until some of the heat was taken off him. So it is the old story, the people with the better gear and aids to catching power will always be better off. I have seen it myself, the *Blair Mhor* of Rosehearty at the beginning of summer off the Cruachan getting one hundred and eighty crans in one ring because she had a good echo meter, these being in their infancy then. It was the *Blair Mhor*'s first summer at the ring net and we did not even know how to handle so much summer herring, as it had to be boxed. There were Clyde boats going around using their wires without catching a scale. The Jacksons of Tarbert, Loch Fyne, became so fed up that they sailed for home and never did any more fishing until they had echo meters installed.

The number of people engaged in fishing around the British coast at one time must have been enormous, for in my time in the Merchant Navy nearly all personnel who were not domiciled in a ship's port of registry hailed from islands around our coast with some sort of fishing tradition. The sailing in merchant ships started in earnest after the First World War when herring fishing was getting bad. The generation who started work before the war and who were too old for call-up did not even know what a merchant ship looked like. True, the *Tea Clipper* crowd before them were away from home, but it was only want that drove them away. But with the start of herring-curing, people did not have to go away from home, so anyone who may think that one generation was better than the other is talking rubbish. The fact is that some were of age when things were more plentiful at home. Some people try to tell you that they went off to see the world because of how smart they were, but the real reason is they went off to see the world because want drove them away from their home.

There was no comparison between the money that was earned herring fishing and the money earned in merchant ships before the First World War. The shares for a hired hand in a drifter when men from my place were going in them were as follows: the expenses had to be taken out of the gross coal, food, and running expenses. There were three men on a weekly wage, namely the engineer, the fireman and the cook, and any money they would make with the 'scumman', i.e. herring falling out of the nets and into the sea to be scummed aboard by one of the crew, usually the engineer. He had to be standing by to keep steam up while hauling, as the fireman was at the sole rope and the cook coiling the tarry spring rope. The hired hands would be in the hold hauling and shaking from the time they went into the swim—usually about one o'clock in the morning—until one o'clock in the afternoon, if the catch was heavy. They were paid the eighteenth share, three shares being made of the money after running expenses and wages came out. There was a share for the boat, one for the gear, and another for the hired hands, mate and skipper. I do not believe there was heavier work done on any vessel sailing on salt water than in a herring drifter. Hauling a heavy catch of spent herring in the hold of a drifter was the hardest job a human being was ever called upon to do. The man further aft next to the cork rope had the heaviest of the lot, as he had the brunt of the weight of the other's herring being sent aft from forward. I heard my uncle Angus through marriage say that the skipper of the *Gamrie Bay* was always in this position next to the corks throughout hauling time.

The herring drifter was a great boat for the work she was built to do but there were too many of them built in the ten years before the First World War. Buckie harbour alone could be filled three times with their own drifters. Space could not be found for them in their own harbour, and so two thirds of them had to be kept in Aberdeen during the off season. The only time their own harbour would see them would be when they were changing gear.

One family who were well known to the Eriskay boys were the Riachs and their five drifters. I think the families who remained level-headed and kept to the one drifter were the ones who survived the hardships and want that came after the First World War. These bad years would have come sooner but the war arrested it for a few years. But when the bad time came a few years after the war neither the herring nor the market was there. This was caused mainly by abuse—too many boats and too few herring. But the money that was made in the drifters' heyday before the war was the kind of money not made in any other job afloat.

Chapter 6

Ships going down—The Scholar Bhain—Local boys made good—Fishing off Tiree and Coll—Purse netting—The Coach: Eriskay's Jonah—Michael Neil Eoin explains whaling to his mother—Michael e Drobhair and the rice pudding—Stories of giants people have seen—Eriskay's strongest man—Uncle Angus and the S.S. Politician—Uncle Iagan and Donal McKinnon get paralytic—Fishing for whisky in the hold—The telephone—Rivalry between Barra and Eriskay

There were always ships going down. There was hardly a bad gale that you did not hear of some ship sinking, usually with all hands, as a stove-in hatch in a tramp steamer with a heavy cargo like iron ore surely meant death for everyone aboard. Ropners of West Hartlepool lost two ships before the war, one in 1933 and the other in 1934. There were a good number of them on the coal run between Sydney, Cape Breton and Montreal, so they would be out there until the St Lawrence froze up in December. This being the worst month of the year in the North Atlantic, the run home would usually be made with iron ore from Wabana in Newfoundland to the Bristol Channel steel ports. By the time rescue reached the vicinity where their S.O.S. was sent from, there were no signs of anything.

Another ship that went down in these terrible gales of December 1934 was the *Blairgowrie*, belonging to Nisbitt of Ardrossan. She was outward bound at the time. Her S.O.S. was answered by the German liner, *Bremen*, which proceeded to her aid but was unable to do anything as the weather was so vicious. She sank with all hands. I know of one woman who was still alive fifty-six years afterwards who lost her husband in that ship.

The following October 1935 the *Valdulia*, one of Donaldson's of Glasgow, sank with all hands west of the Hebrides, bound from West Hartlepool to Newfoundland north about Scotland, a terrible route. Most of the crew were islemen. That gale came early, it was not even a winter gale but one of these hurricanes that starts around the Cape Verde Islands and works its way across to the West Indies. After reaching the West Indies they sometimes curve north or continue on the same route, hitting the Florida Keys and the southern States. You never can tell what they are going to do next. I have had a few anxious moments dodging some of them. But in these southern latitudes they are easily avoided as their speed is usually about ten knots. It is only when they curve and move to northern latitudes that they begin to gather speed. They usually hit the eastern States or Canada or carry on right up to the Arctic. Sometimes the odd one curves towards Europe, September and October being the worst months. It was one of these that caused the *Valdulia* to sink. People who knew her said that she had a weakness at the fore end, a bulkhead that was taken away. With this weakness and the cargo of coal she would not have lasted long. People can only guess as to what happened. They must have known that she was making water when she sent her first S.O.S. saying that she was making heavy weather, and for ships in the vicinity to please indicate. It was not long after that when she sent out another message that they were abandoning ship. This was early evening and that night and the following day it blew a hurricane. All ships in the vicinity would be hove to in weather like that, so there is little that anybody could have done.

When the hurricane passed over and ships started looking for her there was nothing to be seen. No trace of anything was found except a while after a water-logged lifeboat belonging to her was washed up on Barra.

Between ships going down in bad weather and those lost during the two wars, so many ships were lost by this company around the same area that it was known as Donaldson's Deep. It is definitely the worst run in the world for bad weather. It has a special place on the Plimsoll Mark—W.N.A. (Winter North Atlantic). I had an uncle drowned there in 1916 on his first trip on the *Cambotia*, after getting a second mate's ticket at the age of twenty-one. My father was in another ship of the same line, the *Kelvinia*, which was lost there around the same time. They were bound to get it sooner or later, these Donaldson's North Atlantic boats. One of them, the *Athenia*, was the first Second World War sinking. The most vivid recollection of the men who served in them during the First World War is of listening to the trampling of the army horses trying to keep rhythm with the rolling of the ship in the heavy north Atlantic seas. Getting torpedoed in one of these boats was the worst thing that could happen to any seaman, as the men from the prairies of Canada and the States who were carried to look after the horses had never been on a boat before, and were liable to go berserk after going into lifeboats.

Life in Merchant Navy ships before the war was very hard, fed on your 'pound and pint', but some runs were worse than others for bad weather. Any short trip out of Glasgow to Canada, the States or Scandinavian countries was bad. These passenger cargo liners belonging to Donaldson and the Anchor Line had a bad run with wind, snow and ice in winter and fog in summer. I am sure the men with responsibilities aboard them were hurried on to an early grave. True, the ships went at a moderate speed in bad visibility but what was a moderate speed with a schedule to keep and tides to catch?—it was either get on or get out.

Glen's of Glasgow used to leave Glasgow with deck cargoes of coke right up to the bridge, held with uprights and wire netting, and constant shouts of coke going over the side. Then they would leave the Baltic with deck cargoes of timber up to the bridge held together with wires and chains, lashed in a way that it could all be let go at a moment's notice. Deck cargoes of timber were always bad for causing lists. If you met with very bad weather you were liable to lose the lot. It was a common occurence for ships that left the Baltic with deck cargoes up to the bridge to reach their discharging port with not enough left on deck to kindle a fire with. But it was the men who sailed in these coastal tramps who were the real tough breed of the Merchant Navy. How they stuck these kinds of ships that were never in port for one night all these years, from the time they went to sea until retiring age, is beyond me.

The British coast is the hardest coast in the world to navigate with fog, tides, sandbanks and weather. There were some coasters with regular runs doing the same thing for years on end, like the Kelly boats out of Belfast. They had to know only two courses, south east and north west, from Belfast to Liverpool and back. I know because one night in Ma Carroll's pub in Belfast there was a Kelly boat Master there along with a lady friend. They fell out over something and she started to shout, 'Masters they call themselves, south east, north west'. But Masters of coastal tramps were bullied to do things by their owners. I know for I have seen it happen. They would be forced to keep old vessels going that were leaking like buckets, and the pumps would not be able to cope with the rolling, leaving a free surface effect in the double bottoms. Hearing the water swishing back and fore down below and her so loaded to the marks, it was enough to drive anybody crazy. How so many of these small craft survived on the coast for so long is a miracle.

Gardiner's Shipping Company's *Ardachy* survived two wars and she must have been getting battered around for the best part of forty years. I know she was around in the First World War because I was once in one of these big ships out of London. One day a crowd of us were talking out on the hatch, somebody from up north telling how he was shanghaied into the *Ardachy*. The old bosun, a west country man, was listening, and after this fellow finished telling his story says, 'Don't tell me the *Ardachy* is still around'. Somebody says to the bosun, 'You won't know this *Ardachy*, bosun, she usually runs up the west coast of Scotland'.

The bosun says, 'I know her all right'. Then he started to tell his story about her. He was in the navy during the First World War and the naval craft he was in went into Stornoway. They were dying for a pint but service personnel were barred so his mate says to him, 'Seeing there is a slight drizzle on we'll put on oilskins, seaboots and sou'westers, go into the pub and tell them we're off that wee coaster over there, the *Ardachy*'. That is what they did, but as soon as they entered the pub all they could see there were fellows clad in the same rig-out as themselves. 'Well', says the old fellow behind the bar, 'what ship are you two from?' There was a slight pause then it came out, 'The *Ardachy*'. At this, the old fellow started to moan and groan, then said, 'The *Ardachy*, the *Ardachy*, everybody in Stornoway tonight is on the *Ardachy*. She would have to be as big as a Western Ocean Liner before she could carry all of you. I'll give you two a pint, then get out'. The last time I was aboard her was in one of these Ayrshire coal ports. We landed up aboard her after the pubs had shut. I remember her Islay Master, John McNiven, singing 'The Yellow Rose of Texas'. Unfortunately I heard that some time afterwards he was drowned in some coaster that went down at the Isle of Man.

Delivering food and other various necessities of life is one thing, but a word must be said for the people who sell these commodities to the public after they are delivered. Some locations might be better than others for having money to pay their grocer but people living in the country and the islands without regular wages were always at risk of not getting fed. As these people were in funds only at certain times of the year, and even then it was only with luck they would have funds, a grocer's life was one of worry, and sometimes ended in bankruptcy. Both my grandparents on my mother's side were in that kind of business, and even when they went out of business my grandfather was for years travelling for Hamilton, Murray and Co., a Glasgow firm, so most of his life was spent attending to the needs of people.

It is more than likely he had to listen to some abuse on his travels. Travel he did over the Highlands and Islands with poor roads in these days, and sometimes with no roads of any description around the Ross-shire and Kintail area. He had various rest houses along the way. Wherever the Scholar Bhan from Barra was teaching was one, and they would have a bit of a booze-up together. My grandparents were well acquainted with this well-educated man, John Johnson, who was always known to folks as the Scholar Bhan, and it is through them that I heard something of the man's history. I think it would be my grandmother who knew him first, him being at one time a teacher in Mingulay, where the Berneray children had to attend school. I heard her say the Mingulay schoolmaster was bound for Berneray to teach the light-keeper's children when he was pulled out of the MacCaulay's boat and made to stay there. I believe the law would be a bit dubious of going over there to sort them out. They must have been a wild-looking lot, for it was there that Robert Louis Stevenson got his idea for *Treasure Island*, with them looking like pirates. He was over there with a member of the family who was doing maintenance work on the lighthouse, which had been built by the Stevensons. Anyway the next I heard them talking about the Scholar Bhán he was teaching in the Navigation School in Newcastle, for how long I don't know, but he was in my grandfather's territory when he was travelling for Hamilton & Co. in Bracora, Loch Morar, and then for a while on the island of Eigg, this place also being in my grandfather's travelling district. I don't remember which place it was, but they were having a dram one night along with the Director of Education, Mr Morrison, a Lewis man. Gaelic was being spoken and the Director was telling the Scholar Bhán to try and get something into the children's brains, when he replied, *'Ciamar eudal ni mise ruid e dh'fhairaich air dia?'*, meaning, how could he do what God couldn't do? When I knew him he was schoolmaster in Grean in Barra, whose population, according to him, were not well-versed in small boat handling. I heard him on about them a few times. Auntie Bella when she was nursing in North Bay had them in her district.

The other house my grandfather was always glad to go to was Scoppy's house in Bornish, South Uist. Scoppy would guide him to the best chair in the house while the boys would take off his boots and bring a basin of hot water for his feet. Scoppy was another who kept shop at the Castlebay haaf fishing days, having a shop in Vatersay where there were plenty of curing stations. It was not in my grandfather's nature to be severe about paying, but sometimes the firm had to clamp down and it was poor gran who would get the abuse.

He was never happier after retiring than with a pen and ink writing for some geezer who was after a blind pension, or any pension for that matter. There was always a struggle to get pensions as societies were involved in these days.

The people I knew best were at the Balla in Eriskay, and I think everybody there was getting some sort of money, even Masag was receiving the blind pension, but she lost it when she was spied one day at the cattle sale by McColl, the excise man, who was the person taking all to do with the blind pension. Also the three boats at the Balla in Eriskay were in somebody else's name, so the real owners were all paid as hired hands who were entitled to dole money. A fellow in one crew got a bit too greedy and he tried this transitional racket while the herring season was on. If you worked one or two days a week you would get a stamp for the remainder of the week. Questions were asked by the Exchange but he got out of it by telling them that the big boat was out on the bank, and that he was working with the small boat a couple of days a week for carrying the fish to the stations.

Ronald who was the fish salesman, Harbour Master and merchant all rolled into one in Castlebay, was another of the mob from Balla. He was certainly a local boy made good. There were only two places he ever worked, Loch Skipport and Castlebay. He must also have owned a third of the Barra fleet at one time. He had another brother, Neil, who was a Harbour Master out in New Zealand, but the brother who outshone all of them was Eoghain, who was a Master in the Royal Mail. How he ever got his foot on the bridge of one of these ships in these days is something I never found out. He certainly was no *Conway* boy, the *Conway* being the training ship moored in the Thames for the sons of gentlemen. That was one place which was barred to all of us from the islands for the simple reason that nobody had the money to go there. This Master who was in the Royal Mail might have reached a higher station in life than his brother Ronald, but I do not think he would have come up to his standard as far as finance was concerned.

I remember when I started to visit Castlebay in the family boat during the thirties, Ronald's business in Castlebay was a force to be reckoned with. His shop on the street was both the harbour master agency for every steamer visiting the pier, and his fish salesman's office. His fishing boats were away by then but even at that he had to have his whole family around him to run the business. It did not matter what time you arrived at the pier, even at first light in the morning in summer, Ronald was there.

There were big fishings in Castlebay around the early thirties. It is surprising how they could handle all the herring that was landed, considering the work that had to be done processing it in these days. One day alone there were over one hundred crans of an average. Two shots alone came to five hundred and thirty crans: the drifter *Young Crow* two hundred and eighty crans and the *Embrace* two hundred and fifty crans, all from Tiree and Coll.

If Tiree was known at one time as the Granary of the Western Isles, the seas around it could boast the same for fishing. After the end of June, Castlebay fishing was all from Heisker, Coll and Tiree, with the seas around them teeming with fish. Tiree and Coll's curse was that they did not have a harbour. If the weather turned bad during the night's fishing you had to batter across to Barra or else make for Canna, which had the only decent anchorage for these inner isles. The big drifters from the East Anglia ports could fish there in all but the most severe of weather conditions. So it was their sailing with their two crews that did most of the fishing there. Barra was living off the cod end by now, as the fleet was down to four boats.

Around the herring stations it was mostly women's work, so apart from merchants and a few working around the stations and flit boats, not much of this wealth went to Barra. Their young men were all away, mostly sailing out of Shields and the Bristol Channel, where, at the time of the Depression, work was pretty hard to come by.

This big fishing came out of the blue in late July 1932. For a few years before this there was not much late summer or early autumn fishing for a few years on Castlebay grounds. All the herring landed in Castlebay came from the north Minch area and Irish grounds after the end of June. As always with the herring fishing, things looked grim before this, some boats not being near a station since the start on 10 May. The herring breaking out at this time during the season could not have started at a better time for the big drifters. With the long nights coming in, it gave the drifter a better chance to have most of their nets hauled before daybreak, as our part of the Minch was bad for dogfish eating the herring in the nets after first light.

With some of these big drifters working up to one hundred nets and the two-crew East Anglia ones well over the hundred mark, severe damage could be done to the haul if unhauled after daybreak. The Tiree herring were very big and easily shaken out of the nets. The greatest problem was that with this herring being so big, it was liable to drop out of the nets before coming over the rails. It was more or less the same class of herring that was caught on the west coast of Ireland. This Irish west coast herring was so big it had to be counted into the baskets.

The winter of 1932 was very good, with shoals of herring almost going high and dry around the fords between the Uists and Benbecula. I myself, when a schoolboy, saw boats fishing herring in the sound of Eriskay when the school was out for dinner. Low water it was and the herring boats were taking the bottom in the Sound full of herring. It was only when the flood started that they were able to sail for Mallaig. If one of Shonnie Clarke's klondykers was around you did not have to go to Mallaig, you just fished away until you dropped.

My folks with the *Ocean Star* once shot their nets before it got dark. They started with the ring net along with the *St Vincent*, went twice to the klondyker during the night, arrived at the nets in the morning, and only the two anchor-catcher's buoys showing the nets full of herring at the bottom with buoys sunk.

The prices Shonnie Clarke's klondykers were giving was not much— you were lucky if you got a pound a cran for it. Even the ring net was hard work these days—with no spring rope being used, the soles had to be hauled by three men and the herring had to be baled with baskets. Funnily enough, it was somebody who was fishing on the Frazer River in Canada who brought back home the idea of herring being baled by a baler. It would be the Norwegians who used the patent in Canada, as there used to be many of them at the fishing there.

I was one day in Lerwick aboard an east coast purse netter when this old-timer was seen looking down at her with interest. Purse netting being then in its infancy, somebody said to the old fellow how did they like this new net up in the Shetlands. 'Well', he said, 'I don't know if anybody likes this so-called new net of yours, but it's certainly not new to me. I worked that net in the Puget Sound forty years ago. Just wait', he said and off he went like a shot. I could hear these east coast loons talking about the 'feel old yin' who was working this net on some sound. When I heard Puget Sound being mentioned I knew he must have been around the Vancouver area at one time in his life as I had met some Shelties out there along with my own relations. It was not long until he was back with the proof—pictures taken out there in the 1920s of himself aboard purse netters. But give every fisherman in this country his due, they were not the first to start this wholesale slaughter of catching herring this way. They were driven to it, as they could not make a living competing with the foreign catching power that was fishing among them. True, the Loch Fyne men started the ring net but they were forced into that way of fishing because of all the 'fire', or phosphorus, that was in their seas.

The herring that was caught around the Vancouver Island area went only for fish meal. Some of it was kippered or eaten fresh, but salted it tasted awful. This herring and the herring they used to catch in eastern Canada had the same taste, nothing like the European herring. Whether the Gulf Stream or its feeding had anything to do with this I do not know, and why some years were better than others is another mystery. All I know is after giving people despair and anxiety the herring would show up again, drying itself in the pools around the shore. This is what happened in 1933, when the summer fishing in Castlebay must have become one of the best on record, lasting all through the summer and up to the time of the East Anglia fishing in October. A Lewis man was telling me years afterwards that the east coast drifter he sailed on grossed £4,500 for the summer season. She could not have been the one that grossed the most for there were plenty of the East Anglia two-crew drifters there. Sad to say not much of it stayed in Barra, where there was an addition to the fleet of one boat which put it up to four in 1933.

One of the MacLeods of Northbay, the Pol, got this boat new that summer, the *Reul Na Maidne* (Morning Star). She arrived there at a time when the North Bay fleet was away. Nearly all of the Barra fishing fleet was in the hands of shore owners, it being so easy to sell them off. The Eriskay fleet being communally owned, everybody had to be consulted before selling. Most of them were there before the First World War, arriving new under sail power only. It was over the years that engine power was put into them. With bad fishing and men coming back and fore, sometimes to different boats and different men putting something new into them, it would have taken a Philadelphia lawyer to figure out who owned them. But they were always there, sometimes laid up, other times fishing ,and anybody shouting for money for his share out of one of them would be told nicely, 'If you want your share come aboard and work her'.

Eriskay had its Jonahs too, and one of them was a woman called the Coach. This Coach did a bit of travelling, as she had a sister away in Mull where she visited at intervals. The entrance to the harbour in Eriskay is very narrow, with only enough room for one boat to get comfortably between the rock and the shore. As boats left and arrived on Mondays and Saturdays there was not much danger of any boats colliding. But this particular day the *St Columba*, which was working great lines at the off-herring season, was leaving the harbour with the Coach aboard. The *Ocean Star* was in Castlebay on some business and they met in the awkward part. It was a close thing. They were not damaged, managing to shave past each other with fenders helping to soften the collision. So much for the Coach, she went away to Mull, had her holiday and on the night she came back was met in Pollachar by her son-in-law and Shemus, the ferryman's son. About half way to Eriskay in the dark, Shemus was lighting a match around the engine when a fire started and he was pretty badly burned. It was the folks at East Kilbride who saw the fire and before they reached them, half the boat was burned. All they could do was put a big stone through her and let

Mother sitting, aunt Bella standing. Glasgow, 1922.

her sink to the bottom, then make back to Pollachar, as Shemus needed medical attention. The boat was retrieved the following day and the Coach got home, but after this she was avoided like the plague. I think she had some former episodes, but this last tour was exceptional. I cannot remember how she travelled after that, if she ever did, but I do remember the

144

ferryman's wife laying down the law, saying she was not going to sail in their boats again. Eriskay was going to be something like Alcatraz for the Coach from then on.

There were always ones in the islands who were well-known throughout the islands wherever seamen lived. One of these, Michael Neil Eoin from Barra, or Michael Barr-Ach, as he was known to seamen in other islands, was, I think, the most famous. He was one of the Clipper tall ships men who never married or settled down. Not many of these old timers being left, Michael was inclined to get on to the younger generation for not being proper seamen. His first call in Glasgow after breakfast was the Anchor Line ship, *Cameronia*, if she happened to be at Yorkhill quay, to give big Hugh MacLeod, the bosun, another Barra man, his desserts. After a few more calls he would go back to the Broomielaw to give some Barra men a lashing around the shipping office and have some dinner in the sailors' home, making sure he made the sign of the cross before and after dinner, just to see if he would annoy anybody. Before leaving the sailors' home he would give the barometer a couple of taps, shake his head and off he would go once more on his rounds. In his younger days when his mother was alive he used to go home to see her, but like many more of us when the parents are gone the place is never the same again. It does not matter what other people think of anyone there is always a special place in a mother's heart for a son. How often have I heard in a lifetime at sea when something dangerous has passed, 'A mother's prayer'. I believe the loveliest songs in any language have been made for mothers.

Michael and his mother were sitting in the house this day with him telling her what he had been doing since he was last home. He had been whaling out of one of these New England ports. This way of killing whales was practised up to about eighty years ago from Nantucket, New Bedford and New London. At one time before the country was fully developed it was the United States' main industry, but after their civil war, when most of their whaling fleet was sunk by southern raiders, the *Shenandoah* being the most famous, whaling was never the same again. With the discovery of oil in Texas the need for whale oil was not so great but there must have been a few of them ploughing the oceans in Michael's time.

Michael's mother was getting rather interested in how these big whales were caught. Rowing small twenty-foot, clinker-built Carvel boats, would make too much noise through the water, so they would have to glide right up to the whales and stick harpoons into them. After this anything could happen. The whale could go to the bottom or else belt away on what was known then as a Nantucket sledge ride. If the whale was sounding, more line had to be paid out to her, the line having to be wetted, with smoke coming out of it as it was running so fast. If the whale had belted away on a Nantucket sledge ride a turn had to be put on the line and the whale boat would be pulled along with her. His mother, listening to all of this way of catching whales was a bit mystified, so Michael decided to put the theory into practise. His mother was sewing at the time, with the ball of thread on her lap, and had just put thread into the needle. Michael saw the cat going around the floor so he gets a hold of the needle, sticks it into the cat, the cat dives away pulling the thread off the reel and Michael shouts, 'Pay out and wet line, mother'.

Michael spent his last days on this earth in a home for old sailors doing his Bosun there with the wash down every day. Every old sailor they would bring in was inclined to resent taking orders from Michael, so he had a job getting them to do the wash down at first. One day the home was visited by a ship owner, Lord Inverclyde, who owned the Burns and Laird Line. He contributed some money to the running of the home so he wanted to see the old sailors. They of course had been told to be on their best behaviour for this visit. Michael was busy with the wash down and was not paying much attention when Lord Inverclyde walked over to him and said, 'Do you know who I am?' 'No', replied Michael.

'Well, I am Lord Inverclyde.'

Michael, thinking he was another old sailor being brought in, says, 'Oh is that so, well we'll soon knock that out of you!' The response to this was laughter all round.

Castlebay, Barra, was the only place in our southern islands where a living could be made herring fishing. It was also where Alick Eoin Mhor came from to Eriskay to buy calves around the end of spring, when they could hardly walk. He would then leave them for about six weeks until some grass grew, which would enable him to get them in some condition to be able to walk to the shore for ferrying. I remember this well for it used to send the shivers through me when he would arrive over on Saturday in our boat the *Ocean Star*, which was always used for ferrying, with his usual 'carry out'. These shivers were not caused by his 'carry out', but by having the unenviable job of going around the houses to tell them to have their calves at the shore on Monday for ferrying before the boat proceeded to the fishing grounds.

I have had to listen to plenty of tongue in my time but what I used to hear on this round-up was who was going to pay them for feeding the calves for the six weeks. I would then have to listen to the story of the nourishing that was showered on these animals during this period. I would arrive home all in, giving Alick and my grandparents a running commentary on how much they were held in high esteem by the population, granny and Alick being cousins.

Word came one evening that two old sisters staying together wanted to sell some creature that was not going to live when he was over last, but after a few mouthfuls of grass was able to see the summer. The evening was well on by the time the word came about this animal so off Alick went with me to see him. They managed to get him into the byre so Alick would have difficulty seeing him, with one sister on each side to hold him up in case he would go into a coma. With them saying that he was a *Dha Bhlianaich*, a two-year-old, and Alick, half drunk, lighting matches to have a look at him while they held him up, a deal was finally made, but not to their liking of course, which was the way with all of them.

Ones on the west side of Barra called Boreachs had big crofts, but used to come to Castlebay to work during the herring season, usually at the coal hulk, the ones living in Castlebay getting the best jobs. The summer fishing had already started when one young fellow arrived there, as he was late finishing work on his father's croft. I have seen this man, Michael e Drobhair, a few times when he used to come around the fishing boats in later years visiting old ship mates. He did plenty of sailing before he finally fell heir to his father's croft but he never forgot old ship mates. When the cattle sales were on Michael was always giving his mates their booze. This story happened before he ever left home. Arriving and finding all of the jobs taken he was told by somebody that there was a herring drifter looking for a cook and coiler. Michael was one who would have a go at anything, so he goes aboard the drifter and gets the job. Cooking in the islands' boats at this time was very plain, but these east coast men had to be fed a dinner. They were always on at Michael as to why he was not making pudding. He would have heard of this pudding, but how to make it was beyond his skill. Asking the loons about cooking in the local fleet was not much help, as their cooking left much to be desired, being very primitive. But Michael was not one to be beaten. He got talking to some girls working around the houses where lodgers were. For a laugh they gave poor Michael a bum steer by telling him to give the crew plenty of rice pudding. Away to the shop Michael goes for the stores and then asks for a stone of rice. 'A stone of rice?', asks the shopkeeper, 'what on earth are you going to do with a stone of rice, feed everybody in the bay?'

'No', says Michael, 'just these blokes along with me. I am going to make sure that they have plenty'.

The shopkeeper did not say much more. I believe the word was spread around the street that Michael e Drobhair was going to make pudding, the street being a small world of its own where everybody knew everything that went on. The big day arrived when Michael was about to make the pudding. The big pot was ready to hold the stone of rice, as Michael had been told by his 'tutors' ashore. The rice was not on long when he noticed the lid rising from the pot and continuing to rise. Help was called from the deck to find out what was causing this strange phenomenon, these east coast men crowding round the galley door and the rice by this time pouring out on to the stove. They were all shocked at the waste that 'loon' Michael had created, squandering all that 'siller'. I cannot help but admire Michael for his courage in being adventurous enough to tackle anything.

The Coddie bought the flounders caught in the Sound of Barra from the Eriskay crowd, mostly semi-retired men and young ones out of school. He bought most of them but sometimes the haggling about the price would prove too much and they would go to Bruernish to a man called Niall e Garadh, the Cruckil, in Ardvenish, or sometimes all the way to the Allt. The Coddie's favourite saying during the haggling was, 'when were you last at confession?' Once they stood out for the extra penny a dozen, and the Coddie had to give in. Of course he just added on another penny for himself, so that was the price inflated by two pennies.

It started to blow from the south east when this crowd left North Bay for Eriskay. The Coddie was over in Eriskay with tourists a couple of days after that and he met one of the crowd in the boat. He was asked how he got on selling the flounders. 'How did I get on?', says the Coddie, 'I did nothing after you fellows left that day but light candles for you so that you would reach the other side safely, and I also had to listen to the sharp edge of the Calleach's tongue', Calleach being the Gaelic for old woman.

Another time there was a sale of work and the Coddie was busy selling, a job he was well suited for as he was a herring salesman before the First World War. This man from Eriskay, Donnall Cimanach, bought an old sail from him for his own boat. He spread the sail out and right away noticed a hole in it all the way up at the fifth reef. So off he went to where the Coddie was selling his wares, but he had to wait his turn to complain as there was a wee girl ahead of him complaining about a doll she had bought whose legs had fallen off. At last Donnall had his say and started off pointing to the hole, 'Why did you sell this sail, you devil?' The Coddie replied in Gaelic: *'Latha nach cuir u orra ach sinn dhe, she telegrapa gun na siarach h-uit.'* ('The day you will only have to put on that much of it will be a one-way ticket to the other world for you.')

At other times the Coddie would come to Eriskay with a squad of tourists to have tea in granny's house. He would point out to granny who was rich and who was not. Then he would say, 'I've got a very rich one there. I'll send her over. See and charge her plenty'.

There was another friend of our family, the Cruckil, who also had a shop. He had a hard time of it as a prisoner of war in Turkey during the First World War. His ship was caught there at the beginning of the war so that was him for four years away from his family. Turkey had the highest percentage of deaths among their prisoners of war, as only ten per cent of them got home alive. The Cruckil came home after the war and lived to a ripe old age. I know the area he lived in well as my auntie was a nurse there for sixteen years, leaving there to go to Onich, near Fort William, from where she retired.

One night in my father's house in Eriskay the talk started about giants whom people had seen. Lachlan Ian Mhor from Boisdale was staying there as granny had her house in Haun closed, because she was getting old and had to come to stay with my mother to be cared for. Lachlan began first to tell of his giant. The person who actually saw this giant of a man was Lachlan's uncle, one of Eachan Ruadh's boys who was in sailing vessels. This sailing vessel he was in was on a voyage from Australia to Valparaiso. It was a busy, stormy run, that one, at one time, the coal run from Newcastle, New South Wales on the Hunter River, to the west coast of South America. They would have to drop the pilot and start clawing to windward, not being able to go against the trade winds, in order to give the Snares to the south of New Zealand a wide berth before squaring away before the westerlies in the howling fifties. That area must have been the graveyard of a few of them. The vessel Lachlan's uncle was on was well away before the westerlies after making her southing, when one night it started to blow worse than it had ever done before. It was taking all the strength of three men to keep her from broaching to, with her reaping along sometimes at up to eighteen knots in the showers. It was coming to the end of the three men's two-hour stint at the wheel when the Master said, 'If I give you three a tot of rum each will you stay another hour at her?' The Master was hoping after altering course a bit to the north he would work her out of the hurricane. The men agreed, so the bottle of rum was taken up, starting with the man at the lee wheel, then the one in the centre, until they came to the man at the weather side. As soon as this man at the weather side put out his hand to grab the glass, his weight came off the wheel and away she went into the wind until she went on her beam ends. There she was on her beam ends with the mast, sails and yards stopping her from going over altogether. Then, by the grace of God, and some mother's prayer,the wind started taking off until by morning some of the wreckage and masts were cut away and they managed to right her.

The cargo had shifted, so it was down below to trim the coal until she was balanced enough for making passage. After this it can be told in a few words what it took weeks to achieve. Jury masts were rigged and sails got on her until she eventually reached Valparaiso. On arriving there the Master took all of them for a feed, as a lot of their stores had gone bad after her going on her beam ends. The Master says to them, 'Order what you like, boys, it's all on the company'. So they started to tuck in. Before they had finished, a huge man entered the eating house, sat at a table and ordered 'the usual' in Spanish. I believe there were some big, hefty lads among the crew but there was nobody to equal this gigantic man who was sitting at the table. He was dressed in the rig of a country cowboy and so they took it for granted that he could speak only Spanish. So all of their remarks were made in English but all turned in amazement when they saw the food being brought to his table—the hind quarter of a bull. 'The hind quarter?', said all of us to Lachlan.

'Yes', says Lachlan, 'and vegetables too.'

I cannot remember very well how many stones of potatoes and carrots and other trimmings he said were placed in front of this mountain man but he took his time eating all of it. The boys of the sailing vessel were making merry with the local brew after their feed and passing remarks about the man. When he had finished he stood up in the middle of the floor and asked, in perfect English, which one of them wanted to take him on. They all looked at him, stunned. 'Well', he said, 'none of you are up to much, although there are a few among you who could stand a round or two, but I'll give you some advice, never again start talking in a strange place about a stranger when he's around to hear you. I am leaving now and it will be another five days before I'll eat again at my high place in the Andes'. With that he walked out. He was a Britisher.

My father's giant, whom he saw at a Norwegian whaling station in Harris, was as fat as he was tall. Benstack John, six foot five, a cousin from our own island, was with him, and their heights were compared. The top of big John's head was four inches below the giant's shoulder. The ones sailing away from home all their lives were saying that they never saw the likes of this man in all of their travels. They never saw him eating, but I suppose if Lachlan had seen him he would have been tucking into the hind quarter of a whale.

My granny's giant was a local lad living next door to her in Berneray, Barra Head. I do not know just how tall he was, but he was away at the shows. His name was Padruig Mhor Donache Ciobair, Sinclair was his surname. After my granny's people moved over to Castlebay and he was away at the shows he used to visit them, but she said that he ate just like anybody else.

My giant was Angus MacAskill. I never saw him in the flesh, only pictures of him. Many a time when I was in Sydney, Cape Breton, I wished I'd had the time to go and see his clothes and boots. They were kept in a village there called Saint Ann. This man, the Cape Breton Giant, grew up around this village, although his place of birth was Berneray, Harris, which is a coincidence as that is two Bernerays that produced giants. What I could gather about him from the person who was showing me the photographs of him in Sydney is that he was born at a bad time of year in winter when milk was scarce. All the cows had dried up and his mother had died giving him birth, or else she was very poorly. Anyway the only milk available was from a mare that had just foaled, and the mare's milk was given to him. Whether this had anything to do with his abnormal height and strength I do not know, but strength he had, and plenty of it. His family emigrated to Nova Scotia during the Clearances, as did many more families from the islands, when he was three years old. This man in Sydney had a picture of his shoe in which, he informed me, a cat had a litter of kittens, ten in number. He was in the shows in this country. One night he was on the stage in London when Queen Victoria was in the audience. He stamped his foot on the stage and it went a couple of inches through the wood. He did not live very long, as he died in his thirties. He was injured once in New York while lifting up an anchor that weighed a ton. A sailor told him to 'put daylight under it' but the fluke caught him in the shoulder. After this it was a downhill trek for him, and he died shortly afterwards.

Eriskay's strongest man died young. He was found dead in the dock in Cardiff. It was something of a mystery how it happened. He was a cousin of my father. The ones who saw him leaving the Chain Locker pub said he was sober when he left there. How it happened to him can be anybody's guess. His name was MacNiall Bhan Angus MacInnes, on account of his fair hair. I heard while sailing away from home that he would lift three coils of wire one hundred and twenty fathoms each on a steel bar. He once hauled up the mast of one of the fishing boats, the *St Vincent*, on his own. This was an all-hands job and heavier in these days as it was before engine power was put aboard boats. A reef was cut out of the sail when the mast was shortened once engines were put aboard.

We had all seen some giants in our time but nobody's giant could beat Lachlan's. His was the daddy of them all, wolfing down the hind quarter of a wild bull from the Pampas.

Lachlan himself was on a ship over in the United States discharging cargo in some port. At tea time they had some tinned food to eat, but Lachlan and a Harris man were late in coming into the mess where everyone was eating, and of course, as is a common occurence, there was nothing left for them in the kits. So they both went back to the galley, got another tin between them and had their meal. It was not long after they had finished that the boys began to double up with pain but Lachlan and the Harris man were all right. Some union representative or mission man was called in, then a Yankee doctor came aboard and diagnosed the sickness as food poisoning. The Master and the chief steward said that could not be as there were two men who had eaten from a tin and they had not suffered any ill effects. The arguing was going on in the saloon when Lachlan and the Harris man were asked to go over to the doctor that he might have a look at them. The two of them went into the saloon, the doctor looked them over, saw that they were healthy enough and then, as there was a map of the British Isles in the saloon, the doctor asked them to point out where they came from. They pointed to the Western Isles. 'Ah', said the doctor, 'now I know why you two didn't get food poisoning. Do you have a whaling station up there?' Lachlan looked at the Harris man who began telling the doctor about the one near him.

'Now tell me', the doctor says, 'do you go there to get whale meat?'

The Harris man replied 'Yes.'

'Well, that's your answer', says the doctor to the Master and chief steward, banging his fist on the table. Then, looking at Lachlan and the Harris man, he says, 'these two guys could eat as much poison as would kill a dozen men and still be O.K.' So whether the tin they got was all right or whether they were immune to poison through eating whale meat I do not know, but the doctor made the Master and chief steward get rid of the rest of the tins.

The famous *Politician*, of *Whisky Galore* fame, went ashore in February 1941, and from the time he saw her until the time he unlocked the seal to get down the hatch, Uncle Angus through marriage, Aoghais Calumn, was on edge. He could not concentrate on anything else but the *Politician*. He was talking to some of the crew before they left, I think he had sailed with one of them. For a whole month she was left there without any watch being kept on her, and people going on and off, never going near where the whisky was. Angus was fishing with us that winter as their family had no boat, having sold that unlucky boat they had, the *Reul e Chuan*. He was forever at my father to go out to the *Politician*. One day he would mention the shop-keeper, the next the school master, everyone of learning he could think of or who told him there was no harm in getting a few cases of whiskey from her. He would even try to tell you the priest had given him permission just to get aboard her.

At last my father gave way and agreed to go aboard with him. As soon as Angus went aboard he made straight for the chief officer's room and started to go through drawers looking for keys. He did not get what he was looking for so he made for the carpenter's room and after a while he found what he wanted. Only a few cases were taken out of the hatch that night and the locking bars were put back on and secured. The other relations down at Balla were given some of it. Uncle Iagan and Donald MacKinnon on the *Mystical Rose* both got paralytic on the Sunday night, the children wondering what was afoot and telling other children at service on Sunday evening how drink was flowing freely at Balla. These two were at the fishing all their lives, so they did not know how to behave like sailors do when among broached whisky. They said they got it from '*gillean Cnoc Na Luich*' or 'the boys from Brae of Mic', which was their name for upper Balla. On Monday we were away to the harbour and went out fishing with the *St Winifred*. The season was at an end but Angus was saying we were better aboard the bigger boat, as people would not see us coming and going out of the Haun, with him now being in possession of the keys to the hatch of the *Politician*, and as happy as a dog with two tails.

Our relations from Bunivulin aboard the boat were not believing us when we told them that we got some of the whisky at the weekend, until Angus started showing the keys, holding on to them like grim death. We left the harbour, shot the drift nets, anchored them and then proceeded to go trawling in the Sound. We were seeing people aboard the *Politician* but they were only scouting around, taking odd bits of rope around the deck. Nobody was tackling the hold. Approaching midnight we saw a wee engined boat nearing her from the Lochboisdale area, going alongside her and boarding her. We then got the trawl up and also went alongside. On boarding her we found they had broken the seals. After this she was left free to all comers.

I think people did very well staying away from the whisky hold for a whole month, angels would not do better than that. What was going to happen after this was not the shame on the people who took the whisky, but shame on those who were forever reporting to the police when they were not aboard her themselves. Slippery as an eel she was, with her bunkers burst. She had landed at the door of people who were more capable than most to fish the cargo out of her, but this was not an easy task. Eriskay got most of the blame, that is true enough, as they did take more out of her, but they did not drink all of it themselves, as all the elderly people from other islands had to depend on Eriskay to fish the cargo out. This needed some expert skill, as you had to stab the cases with the grain of the wood or the wood would smash with the bottles. We used to have a knife at the end of a long pole with a notch in it. Once the knife went through with the grain of the wood you had to give it a slight twist. It was then hooked and you had to take it gently out of the stow, loft it all the way up until it broke the water surface, then somebody standing by had to put a hook inside the wire that was around the case. How some did not get killed is a miracle, as there were some panhandlers going aboard her who never were afloat in their lives other than the passage out to her. One night I saw three of them walking into the lower hold thinking it was solid, as there were hatch covers floating on the surface. They had to be fished out with the fishing poles we used to retrieve the whisky cases.

All this retrieving the whisky from the lower hold was to come after what was on the twin deck was finished, the twin deck lasting about a week. When we boarded her that first night the ones in the small boat had broken the seal so that there was no use for uncle Angus's keys any more. From now on number five hatch was open to all comers, and they came in their hundreds. Aoghais Ruadh, Aoghais Ian and his brother Roderick, 'the Case', were the ones in the small boat from south Lochboisdale. They were working at her when the first salvage tug came with Donald Ferguson, who was one of Lloyd's agents at the time, on board.

I remember them drinking whisky with tea for chasers in our boat and Aoghais Ian telling us how much whisky was aboard her, as he had seen a cargo plan. With the drink in abundance he got a bit mixed up with his figures. At last he said, 'My figures are getting as bad as the old woman's who was staying at the back of Ben Mhor who had a small croft. There was a quota of a few sheep to every croft and the man who made sure you did not exceed your quota was the manager, Glas. He paid this old woman a visit this day to ask how many sheep and rams she had. She told him that she made three yards of special cloth with the precious wool that came from around the rams' testicles.'

Roderick 'the Case' said, 'The man should have taken a mathematician along with him'.

Aoghais Ruadh said it would take more than a mathematician to solve the problem.

Eventually when the whisky finished on the twin deck and they started to fish for it you could hardly get around the hole with the crowd who were fishing. Uncle Angus was saying this day, 'We'll have to dig and get into the manhole at the back'. My father replied, asking if he had not had enough yet. 'No', said uncle Angus, and informed my father that the schoolmaster was telling him that the tilley lamps were in good order that night, so they had better have a go at the manhole.

These tilley lamps were used when dances were held in the school, so we had the use of them as the schoolmaster was in our crew. Angus was getting everything ready, including picks and pinches, as there was a lot of digging to be done to get into the manhole. When we went aboard that night there was the usual crowd around the twin deck, every party with a couple of poles, but they were not getting very much as it was harder to reach the centre and getting deeper. Our own relations from Glendale were there. I remember I was the first from our party to go down but I just stood at the bottom of the ladder waiting for the gear to appear. When my uncle Alisdair saw the gear that was sent down, the shouting started, 'What is that devil Aoghais Calumn going to do now, is he trying to break her up and take her home with him?'

We were not long digging when snoopers started coming around and others coming from a long way away who were not acquainted with the working of her, and who had no fishing gear. At last, after a struggle, as most of the rubble removed was bricks, the goal was reached, the hatch opened up, and what a sight met our eyes! High and dry to the top. I am sure three hundred cases came out of that manhole that night, as much as they could carry. One boat from North Bay, the *Watchful*, had, I am sure, sixty cases. She was a big engined boat. It was the time of year when people were home to do their spring work as more work was being done about the crofts. The ones with bigger crofts who had ploughing to do were beginning to suffer, as that kind of work needed sobriety, but as we in Eriskay were turning the ground with spades we could manage so long as nobody fell down. The schoolmaster was our biggest worry, as he was getting worse than uncle Angus for making plans and getting tilleys ready.

I remember one day passing the school house and there was uncle Angus chasing around the garden. Thinking that he had gone round the bend I went over to find out what he was up to, chasing the big boys and trying to get them inside after playtime. I asked him where the schoolmaster was. He pointed to the house, then once he had bullied the boys inside the school he went into the house and there was the school master playing away at the piano along with Oisean, another local worthy, singing 'Maxwelltown Braes'.

Angus was nodding to the two of them, saying, 'It's going to be Rotain and his wee chain yet', Rotain being the one who used to take people away to the looney bin. He had a wee chain for chaining them up, so Angus was saying.

The only other night there was any excitement out of the ordinary was the night the money was discovered, three big boxes of it. Some crew must have had their quota early and gone down number six hold where they came across it. I remember somebody coming to the coaming of number five hold and shouting, 'sub up', then throwing a handful of the money down. Everybody began to crowd around number six to go down for some of the money. I heard someone else shout that there was plenty for all, as there were another two boxes of it, then another voice was heard saying the money was of no use as it was all West Indian ten shilling notes. Others then began to name money changers who would cash them, from George Robie in Port Said to Frisco Paddy in San Francisco, not to mention 'Kate Mhor' in Barker's shop on the Govan Road in Glasgow.

At this time in 1941 British money was not worth much in any country. Nobody wanted to know us or our money. What was left of the free world was hoping, praying and preaching isolationism, but apart from some comforts and lease lending which had begun about this time no one wished to know us. All they got out of the *Politician* was a load of booze. People call it thieving, but every bottle salvaged was put down the drain in Greenock. Also there was a signature missing on the ten shilling notes, something that anyone would have noticed at a glance. The other luxury goods aboard were to pay for everything she was going to bring back with her, Britain being the workshop of the world at that time. There were not many who could afford luxury goods in this country then, as few of the population had even a bath in their own homes at that time. Perhaps the *Politician* was sent by Providence to boost up an ageing population as things looked pretty grim with hardly a day going by without some tragic happening, and someone being drowned or killed. Some families had two or three missing, not knowing whether they were alive or dead. The ones who turned up alive were in prisoner of war camps, their families having had to wait over a year for word.

I was out at the *Politician* one day in our boat together with Oisean and the island schoolmaster. There was a large box filled with telephones aboard her but everyone there was interested only in the whisky. However before we came out of the hold Oisean was handling one of the phones, and when asked what he was planning to do with it he said that he was taking it home to his father to phone Mari in London. We left the *Politician* but not before Oisean took with him the plates that were lying unwashed in the mess room for over a month, having been used to eat some sloppy hash. We arrived in the Haun and shared out what we'd got, Oisean still with the plates and phone in a bag. He called in at my granny's house. My mother was there and Oisean there and then gave my mother and granny some of the plates,

A crowd in Eriskay, with the car ferry at anchor in Haun Bay, and the tip of Calvay marked with an 'x', where the Politician *went ashore*

telling them how kind we all were when we took him out to the *Politician* in our boat. Granny took one look at them and raised her hands in horror when she saw the unwashed plates which were by this time full of oil, as everything aboard the *Politician* was saturated with oil from burst bunkers. Then the schoolmaster and myself went with Oisean to his father's house, where, after giving his father Lachlan a few scoops out of the bottle and getting him into a merry state, Oisean began again to excavate in the bag, taking out the plates and presenting them to his mother-in-law, leaving the phone until last. When he brought it forth he handed it to his father telling him he was now just as well off as all the neighbours, since he now had a phone in the house to give Mari in London a call. Lachlan took hold of the phone and started shouting into it, with Oisean telling him to shout louder so that Mari would hear him in London.

Oisean had full-time employment with the man who had the shop on Eriskay. The shopkeeper was glad to have him as the shop was a good bit away from the shore so Oisean had plenty of lumbering to do, carrying things to and from the shop. He was a very honest man who just had a habit of shocking some good-living ones.

Oisean was always praising this man Belford who had the shop, and he deserved praise too, as Belford would go out of his way to get anything you asked. This day Oisean came to granny's house carrying a bag of some stuff. Right away he started to praise Belford and the new stuff he was after getting to sell in the shop, some powder he was telling granny which you used and did not need to wash for a month after. Granny was all mystified about this until Belford's wife came to the house one day, and granny asked her about this new powder they had in the shop. It took Belford's wife some time to figure out what granny was talking about till at last she screwed up her face with laughter saying, 'Oh, he must mean the D.D.T.'.

There was a time before the *Politician*, around the middle 'twenties, when barrels of 'hooch' were coming on the shore and one of them landed on the same stretch of sand that Prince Charles Edward Stewart landed on in 1745. There was a gathering around the barrel of all the locals but no one wished to be the first to taste it. My old grandpa and a few of his cronies from Balla got to hear about it, so off they went to join the brigade around the barrel. As no one wanted to be the first to taste whatever was inside it old grandpa had a solution to the problem that saved the day, and that was to try it on a dog someone had with him. I was telling this story to a Rhuach from Lewis I once sailed with. 'Well', he says, 'I'll tell you a better one than that', and so he began that they had got a barrel around their shore at Rhu too, and, as in Eriskay, they were all dubious about tasting it. Then this hard case who had been away from home most of his life over in the United States happened to be home at the time. At home also was a brother of his named Colin, who was not very bright. Well, this fellow arrives on the scene with a bucket, which he filled from the barrel. Seeing he was a man of the world, someone asked him what he planned to do with it. He replied that he was going to make his brother Colin drink it first. Colin survived the test with no bad effects, and then everyone joined in, mixing it with cold tea to give it a bit of colouring. As it turned out the contents of the barrels was wood alcohol, white in colour. It did not do them much harm. In our place they only got one barrel of it but I heard an east coast fisherman say that a couple from his village died of it. They had been lying for the weekend at some island and they must have had too much of it. They reckoned it came from some ship which had been sunk during the war and had taken all this time for the hatches to break up, so releasing the barrels to the surface. Every island got a share of it.

Old people who could not go aboard the 'Polly' were descending on Eriskay as everyone had relatives there, especially at that time. They would go away with some of the loot then start calling the ones in Eriskay a crowd of thieves and robbers for looting the Polly.

After being left there all that time with no one to worry about her the wreck of the Polly was sold to Arnott and Young of Clydebank. They started to salvage her, taking more of the whisky out of her to lighten her, then filling her up with compressed air before taking her into a safer place in the Sound, where she sank. I was not around at the time but my father was for eight years working for this salvage concern during and after the war, until he started fishing again in 1949. I do not know what went wrong when she was brought into the Sound, something to do with compressed air inside her, however when she sank they had to cut her in two. Taking away the fore end in one piece and with the after end where the whisky was cut down to low water mark, they towed the fore end to Rothesay, eighteen months from the time she went ashore, where she was broken up.

While the booze lasted people just drank out of any vessel that was handy. I remember one morning a relative of ours whose job it was to look after the bull in winter came to our house after letting the bull out. As it was a bad, wet morning my mother said to the man, 'Colin, you had better take a drink of whisky to warm you up'.

'No', says Colin, 'I'm afraid to drink any more in case I get drunk. I had a full milkpot of it before I left home.'

There is only one other thing to tell about the *Politician* and that concerns the big box of sandals which was found on the twin deck in the whisky hold. They were all left foot sandals and most of the children on Eriskay were going around wearing these left foot sandals on both feet. This was the first summer children there wore anything on their feet, as it used to be bare feet for them from May until October. The box containing the right foot sandals was put aboard another ship to stop the dockers and crew from broaching them. Perhaps that box landed at the bottom of the Atlantic as plenty of ships were lost through enemy action in 1941.

Chapter 7

Spring work—On the Atlantic convoys—The bright lights of New York—At St John's, Newfoundland——I join the Murena—We are torpedoed, but remain afloat—I try some soothing words of Gaelic on Jiff, the frightened dog—No wonder I was an alcoholic... —I defend the honour of the Ladies from Hell—Heroism and horrors of war—New Year's night customs—Drinking day and night in London docks—In the Pitcairn Islands with the descendants of the Bounty mutineers

The *Politician* and the spring work came to an end at the same time. All those at home doing spring work had to leave as usual to earn their living. The Merchant Navy Pool was not yet in operation and so people could stay at home for a couple of months to help out, as the old people needed their services to survive. In Eriskay seaweed had to be cut from boats, and all the ground had to be turned with the spade, peat being cut where boats had to be used for ferrying the seaweed. People had by now been staying in Eriskay near enough to one hundred years, but the spring of 1941 was the last spring that people were around in numbers since the island was first settled.

The Merchant Navy Pool started in June 1941, not that it made any difference to anybody in Eriskay as they had to go to sea to earn a living anyway, but from now on, and for the duration of the Merchant Navy Pool, people had to go home and back when there was leave coming to them. With people away from home tied to their jobs and the people at home fishing herring out of season, their way of life died out forever. With all the spring work and the Polly finished, people began to drift away, some of them never to return, as they were killed in enemy action.

The first ship I joined in Glasgow that summer of 1941 things were pretty bad. Convoys had to go through the Minch up to Iceland and down by the Greenland and Canadian coast until the convoy was dispersed when past the war zone. The first day after leaving Glasgow and going through the Minch I nearly started a fight aboard. I was keeping watch on the bridge as all radio officers had this duty. The only ship in convoy keeping radio watch was the commodore ship, as submarines were able to pick up radio oscillations if all ships had their radios going, and so all messages were passed to ships in convoy by a commodore ship through the international code of signal flags, semaphore or morse lamp. So much for all my months in wireless school, but the morse came in handy for the lamp. I was keeping watch anyway with an old Geordie mate who was back at sea after a few years ashore being warder in a prison, having had to take what was going during the Depression years. I started to tell this old mate when passing Loch Dunvegan what I knew about the Fairy Flag that was in Dunvegan Castle and was said to have been given to one of the MacLeods of Dunvegan by a fairy. He was listening to the Fairy Flag story and, I believe, saying to himself that this was another load of bull from the heather, when he was relieved to go for a meal. Going down to the saloon he began to retell what the stupid fellow on the bridge was saying about fairies, but of course one of the fellows in the saloon was also a believer in fairies. Then a fight almost started there in the saloon between the chief engineer and the mate because of the fairies, the old Geordie mate shouting about people in the twentieth century believing in that kind of tripe. The chief engineer's granny being Highland must have filled him with fairy talk as he was definitely a firm believer.

We were hardly north of the Butt of Lewis when we started picking up survivors. With the long summer days in these northern latitudes you never knew where an attack was going to come from, air or sea.

This detour up to Iceland and Greenland must have added another fortnight to the passage. The convoy was forever changing course with bad weather and fog being worse when the only thing you had for a guide was ships blowing their numbers in the convoy, this and a fog buoy which was streamed behind you for the ship astern to keep her distance from you. If you had over ten columns in the convoy that was three figures you had to blow, and there were ones in their watch below trying to sleep.

Men were still working 'field days', in other words, continuous shifts, up to 1942, until the ship owner was compelled to do away with them forever. Anyone working these kinds of hours was dead beat at five o'clock when the day's work finished, after keeping a watch the night before. Ships were most at risk at daybreak and at dusk of being torpedoed, and anybody going into a lifeboat after a dusk torpedo was usually dropping off his feet for lack of sleep.

Before approaching the United States coast the convoy dispersed and ships proceeded to individual ports. The dirty job of discharging ballast then commenced, a job for all hands and the cook, and anybody willing to earn a few shillings during their watch below. Ballast had to be carried in lightship vessels to keep the screw under water in convoy in case of any tell-tale signs being left behind.

It was a Sunday morning when we finally dropped anchor off New York and all pleasure-seeking folks were out in their yachts and speed boats. This was a different sight from the one we left behind us at Dalmuir, Clydebank, Port Glagow and Greenock where whole closes and families were wiped out in some parts as in other towns in the country. Here we saw fun-loving, well-fed people rather than the half-starved ones at home who had to queue for almost everything. It was the first time I ever saw a town lit up, as the blackout was on at home before I ever left to come to the city, and I must say New York lit up is some sight for someone who never saw anything brighter than a tilley lamp.

We went alongside on the Monday morning and the usual crowd came aboard, namely customs, doctors, immigration. Passing the customs was easy enough, as coming from the U.K. nobody had anything to declare. But the doctor was a different matter. Everyone had to line up and pass through the saloon, in one side and out the other. This was my first experience of life in the raw, as all hands except officers were required to drop their pants to let the doctor see their private parts. When my turn came I was told I did not have to drop my pants, and when I came out on deck I was a bit bewildered by it all until I heard someone mumbling, 'That bloody officer could be poxed an' all'. So that was my first experience of rank. There being no apprentices aboard, no one my own age was amidship. The nearest in their early twenties were the third mate, a Geordie, out of his time in Ropner Shipping, and the fourth engineer who hailed from Anderston Cross in Glasgow. So I had to go ashore on my own to one of the dockside cafes as I did not want to go too far away from the ship. I was drinking something in this place when I was approached by this person who, after talking to me for a while, invited me up to his house. Thinking he was being hospitable I went with him, but on going into the house I was surprised to see that there was no woman in the house or family there. I had hardly sat down when he sat down beside me on the sofa and started to kiss me. I do not know what I must have heard about his kind but I made for the door there and then.

I was telling the third mate about my experience the following day. He told me I had been lucky to get away as there might have been more than one. He called the fourth engineer in and explained how I had been 'picked up by a queer' the night before, and so it was decided then that I should go ashore with them that night, as I would pass for eighteen to get into the bars. We worked our way up to Times Square where all the life was, and landed in one of these night clubs with a floor show. The fourth engineer was carrying a bit of an old shirt with him for devilment and during the times the girls in the floor show were kicking up their legs he started to tear the shirt, which brought the floor show to an end. All the girls began to look at their scanty clothes to see if any part was torn but found nothing out of order. It was then that somebody pointed to our table, and the next thing I remember was these three bouncers getting hold of us and marching us to the door, where the three of us were given one good heave which landed us in a pile on top of one another on the pavement. We must have been the biggest hit on Broadway that night.

After a week we were fully loaded and ready for sea, heading for the convoy port of Halifax, Nova Scotia. All ships en route from anywhere in the western hemisphere to the U.K. gathered here before trying their luck with the North Atlantic. There was more than enemy action to contend with in the North Atlantic, the worst being fog and the approaches to the bad coast of the west of Scotland. Being days, and sometimes weeks, without a sight, with fog and convoys zig-zagging to keep away from the enemy, and then losing the convoy altogether, was a common occurence. The best you could do in these times was to call up a shore station and ask him to take a bearing and strength of your signal, then transmit it back to you. But you would have to be really desperate before breaking radio silence, as an enemy submarine could be listening in and could pinpoint your position.

This was the way of things with us one day after being a couple of weeks without sights and having lost the convoy through fog a couple of days before. We knew by the back-breaking sounding machine that we were on soundings but the question was where, as the edge of the Continental Shelf is more or less the same depth all over. I went on watch at noon as we were keeping radio watch, and the chief radio officer said to me that I was wanted on the bridge to see if I had any idea what place it was they were seeing. We were bound for Oban and I was hearing a few places being mentioned when I went on the bridge, places like Tiree, Colonsay and Tory Island. The Geordie mate was saying it was Tory Island, the Master arguing it was not, as Tory Island was one island. There was nothing like these islands we were seeing in our Outer Isles, to my knowledge anyway, but I had seen St Kilda a few times from the top of our own hill in Eriskay on a clear day. The fog had cleared a bit by now and I was seeing these sharp peaks better and, as far as I could remember of what I had seen from the hill at home, St Kilda had these sharp peaks. So when the Master asked me abruptly, 'What do you think they are?' I, to add confusion to chaos mumbled, 'St Kilda'. Before I let the words out of my mouth the Geordie mate pipes up, 'St Kilda! Get that stupid booger off the bridge'. The second and third mates were looking through the West Coast of Scotland pilotage book. They leafed a few pages until they came to St Kilda, then one of them said, 'Well it does look like St Kilda, all right'. So it was decided to have a sail around it, keeping a good distance off to look for a village, for we knew that even if it had been evacuated the houses would still be up. Before long the houses came into view and we managed to get our first proper position since we left Halifax. As I was going down to the wireless room I was hearing the chief mate and the chief engineer at it, the chief engineer telling the mate, while pointing to the cross-eyed galley boy who was outside the galley peeling potatoes, that he would have navigated her better, and that he had better go back to being a prison warden where he belonged, the mate being forever laughing at him about the fairies.

There were a lot of ships going ashore around the west coast of Scotland in these years, as nearly all traffic coming and going from U.K. ports had to pass by. In peace time not much traffic came this way so merchant seamen from southern ports were not very well acquainted with the coastline. I believe fishermen and those with local knowledge helped, as fog can be very deceiving. I heard my own folks saying they were one morning stopped in clearing fog at the back of Fiary at the mouth of the Sound of Barra arguing as to what places they were seeing within sight of their own homes as they were coming in from the Haaf.

For most of 1941 and 1942 the majority of British ships were sailing between the eastern seaboard of the United States, Canada, South America and the Colonies. But for the tramp ship it was either back home or load for Suez Canal by way of the Cape of Good Hope, as going through the Mediterranean from the western end was suicide. The month of December 1941 we were outward bound for St John's, Newfoundland, when on the 7th the Japs attacked Pearl Harbor, so there was no choice left to the Americans but to come in along with us. The month of December can be bad anywhere, but is even worse in the North Atlantic, with hurricane-force winds, snow, ice and short days. This was the state of affairs for us after having to leave the protection of the convoy one terrible day towards the end of the month. Not being too sure of our position when we left the convoy, as it was sailing on dead reckoning all the way across with a blizzard blowing every day, we were approaching a dangerous coast. At last, in desperation, we were forced to break radio silence as even a submarine would not be able to pinpoint you in this kind of weather. The shore station sent back our bearing and strength of signal which gave us a fix, and we were able to alter course for St John's, where we arrived soon after. There was not much of a welcome waiting for us here. The harbour was chock-a-block with disabled ships. The corvette that came up within hailing distance told us we had better get the hell out of here as a submarine had fired a torpedo through the harbour's narrow entrance and hit a ship. He was told that we had a coal cargo for the place but he just went away firing his depth charges. The submarine, as far as they knew, was hiding against the shore. It was daybreak before they made up their minds what to do with us, having been all night rolling her guts out off St John's. The place they picked for us to await orders was a wee cove south of St John's called Bay Bulls. They found a place in the harbour for us after a couple of days so we went in there.

It was some place, St John's, in the year of 1941. There were tiers of disabled ships, some which had just managed to get in under their own power, having had to burn their twin deck hatch covers in the process. Others had to be towed in by a fleet of rescue tugs which were available there to do the job. Our coal was badly needed as there were ships there with empty bunkers, but the harbour was all activity, with ships licking their wounds and making ready to have another bash at the North Atlantic.

The ship that caught the torpedo was the *Antarctic*, old *Terra Nova*. Being used as a sealer at the time, she was laid up in the harbour until spring. Whether she was placed inside the harbour entrance for such a purpose is questionable, but it was a good job she was the one that caught the torpedo as there were a few ships with dangerous cargoes inside.

These Newfoundlanders used to have a few of these old sailing ships used as sealers at this time. Once the spring came and the ice started to break up they were crewed with anybody who could carry a club. Nobody seems to have been turned away, and there would be up to a thousand men aboard. Newfoundland was very poor at the time, being a colony on its own. It was after the war they went in with Canada. The only occupations they had besides logging were the spring butchering of seals amongst the ice floes and fishing on the banks during the summer.

A hard life they had out on the Newfoundland banks, a bluenose mother ship lying at anchor and dories fishing away from her. They would be out there in these dories with a fog horn tied around their necks, usually a ram's horn. The banks were usually in the track of these terrible hurricanes that came roaring up from the West Indies. Sometimes they curved before hitting the States and would go up the eastern seaboard, gaining speed with latitude. By the time they reached the banks they would be travelling at forty miles an hour. It was not easy for these bluenoses to gain land before it was on top of them. That must have been the reason why three hundred Newfoundlanders were drowned one night in 1921, a disaster I used to hear their seamen talking about when I sailed with them a good number of years afterwards. There were other nationalities on the banks using dories, namely French, Spaniards, Portuguese, as well as men from Lunenburgh, Nova Scotia and Gloucester, Massachusetts, all the fish being cured aboard the mother ship.

The harbour of St John's was surprising in how much shipping it could accommodate once inside the narrow entrance. In the town itself you were forever climbing if you wanted to go from one street to another. The first street, Water Street, was where a seamen's mission called the Caribou Hut was situated. It must have seen a few nationalities through its doors that year of 1941. There was some loss of life in a dance hall in 1942, with local girls burned to death there along with sea-going personnel, but being war-time not much was heard of it.

I called there a few years after the war. It looked so different. Not one ship at anchor where there used to be tiers of disabled ones lying. The busiest years of its life must have been 1941-1942 when many a seaman was glad to see its high cliffs after anxious times battling with the North Atlantic in disabled ships.

After Pearl Harbor the war at sea was fought further south. It was going to be the biggest slaughter of the war at sea. By the time convoys were organised down the eastern seaboard of the United States there was heavy loss of life, especially among tankers coming up from the Gulf of Mexico ports. With every town lit up and all aids to navigation in operation the submarines could not go wrong, and they were picking them out to their hearts' content. It took them a while to get things organised, redirecting traffic through their canals and mining certain points of their coast. Up to now their canals, built a long time before between Chesapeake Bay, Delaware and the Cape Cod Canal, were hardly ever used by deep sea ships, but they were certainly going to prove their worth in stopping this heavy loss of life on ships that had descended on the eastern seaboard of the United States .

The fellows in these submarines must have had nerves of steel. I believe some of them must have cracked under the heavy strain they had to go through. Remaining surfaced in the middle of a convoy, in case the sonar would pick them up if they submerged, must have taken some nerve. But seamen who had a cargo of T.N.T., benzene, iron ore, coal or any other dangerous cargo that would send you to the heavens in a flash or to the bottom in one plunge, had no chance. Having no chance, and being resigned to your fate, there was no need to turn in with your clothes on. On lightships or ships carrying a cargo, where you did have a chance to reach the lifeboats, men were always lying in their beds off watch below fully clothed, as going into a lifeboat otherwise was more or less like signing your death warrant.

Even before the United States came into the war we would never have managed without their help, as any vessel in trouble or damaged through enemy action was sure of a welcome by the majority on reaching their shore. True, there were ones who wanted to keep out of it, preaching isolationism, but that was only to be expected from a country which kept open door for every country in Europe. It only stood to reason that each one of them had a weak spot for the old country which they or their forebears had left behind, but once the U.S. was attacked and on a war footing they were friendly enough towards us. There was only one old country then and that was Britain.

People were always hard on you coming from the Highlands and Islands of Scotland, and would nod their heads in a knowing way when you were introduced. And of course my English at this time left much to be desired. (It still does). The old Geordie Master I sailed with as Deck Officer at one time came aboard one day in a port in Mexico. He was all muddled up about a place he was told to proceed to, as he had never heard of it. "Did any of you hear of it?', he asked.

'No', was the reply.

So it was out with the charts and catalogues till at last we had every bit of paper spread out over the wheelhouse. But it was no use, we could not get a scrap of information as to where the place was. Somebody suggested asking the office but decided against that as it would make us look kind of foolish. So the four of us were standing looking at one another in the wheelhouse when I spied this Mexican going past on the quay. With nothing better to do I went out onto the wing of the bridge and began to shout to him in Spanish, asking where such a place was. The old Geordie Master was out like a shot after me, telling me to shut up before the crew heard about it and we would be the laughing stock of the ship. 'You booger', he says, 'you can't even talk English, never mind Spanish. The only place anybody could understand you was that port in Nova Scotia where they spoke that wild language of yours.' So it would seem that this is the old story, people consider themselves better because they were brought up in a more modern community than others.

Well the Mexican on the quay started pointing up river and repeating the name of the pace we had been trying to find all afternoon. It turned out to be a small jetty further up the river which was used for a lay-by berth.

Young fellows from the Highlands were treated rather cruelly by ships' officers when looking for jobs. Poor souls with fishing discharges were told by some smart Alex, 'Sorry, we don't fish here'. The Skye boys could go one better by being a bow rope on the paddler *Talisman,* or a discharge out of the dredger *Hopper* number four, and being told to 'Hop to hell ashore'. If it had not been for men from their own part of the world being around before them, they would stand a poor chance of ever getting a job.

Once the Americans were in the war we never looked back any more, having the richest nation in the world on our side. It must have been madness for the Japs to attack a nation like that, with half their soldiers fighting in China. It was all to our advantage. The majority of them would have been in before that, but for the crowd preaching isolationism. However the Japs and the Germans settled the question by declaring war on them.

After sailing for over a year as radio officer and having crossed the Atlantic eight times, I decided that the radio was just not for me. I could not see myself at the job for the rest of my life. It was not too bad during the war in convoy when the only ship keeping radio watch was the commodore ship, which relayed messages to other ships in convoy through flags, semaphore and morse with aldis lamps, but I could not picture myself in peace time on my own in a radio room. I had my heart set on being a deck officer, so towards the end of 1942, after I signed off, I resigned from Marconi and went to the pool in Glasgow for a job as ordinary seaman. The pool in Glasgow at the time was on James Watt Street. Down below was for deck hands and upstairs was for officers. I went down below to the deck hand pool. It was all right with them, but I had to go upstairs to the officers' pool to ask them to release me for downstairs, but the answer was 'no', as they just had the job for me—to go to Spain for a trawler to be delivered to the navy for mine-sweeping. I tried everything and others sailing on deck tried, but the officers' pool would not budge. After a fortnight round the Broomielaw and no money left, somebody said to me: 'You had better go to the corner of Plantation Street and get a job in one of the rigging gangs. Once you're in the docks you might get a pier head jump on some ship sailing short-handed'. For a couple of months that is what I did, but I found that ships sailing short-handed from Glasgow usually spent some time waiting for a convoy, and they had a pool in Greenock for pier head jumps. At last I had to give up and go to the officers' pool where I was welcomed with open arms. They were asking me where I had been, thinking I had been in Hawkhead Asylum, as they thought nobody in their right mind who had a radio ticket wanted to sail as an ordinary seaman. 'We have just the right job here for you, sailing as second radio officer in a Dutch tanker which is just now lying at the Tail of the Bank. She is sailing tonight in convoy. Go home, get your gear, and take the train down to Gourock where a launch will take you out to her.'

So that was me in a worse state than I was before. At least with Marconi I would sail on a British ship. My only memories of Dutchmen was as a boy going away on the family fishing boat, *Ocean Star*, and going alongside their boats which used to lie in herring ports like Castlebay, Barra, to sell them baskets of mackerel which had swum into the herring nets and were not very welcome.

These Dutch and Swedes would give us half a crown a basket and drink some mahugram, white stuff which I remember getting a mouthful of one morning and I was spitting for a week after it. I also remembered the clogs they were wearing. These were my thoughts going down to Gourock. Eventually I arrived there and got aboard the launch which was ferrying out some Yanks who were drunk. These Yanks were originally from every European nation, as from their conversation I was to hear a few countries mentioned, but they just took it in their stride when being addressed by their country of origin and 'b——' after it.

At last I was alongside the *Murena*, but before I got on the ladder another fellow was down like a shot when he saw me on the verge of going up. He said, 'You don't belong to this ship', and when I explained who I was he answered, 'The best of British luck to you'. Then, shouting up to the one who was giving him a hand with the luggage he gave me some introduction. The one who was in such a hurry to get out of her was a cadet out of the P&O who had made a trip in her as 4th mate after failing for his ticket. The one who was waiting for me at the top of the ladder was the new 4th mate, his name Anthony Winstanley, who, apart from the gunners, was the only Britisher aboard.

Anthony F Winstanley was a proper gentleman, a product of Laxton Boarding College run by the Dominican Fathers. His reason for being here was that enough of his grandmother's money had been spent on him and it was decided he should go to sea.

Where I came from ones had to go to sea to earn a living or else starve, so there was a big gap between us. Anthony knew plenty of elderly men from the Hebrides, quarter masters in Paddie Henderson's of Glasgow, who were using well-spoken English boys for their ships as cadets, as their ships were running out east in the passenger trade.

About five months of my life were spent in the *Murena* along with Anthony Winstanley, him leaving the *Murena* in Loch Ewe to have another go at the second mate's ticket. All these years later, fifty four of them, I did not know whether he was alive or dead until one day I was visiting another shipmate of mine, Captain John Donald in Greenock, a gentleman who saves up copies of the maritime magazine *Sea Breezes*, and who gave me some to take home. In the first one I read, towards the end, the names *Murena* and *British Fortitude* caught my eye, and there was Anthony's name with him looking for information as to whether any reader knew anything about what happened on 23 February, 1943. He was by now domiciled in Victoria B.C., Canada. It did not take me long to write to him Airmail, and he was just as surprised to find me alive, there not being many left of us now who have seen any war action.

Meeting me at the top of the ladder he took me and introduced me to the Dutch officers who were having a party, and one of them handed me a drink. It was Bols gin and tasted better than the stuff I drank in the Dutch mackerel boat in Castlebay, Barra.

We sailed the following day, 14 February, 1943, in a convoy of sixty ships escorted by twelve British and American destroyers and sloops, bound for Curaçao in the Dutch West Indies. As we sailed south, ships bound for the U.S.A. and Canada left the convoy, until by 23 February there were only thirty-two ships left in the convoy. We were then two hundred miles south of the Azores, and it was after dark that night when we ran into trouble. You could tell there was trouble in the air, as our escorts were letting off depth charges in the convoy, but we were not unduly worried looking at the destroyers and sloops circling the convoy. By nightfall, the depth charging had stopped, so everyone started breathing more easily, but it was the calm before the storm. We were not to know that four submarines had penetrated the circle of protection around the convoy, and that they were hiding under the hulls of ships, ready to pounce.

The trouble, or what caused the trouble that night of 23 February, started that morning, fourteen hours before the main attack at 05.30 G.M.T. (07.30 C.E.T.) when U-522 sank the British motor tanker *Athel Princess*, which was the first casualty of convoy U.C.1. U-522 was sunk by H.M.S. *Totland* that morning and this must have been the opening that the other four U-boats needed to get into the convoy. It is terrible to think that one of their own, along with its crew, had to be sacrificed to get what they wanted. It is also hard to imagine how they waited all day for fourteen hours, hiding under the hulls of the ships in the convoy to escape the depth charges, and how they managed to escape when all hell broke loose that night. Even then they had another couple of tries to get past the circle of protection of the convoy two days in succession.

The submarines that attacked convoy U.C.1 that night were: U-382, U-202, U-569 and U-558. They attacked the convoy between the hours 22.14 and

23.45, Central European time, that being local convoy time 19.14 and 20.45.

Our *Murena*, the Dutch tanker, was the first to be hit, at 19.14 by U-382 but remained afloat. An unidentified Norwegian motor tanker was hit by the same sub three minutes afterwards. At the same time the British steam tanker *Empire Norseman* was torpedoed by U-202, as was the British motor tanker *British Fortitude*, which remained afloat. The American steam tanker *Esso Baton Rouge* was torpedoed at 19.21, also by U-202, and sank. The British steam tanker *Empire Marvel* was torpedoed at 19.30 by U-569 and sank. The *Empire Norseman* was torpedoed again at 20.45 by U-558 which sank her. She had remained afloat after the first torpedo from U-202.

Our *Murena* being the first to get hit, we had no inkling of what was to come. A flash of lightning, a loud roar, water shooting skyward and the ship taking a heavy list to starboard were our only warnings. Every article like tables, chairs, and anything loose, was thrown all over the place. Glass was broken and crew injured by the terrible shock of the torpedo. The ship was listing to starboard, as all starboard side tanks on the fore-end were smashed up and open to the elements. Men were having difficulty walking on deck with the heavy list and down by the head.

Well, a lot of unkind things have been said about the Dutch by other nations, things like Dutch uncle, Dutch courage, Dutch this, Dutch that, but their courage in this situation was exemplary. After the first shock of torpedoing was over, and it was seen that she was not going to break in two, the engines were stopped, men remaining at their stations in the engine room. The Chief Officer, or, as they called him, 'stiurman', a calm, intelligent man, went forward with the Chinese carpenter, something it took plenty of courage to do, and by their brave action in opening other valves on the port side, they brought the ship slowly back on an even keel.

The ship was stopped all the time she was coming back on an even keel. Also the after tanks on both sides had water run into them to get her trimmed by the stern. During this time, with the language difficulty, the Dutch and the Chinese talking in their own language, the only one I knew as frightened as myself was the Master's wee white dog, Jiff, who was barking furiously and biting anyone coming near him, understanding only a smattering of Dutch, and his master busy enough trying to save his ship.

With more ships getting hit, one tanker which must not have been gas-free disappeared in a flash, and other ships in the torpedoed ships' columns nearly collided, before evasive action was taken. Ones were blowing on their whistles and sounding their sirens in the dark to signal their intended actions. Things looked ugly for a while until the hurt ones either sank or dropped out of the convoy. There were also depth charges being fired by escorts.

We managed to drop out of the convoy after the ship astern nearly collided with us and were lying stopped for a while until some trimming was done. With wee Jiff going off his head barking and biting, I tried some soothing Gaelic words on him. Well, whether he mistook Gaelic for Dutch, or whether it was hearing my young voice, I don't know, but he calmed down and came over to me and let me lift him up.

There were three or four tanks on the starboard side open to the sea. The explosion had loosened soot, and this caused balls of fire to come out of the funnel, so the sooner we would get going the better, for if we had stayed any longer we might have been sunk like the *Empire Norseman*.

We managed to catch up with the convoy before dusk the next day. In the morning a British sloop came within hailing distance, wanting to know how we were and did we need any medical assistance, but we said there wasn't anything we couldn't cope with ourselves. I think Jiff caused the most injuries, having bitten a few of the crew.

The *Murena* and her crew were lucky. If that torpedo had hit a bit further forward, the Chinese, whose living quarters were under the fo'c'sle head, would have been hit. If it had hit further aft the officers below the bridge would have got it.

The following afternoon, along with the *British Fortitude*, we were treated to a bit of cheering from other ships while sailing through the convoy to take up our original positions.

After taking up our positions, a U.S. destroyer came within hailing distance, also wanting to know if we needed any medical assistance, at the same time telling our Master in Yankee slang, 'You got a nasty gash there, cap'. A sixty-five foot 'gash' it turned out to be. I was on the bridge at the time attending to some flag signalling when I overheard the Master and stiurman saying something about 'yankee bull'. When I joined them they started in English, pointing at the damaged fore-end at what the Yank called a gash, and the Master taking off his cap and demonstrating what he had been called—a 'cap'. Then the stiurman had us all in gales of laughter at the Yanks who were now falling in for their 'gum and candy', adding that he must have thought he was talking to one of their shoe-shine boys back home. Falling in for 'gum and candy' was a joke among other maritime nations, all booze being banned aboard yankee naval ships then. Seemingly a few years before the war, while on manoeuvres off the Californian coast, a few of their ships piled on the rocks, booze being blamed for it. Whether this rule still stands or not I don't know but I know they did not have much success with their Prohibition ashore. That lasted twelve years. I was shipmate along with a Norwegian who was always complaining about his bullet wounds, which he said he received in the booze launches that used to run the gauntlet from big ships outside territorial waters.

Having got into our position in the convoy we were sort of getting back to normal. Our badly damaged fore-end was still with us, and we were two hundred miles from the nearest land, which was the Azores islands. The next nearest was the island of Madeira, which was eight hundred miles away. Both places had no facilities for repairing our badly damaged ship. Our destination, Curaçao in the Dutch West Indies, was three thousand miles away. Our only hope was to stay with the convoy, hoping she would remain afloat, to reach Mona's Passage in the West Indies, where the convoy was bound for. The U-boats tried to get into the convoy that night and the following night but had no success. Of the U-boats that attacked our convoy that time, none of them survived the war, and before four months elapsed three of them were lost. In the mid-Atlantic, aircraft from the U.S. escort carrier *Bogue* sank the U-569 on 22 May, 1943. South west of Iceland the sloops *Starling, Wild Goose, Kite* and *Woodpecker* sank the U-202 on 2 June, 1943. In the Bay of Biscay U.S. aircraft sank U-558 on 20 July, 1943. U-382 was sunk in a collision with U-673 north of Stavanger on 24 October 1944.

To give them their due, the Germans who manned these U-boats must have been courageous men. It was bad enough below there in these steel coffins but being depth charged to kingdom come was something that only the best of the Germans could cope with. There were also the long waits they had to endure, hiding under ships' hulls in convoys after penetrating the circle of defence given by escort ships, and waiting for their chance in the dark. Surfacing to attack was something that any human being was called on to endure. I could never get myself to hate Germans, as it was their buying our herring was the saviour of our island.

We carried on with nothing much happening, except when all the convoy ships had their ensigns at half mast a few times for burying at sea. There would also be signals from the commodore ship to see if any ships had room for survivors picked up by escort vessels. The night time was worst, as after the bad shaking up we had it was hard to get to sleep with four of her tanks open to sea.

One thing in our favour was the weather, which remained good. The hurricane season was still to come and we managed to keep up with the convoy which was doing eight knots. After ten days from the time of being torpedoed, land was sighted ahead, which proved to be the entrance to Mona's Passage. It was not long after that the commodore put up a signal for us and the *British Fortitude* to proceed under escort to the United States naval base in Guatanamo Bay, Cuba. After arriving there we were safe at last in yankee hands—we could not have been in better. Their navy divers went down to inspect the damage and reported a sixty-five foot hole in the side. With the mast out of place it's a wonder it didn't fall down altogether, as the big raft attached to the stays on the starboard side was blown to kingdom come. The following day we were at sea again, along with the *British Fortitude,* and it wasn't long after sailing along the north of Cuba that we were anchored safely in the calm waters of Key West, Florida. At last these Dutchmen could hold their Bols gin party, and the Master, a man of few words, could praise the crew. The engineers especially deserved praise, having been stuck down there in the bowels of the ship never knowing when another torpedo might hit the engine room and kill or drown the lot of them.

A couple of days in this safe haven and we were given our orders, the *British Fortitude* for Tampa, Florida and us for Jacksonville, Florida. So that is where we had to say goodbye to the *British Fortitude*. I have never met anybody since who sailed in her during these anxious days we were in one another's company.

The short run in a small convoy from Key West to the mouth of the St John River, with the town of Jacksonville twenty miles further up, did not take us long. The town was within walking distance of the shipyard. We were the second ship into this new dry dock and there were also liberty ships in a shipyard in various stages of construction. They used to come to the shipyard in big pieces from inland and be put together in six weeks, from the laying of the keel to the finish.

Once the water was pumped out of the dry dock all hands went down to see the damage to our hull. Looking at the tangle of broken steel and damaged beams we were shocked to see the destructive power of a torpedo. Also I saw some naval personnel conferring with the Master about some steel they found entangled in this mass of wreckage. It turned out to be parts of the torpedo. All the crew members were just fascinated at the sight of the damage, all of us wondering how we managed to sail over the many miles of ocean in this state.

The activity going on around us was out of this world. In dry docks in Britain things remained unchanged, with people having to go ashore to a dirty shore toilet to answer a call of nature. These Yanks welded pipes to the scuppers, hence saving us a trip ashore. It was in that dry dock that I saw my first rust-chipping machines, also machines for spraying paint, and it was the first time I ever saw ordinary working-clothed men walking into parked cars. Our dockyard manager, Mr Campbell, a Scot, was saying, 'We think of everything in this country', adding that the country he affectionately called 'the old country' was fifty years behind the times.

So there we were. You heard Yankee bull, and them on their naval ships falling in for 'gum and candy', but we had the greatest, richest country in the world on our side as those fighting against them found to their cost.

There is a joke about the Glasgow clippie who was putting the Yank off the tram because of there being too many on it, and the Yank saying, 'How can you do this to me when we have been feeding you all these war years?' The clippie answered, 'If you mean spam and dried milk, you can keep it'.

The activity ashore was much better than in the dock. Women of British origin had started the Daughters of the British Empire and we got invited to homes and bingo clubs. Being only just turned eighteen years, I took a seventeen-year-old girl to the pictures, but my friend Anthony had an eye for the ladies, and was not long in dating one when he spied another one some night we were playing bingo. These girls were all daughters of the women who were called the Daughters of the British Empire. This girl I remember was called Diane, and how to get her phone number was a problem

My shipmate from the Murena, *Anthony Winstanley, with his girlfriend Diane in Jacksonville, Florida, April 1943*

for Anthony. At last he decided, on my advice, to tell the mother of the girl I was going with that somebody was interested in Diane and to ask for her phone number. Anthony was so crazy about her that fifty-four years later after, I got in touch with him through the magazine *Sea Breezes*, and him residing in Victoria, British Columbia, I thought she was his wife until I received a letter from him.

With these shore parties and the Dutch holding Bols gin parties, it is no wonder I was an alcoholic by the time I was forty. Also with the *Politician* coming ashore where I was a couple of months working, and having a hand in all the looting before the salvage team took over.

One night in particular with a party going on and the Bols gin flowing freely an argument started between Anthony and the third mate. This third mate always had a knife against anything British. Myself being raised in the Highlands of Scotland in the belief that there were no soldiers like Highland soldiers, 'the Ladies from Hell' and so on, I was expressing this point of view, and adding that as soon as the Germans crossed the frontier into Holland the Dutch put on sand shoes and started running. After the party I was hearing drawers being opened in the stiurman's room which was beside mine, and the next thing I knew he was standing with a revolver in his hand demanding me to repeat what I had been saying about his countrymen. Instead I started to say, 'Dutch very good, very brave, don't shoot, stiurman'.

'I am going to drill you and that limey friend of yours full of hot lead', he replied, these things he had heard in wild west movies.

'Don't shoot, stiurman, don't shoot', I was begging him.

At last he had second thoughts about it and came into the room to yarn about his days in Scotch sailing ships. In his young days at sea a good half of the world's merchant fleet was owned by Britain. They had so many ships, that, along with the numerous fisheries around their shores, they did not have enough men to crew all of them, and so it was men from other European countries they had to turn to. These men, whatever country they came from, were known as 'square heads'.

It was in one of Glasgow's sailing ship companies that the stiurman was sailing one of Tommy Law's 'shires'—all of these vessels being named after Scottish shires, such as the *Nairnshire*— when, this bad day rounding Cape Horn, it was decided that the time had come to do something about the food, or lack of it, with them hardly able to walk, never mind do their work. They all trooped aft to the break of the poop and demanded to see the master. It was not the master who came but his wife, Maggie, threatening them with, 'If I hear any more complaints from you square heads, I'll shoot the lot of you', and, to emphasise the fact that she was not kidding, she put her hand under one of her many red flannel petticoats and pulled out a revolver saying, 'You will get your whack and nae mair'.

The best day of the lot on the *Murena* was the day two of them went ashore in the afternoon and came back married before tea time. Thinking they had gone for a stroll on their afternoon off, we were shocked, I was anyway, but I don't think anything would shock these Dutchmen. The second mate and the third engineer were the two who got married to these two girls they had met a couple of weeks before. There was shouting and laughing, half Dutch, half English, when they came back,. The stiurman spied me anyway, and shouted, 'Come on Angus, come and kiss the brides'.

'The brides!', I said.

'Yes', he replied, 'the brides'.

Then, calling them by their christian names, he told me that they had married since they went away a couple of hours before. Then I was introduced to these two brides, the stiurman adding that I was one of the hillbillies of Scotland.

'Oh yes', they said, 'we know, one of these mean people who goes around dressed in skirts playing some wild music. '

They, too, had been to the movies! I think there was a movie showing about this time called *Bonnie Scotland*, with Laurel and Hardy dressed as Scottish soldiers in India. Also, Harry Lauder didn't help Scotland's image with his jokes, the stiurman saying we would have to have Angus dressed up in a skirt to give them a hillbilly fling. Then the chief engineer began to show off his knowledge of Scotland by saying it was not skirts that were worn, but kilts, and that he had worn one while he was on holiday up in Aviemore. Anyway they all agreed that it would call for a party. I could hear them calling for their boy, after which a wrinkle-faced sixty-year-old Chinaman appeared, and was told to get things organised.

Looking at these to two good-looking girls you could not help but marvel at their courage marrying men they hardly knew from another nation. I remember two old spinsters who lived next door to my father's house in Eriskay. They used to go to the gutting in the Shetlands in their young days. Caorstidh Nighean Ian and Peggi Aoghais Ian Bheag were their names. This Sunday they decided to go for dulce seaweed around the shore. About this time, Dutch herring fishermen used to fish in the Shetlands, but were also enjoying a Sunday off. One of the Dutch boys started to climb down to where the two were, and Peggi and Caorsdith started screaming blue murder, with the Dutch boy shouting, 'No touch fraus, no touch fraus'.

This marrying business, too, had me baffled. It certainly was different from Eriskay, where they had to be called in their own church three Sundays in succession after what they called a '*reiteach*', and that was not all. The couple had to go to the main island of South Uist, where their names had to be put on some table in the protestant church. One character, Ian Roshinis, had his name on the table in the protestant church for fifteen years after he took Walker's bus, and never came near Eriskay all that time, sailing the oceans of the world, he was.

By the beginning of June the repairs to the *Murena* were nearly finished. It had taken them longer than expected. True, they could put together a liberty ship in six weeks, but our *Murena* being a riveted ship, it took them longer than welding them together.

At last the day came when everything was in place, and they started flooding the dry dock. We would soon find out if the repairs were a success, and they were. Soon it was time to say goodbye to the ones ashore and head back down St John's river for the open seas again.

Our destination was Bayonne, New Jersey, where she was loaded in a day, ready to have another go at the north Atlantic. Then we would find out our destination before arriving in the U.K. A day out and we got our orders—the naval base of Scapa Flow in the Orkney Islands, where our oil was required for Russian convoys. We were not at anchor there very long when the R.F.A. (Royal Fleet Auxiliary) tanker, *Blue Ranger*, with half her deck crew belonging to my part of the world, came alongside. It was great to hear Gaelic being spoken again, as the language I heard most for a while was Dutchmen talking to Chinese in pidgin English. My first cousin, Michael Ruadh MacPherson, was one of her crew, and I was to hear the first song he composed. He must have composed hundreds afterwards, but this one was his first after being in a Russian convoy.

After a couple of days the oil was out of her, and we got our orders to proceed to Loch Ewe to pick up a convoy. It was only a day's run between the two places.

We were going to get changes in our crew. Anthony was leaving us to have another go at his second mate's ticket. The Master was also leaving us, having been promoted to Superintendent in the Dutch Shell London office. He was also going to meet the Dutch royal family to receive a decoration. The stiurman was promoted to Master, promotions they both deserved for saving their ship during atrocious conditions. I can still remember waving to Anthony aboard the launch, not knowing it was going to be another fifty-four years before I would hear his voice again on the telephone, with an ocean and a continent between us.

There was also wee Jiff alongside his master, barking away furiously, sensing I believe, that he was never going to see any of us again lining the rail to give them a send off. I believe the most hair-raising experience of Jiff's short life-span was with us in the *Murena* that horrifying night of 23 February, 1943.

We had been made most welcome in the dry dock at Jacksonville, as ships in trouble through enemy action were given all the time they needed to repair their damage. Some of the little rescue ships used in convoys during the war landed up on that eastern seaboard of Canada and the U.S.A. after the war, never, sad to say, being able to pick up their pre-war trade. Some trades like the Dundee-London run or Curries of Leith's German run with the salt herring from isolated Scottish herring ports, were no longer there. Clyde shipping cattle boats, although not out there after the war, their trade to the Clyde was never going to be up to pre-war standard again. They would always earn money for their owners but not on the runs they were built for. What these small plucky rescue vessels went through during the war with bad weather alone was some feat. Vessels in the convoy like the wee *Melrose Abbey* bobbed up and down on the waves like a seagull. Some of them were lost through capsizing, and there was terrible loss of life aboard one of them which was carrying a few rescued crews when she was sunk by bombing. Sadly, burying at sea in convoy was a common occurrence, when all ships in the convoy would lower their flags at half mast. Never in our island maritime history, in my opinon, was there such good and dangerous work carried out, as the convoy, through necessity, would just steam on, leaving these small vessels to the dangerous work of rescuing. After the rescuing was finished they had to steam like hell to catch up and get into whatever safety the convoy had to offer. Many a poor, injured, half-drowned and half-frozen seaman was glad to get onto their rolling decks.

The colliers were not used in these Atlantic convoys except in exceptional cases, as there was enough work for them on the terrible east coast where they had to deal with E-boats. One of these E-boats shifted one of the sand buoys one night, sending the whole convoy piling onto the sands. One fellow I knew spent the entire night clinging to the mast of his sunken ship. Another time one collier was used in a Russian convoy and was saved because one of the firemen was deaf. They were on their way back from Russia when the convoy was attacked by German bombers. With the convoy route being near the Norwegian coast it was bombed more or less continually. These two firemen were on watch in the stockhold and one of them decided to have a blow of fresh air on deck, the deaf man being left below. While the fellow was on deck a bomb fell on the deck, but it did not explode on landing, so it was decided to abandon ship. Abandoning ship can be a harrowing experience at the best of times, but with an unexploded bomb around, and space limited as the ship was small, it would be done even more quickly, as the bomb was liable to go off at any minute. The crew were picked up by the rescue ship and the navy informed. They went aboard to see if there was anything that could be done in case the Germans tried to salvage her. One of the navy boys, on going down below and wandering into the stockhold, must have thought he was seeing a ghost when he saw the deaf fireman sitting on the coal rolling a cigarette and asking the navy fellow where he came from.

The bomb was defused and the crew driven out of the rescue ship and back aboard. The deaf fireman appeared at the end of it all in Buckingham Palace to receive the D.S.O. from the king.

There were plenty of fellows during the war who did heroic things but no one was ever around to see them do it, hence they got no medals for it. After the invasion of North Africa the Mediterranean was going to be the hub of activity, except for the fighting on the Pacific Islands and Russia. These poor soldiers known as the Desert Rats must have got it worse than anybody these years fighting in the desert, with sand for breakfast, dinner and tea. After this they had to go through the invasions and more fighting in Italy, then being called back home for the Invasion of the Continent. Fighting all the way from Normandy to the heart of Germany where, I was informed by some of them, there were castles with the best of wines, so thick that they had to use spoons to drink it. They certainly deserved any feast they got after their long hike from the time they broke through at El Alamein until they reached the heart of Germany.

The Mediterranean in 1943 was where it was all happening, the biggest bang of the war, apart from those bombs they dropped on Japan, happening there. It was towards the end of 1943 at Bari in Italy when these ships blew up, causing a great loss of life. It is a wonder to me how there were no bigger bangs during the war when you think of all the stuff that was carried in ships. I think they could call themselves very lucky.

In Halifax, Nova Scotia, in 1917 there were only two ships—a French and a Norwegian—involved in the collision which caused the explosion that resulted in a great loss of life to the population ashore. It might have been because the town was built with too many wooden buildings which caught fire and got out of control. The explosion was such that an anchor belonging to one of the ships was found miles inland. The explosion at Halifax being well away from the scene of battle and happening on another continent, people would hear more about it. But the Bari explosion happened more or less on the battlefield, where death was an everyday occurence, and people never thought so much of it. I believe people who were around this war zone at the time would see it as the worst in history.

Apart from all the wounding and killing, the starvation amongst the civilian population was something people had to see to believe. There were people coming down around the dock area rummaging in galley slops and everywhere they thought they would get a bite to eat. There were religious people begging for starving children in orphanages, workers aboard ships coming out of the hold with lumps of frozen meat which had been hacked off a carcass with an axe, throwing it on the red hot galley stove, giving it only a few sizzling turns, then wolfing it down. But even through all of this upheaval, people sometimes got laughs, like the evening a crowd of us were going ashore each carrying a pillow slip with a few pounds of brown sugar inside. There were always burst bags and hold-sweepings, which both crew and dockers thought were rightly theirs. After getting through the dock gate—for a price, as some of the sugar had to be handed over—we were set upon by a crowd of young boys, not one of them more than ten years of age, and each one brandishing a revolver. They made off with the loot, laughing their heads off, and left us standing there flabbergasted. There was nothing else for it but to go back for more sweepings, telling the fellows at the dock gate of our predicament. They promised us police protection next time until a deal was made. Of course when we went aboard we were the laughing stock of the ship, getting held up by a crowd of kids. But around these areas at that time life was very cheap, with plenty of guns and bullets changing hands and I believe these same kids knew how to use them. For boys in their teens this kind of thing was turning out to be a way of life. People ashore would accost anyone for any article of clothing, bargaining being known as 'changie for changie', but the only thing they would have to exchange would be their local brew.

I remember once I had an old pair of 'John L' pants, named after the boxer, John L Sullivan, someone at home had knitted for me as a present. These home-knitteds were common in the islands in my young days. I got them out from the bottom of the bag, red in colour they were, and exchanged them for the local brew. The following morning one of the boys was standing looking through the porthole at some activity going on out on deck when he suddenly burst into fits of laughter. Thinking he had gone bomb-happy, as this was common around this time, we made for him, but all he could do was point out to the hatch, where the fellow who was directing the cargo coming from the hold was standing wearing my John L's and nothing else, the sight of which sent everyone into fits of helpless laughter.

The way folks dressed in Eriskay was, for the men, a home-made pair of pants, a jacket which would normally outlive three pairs of pants, and would probably be the wedding jacket, and a home-knitted jersey. The women would wear a hat on the first Sunday after being married, thereafter a knitted shawl would be the usual style for the rest of their days, until squares of material came into fashion.

Those wearing the John L pants must have had the constitutions of horses. Even with the ravens' tongues hanging out with thirst it was a common thing for two pairs to be worn by these old fishermen in Eriskay. I remember a group of houses in Rhubhain near to my grandparents' house where the occupants, Duncan, Ian Ruadh and the Cummings, were always visiting us for a ceilidh. The young one, Donald Cumming, died there after collapsing one day coming from the post office. One of these frequent visitors of ours, Ian Ruadh, was not married, but stayed with his three sisters who were always bullying him into wearing more clothing in case he would catch a cold. One sister, Mor, was the star bully, and would start on about Ian going away to sea wearing only two pairs of John Ls.

I can still see Mor on New Year's night when the children used to go from door to door collecting. This was known as the *culleag*. Girdle bread was the commodity which was always collected. You received three of them then gave one back. Mor always made sure the one she got back was not broken, then she would ask who had baked it, giving a running commentary of all the ingredients she put into her own girdle bread. Then what was called a *casain* would be passed around. This was a bit of canvas rolled and dipped in paraffin which was lit. The person using it would make the sign of the cross with it, then wave it three times around the head. Woe betide anybody if the light went out in the *casain* when the operation was taking place, as all hands would stand stunned, something similar to a court room when a judge would put on the black cap. The person holding the *casain* when it went out would be under a death sentence until the next New Year, and people were always making sure, especially Mor, that it was well dipped in the paraffin before use. Then some old geezer would start complaining about the size of some of the boys at the *culleag*, as in his young days everyone who wanted to get into the big collector's *culleag* had to lift a stone of some weight above his knees before being elected to the elite.

⌒

Apart from occasional squabbles around the crofts, everyone looked content enough as they did not have to worry about rents, mortgages, etc. as long as they had flour, tea, sugar, potatoes and fish, which could be had from the rocks if the weather was too severe to go out in boats. Everyone had hens and sheep. Our folks over in Glendale had a few hundred sheep. In other words, if everything else failed, I do not think they would have starved with the sands around them full of shellfish. As well as that nearly every house had a gun for shooting ducks.

City folks were inclined to look down on people living at the back of beyond, but when you got talking to some of them they themselves had some sad stories to tell of the hard times they had bringing up their families.

An Irishman I sailed with was telling me before the war he was ashore on the means test domiciled in the north east of England. His wife was in hospital and he was doing the cooking and bottle washing. This particular day all the money he had was just enough to buy a rabbit, so he managed with some vegetables, to make some kind of a meal for the family. The time came for taking it off the fire. The family began to crowd around him, each one holding a plate and saying, 'Give me a wing, daddy'.

He got so fed up that he turned on them saying, 'By heaven what do you think I've got in the pot, a bloody spider?'

The Irish, like our own crowd from the islands of Scotland, were usually in the hardest and poorest-paid jobs and had left their homes for the first time taking with them a cooked old hen, their bare fare and a prayer from the ones at home. If they were lucky enough to find a job, a remittance sent home was the difference between starving or surviving.

War or peace did not seem to have made much difference to the lifestyle of these people, especially the ones at sea. Only with the Irish it would have been so easy, with all the danger around, for them to have stayed at home. But no, they were back more promptly than their shipmates on the other side. When somebody asked the cockney who was along with him aboard ship, he replied, 'Oh the usual mixture, Stornoway, Irish and Maltese'. It did not matter which island you came from up north you were still from Stornoway as far as the cockneys were concerned. The best memory I have of sailing with these fine, inoffensive people is the way you could leave your belongings without locking them up and nothing ever went missing. Nobody interfered with the religious beliefs of anyone else and padres from missions of various denominations who used to come aboard were all treated with respect. Often there was a sense of humour, as when the padre was going to the galley, the place where everyone went to for information, and the cook was perhaps in a bad mood through someone getting on to him about his cooking, and was saying to the padre that if he was looking for converts to start converting his galley from coal to oil.

These London ships were mostly frozen meat boats running down to the Argentine and up the west coast of the United States and Canada, but

Myself sitting on rail on far right, next to Donald Morrison from South Uist and John MacInnes from Sleat in Skye, sitting down, second from right. The rest cockneys.

the majority of them ran to Australia and New Zealand. It was amazing the amount of trade that went to New Zealand, and yet these two islands looked so small on a map of the world. The Canterbury Plains must have had a lamb to every square foot.

These Federal ships or Harland boats as they were known in our islands, Harland their superintendent being a household name there at one time, were the ones all the boys were after. It was between the Harland boats and the whalers that all the big pay-offs came from, but speaking for myself, I never got any of it, and maybe it's just as well, as I might not be alive today. Some of the boys were wise and looked after their money, others were just as well not getting it. Around the London docks it was all drinking, from the time the pubs opened for the dockers at six in the morning right through until six the next morning, landing up around Billingsgate in the small hours, drinking along with the fish lumpers. You could not survive living this way for long, a fortnight at the most, before the money would run out. Then you would have to sail to earn more and most of that would go to the pubs in Custom House. Some fellows never went any further than Custom House, maybe up to the Abbey Arms for a feed or to cash an advance note at Wolfe, the barber's shop. The surprising part of it all is that people living this way of life are living to a ripe old age. One of them I saw not so long ago, Tamaruish from Back Lewis. He was a proper gentleman boatman on the Clyde, and before that had another home job on the river oil tanker, married and became a regular in the church. Sadly, Tamaruish is not with us any more

Shaw Savile shipping line jobs were not sought after, as the overtime which they were all out for was not there. Crews were sent aboard the *Dominion*

Monarch and the Bay Boats right up to sailing time. But there were still old timers, like Sandy Ian Bard from Ness, who was devoted to Shaw Savile. I have seen Sandy over the side at sea leaving Curaçao, cleaning the white after the usual overflow of bunkering oil. He could not ask a crew member to do it at sea, and you would not dare go near to help him. There was not much to break the monotony. Curaçao, Panama and Shaw Savile had the mail contract for Pitcairn Island, where the descendants of the *Bounty* mutineers resided. The ship would lay off the island for a couple of hours and the natives used to come out in their longboats singing eighteenth-century hymns until they came alongside. Then they would climb up ladders to get aboard, men and women, to sell their wares.

It would have been quite a thrill for these passengers, some of them emigrating and never having seen much of the world, to be suddenly in the midst of a piece of history. I do not know what kind of service these Pitcairn Islanders have today, but over thirty years ago they had a great service, as besides the Shaw Savile mail contract, other ships used to call there out of curiosity, and also to break the monotony on the long haul from Panama to the Colonies. Once you were out in these colonial ports you discovered they were all more or less the same, as what I can remember about them was men rushing ashore at five o'clock to get a drink before closing time at six. Then after closing time it was sly grogging around most of the pubs' back doors which were open, this being a very unusual way to live for anybody from any other country.

Scotland was being blamed for this way of life, as it was the strict religious beliefs of the early colonists that started it all. I can still see the crowd of sailors waiting to cross the street to get into the Waterloo in Wellington at five o'clock with cars driving by. They tell me things have all changed out there now. They are keeping civilised hours, but these hours did not look to me to be the best way to make people stop drinking. People who want to drink will always find a way, regardless of laws made to keep it from them. It has been tried in Scotland with Temperance Societies and towns going dry. The United States had it for twelve years from 1920 to 1932 and I believe it caused more law-breaking and killings on land and sea than at any time in its history.

Chapter 8

*Jumping ship in New Zealand—I am carted to the calaboose in Buenos Aires—
Long runs on the tramp steamers—Saite from Barra comes back from the dead—
Smuggled kippers for breakfast—I am paid off, having drunk my week's wages—I
am shanghaied on a Geordie collier bound for Canada—Wishing myself on Eriskay
—Amongst the Gaelic speakers in Nova Scotia—Dr Kissling, a nice man of
noble birth—Donald Ferguson, prince of finance—The sea: Eriskay's saviour*

You could see the size of New Zealand's two islands on one chart but when
you looked around its ports and saw all the ships, nearly all of them loading lambs, you could not help but wonder where they were all coming from.

I remember one year the whole Argentine fleet was there after having
spent weeks at anchor in the River Plate. As the country was having one of
its many disputes, they had to leave and batter around Cape Horn to New
Zealand. Houlders Brothers, Donaldson's of Glasgow, and companies running to the Argentine during the companies' lifetime, were landing out in
New Zealand and getting their holds filled like the regular traders. There
was a strike in New Zealand that year—1951—that lasted for a few months
and held up exports and affected their wool-clipping season after the strike
when they probably needed all the ships they could get.

Seamen were always tempted to jump ship there as it was so easy for a
seaman to enter the country. Once you did a month in prison for illegal
entry, that was you in. But getting out of there again was a different matter.
If you were not squared up with the income tax you were never allowed to
leave. I have been tempted to jump myself a few times but there was always somebody to throw cold water in your face putting you off. So, with
the more sensible ones putting you off, and seeing the certain element around
the ports who had no intention of making anything of life, I decided to stay
where I was.

It is strange about people emigrating from country to country looking
for a better way of life. Maybe there are some countries where you eat,
drink and play better than in others, but that does not say you will be happier. Some of the happiest people I have met in my life were the ones who
were not too sure where their next meal was to come from. There is a brother
of mine buried out in Auckland. He died through an accident aboard ship,
just like plenty of others from my part of the world. Hardly a family was

left untouched in this way, some member being buried in a foreign land or at sea through drownings or other mishaps—that is the lot of the seamen. There was always a seamen's plot in some graveyard in every port wherever you went in the world.

The Argentine fleet being out there was a surprise to everyone, as these ships never usually strayed from their run in a lifetime. It was usual on seamen gathering together and swapping yarns that they all had one thing in common, and that was having spent a night in jail in Buenos Aires. This is what happened to me once having arrived there to top off after loading in isolated places down in Patagonia and the Falkland Islands. These frozen meat boats usually carried twelve passengers. For anything over that number a doctor would have to be signed on.

Loading down south was usually done at anchor, with nobody allowed ashore, so the boys had a good thirst on by the time Buenos Aires was reached. I was around the gangway until about ten o'clock having had to wait for my relief, who arrived sozzled by that time. During the time I was at the gangway the Mate came around with a passenger who had boarded her down south and was on his way home to Britain, a middle-aged man looking for a tow to take him ashore. I was not too keen on having someone to tow around, as my own thirst was rather great by this time, but the Mate began soaping me up saying that I used to be somebody of his own clothing, and that I was only on deck to get time in to go for a deck ticket, and so I finally agreed to the tow. I had all good intentions of passing the First and Last bar but was spotted by somebody inside, so that was me in tow and all.

The passenger thought this was great, being one of the boys, and, after a few scoops of the local mahugram, I thought the same. But we were not there long when trouble started and the Vigilantes came and carted the lot of us to the calaboose, including the passenger. I would have given anything to have been blind drunk that night, but being sober I could only listen to a drunken crowd of seamen threatening the Vigilantes with all sorts of retaliation. Some were for sending out their own local militia at home to blast them off the face of the earth. An old Irishman was going to write to de Valera, the prime minister, about sending out a destroyer to deal with them, while someone else started shouting to him, 'You haven't got a bloody navy, all you've got are canvas boats for taking you through the bloody bogs'. All of which started up another rumpus. A Norwegian crew was also in there. I remember a young one of them, who could not have been more than sixteen, shouting at the Vigilantes that this place was the arsehole of the world. Very early in the morning there were all hands on deck letting us out, as the ship had to be shifted before the dockers started work at eight o'clock. So with hardly any crew aboard, where better to look than the calaboose, with the result that some of the ones aboard were up with some bribe to get us out in a hurry.

It all passed off as another shore escapade except for the chief steward mumbling about putting us on half rations on the way home, the bribe having been some of his stores. Nobody was carpeted for it except me, because of the passenger. I was called to the Master's room shortly after breakfast time. All my seagoing career I never seemed to belong fully to any department, any trouble afoot and the culprits all seemed to be from my crowd. I believe that is why so few people change the kind of work they initially start on. They would rather go through life miserable, hating the kind of work they were doing rather than change. Anyway this carpeting usually happens after breakfast when people are fed, and when everyone is at his best, everyone that is, except the poor soul who is on the carpet, which is regarded as being more or less as sombre as a religious service. The carpeting talk is the usual about being shocked by the behaviour of somebody who had been entrusted by the Mate with one of the passengers to be taken ashore to see the city sights, but instead was taken by me to the First and Last amongst the dregs of humanity. Also at the end of the trip he would have second thoughts about giving me a reference which I would need for going to school, as, in his opinion, I would never amount to anything in life. The passenger was thrilled by it all. This might have been one of the greatest escapades of his life, something to tell his friends about at the local club, his night in jail in Buenos Aires.

I remember another trip when we were loading sugar in the Reunion Islands off the east coast of Africa. One night the fourth engineer was taken to jail for causing a disturbance. I went up to the jail and started to argue with these French police, saying that I wanted him out to take him back aboard ship. They took me over to the cell where he was and I thought they were going to let him out, but instead of that, when they opened the cell door, they pushed me in along with him.

These tramp steamers sailing to every port or creek in the world, loading almost everything, were the ships to be in for anybody who wanted to see the world. The long runs these tramp ships took from loading to discharging ports and vice versa used to be over two months sometimes, with maybe a few hours in a bunkering port to break the monotony. Sometimes if a lightship coal-burning tramp was sailing from a port where coal was cheap, enough bunkering coal would be taken aboard to take her to a loading port with only a flashing light on some cape to be seen during all of these monotonous weeks. Two years was the limit for keeping ships away from their home, but it sometimes went over that period if a cargo was picked up, which added another few months, as these old ships could not do more than seven knots, and that with everything in running order. The *Dalton Hall* was away from May 1937 to March 1940, two years and ten months, a long time for married men to be away from their families.

A favourite loading place for a tramp steamer leaving the U.K., having battered across the Atlantic lightship with after holds flooded as a last resort to give her steering way, was Norfolk Virginia, to load coal for anywhere, but mostly for Japan. I don't know whether these mines out there were heavily subsidised by the government, but it being bad burning coal none of the countries we were taking it to were very keen on having it, even though they were getting it for next to nothing. I have seen us take a cargo of it to Ireland.

Between the Panama Canal and Japan lies Honolulu in the Hawaian Islands, a bunkering port where we arrived once on New Year's Eve. There were three policemen patrolling on the quay opposite the ships, one at the fore and after end and one at the gangway, with orders to arrest anyone sneaking ashore. We had loaded her in Norfolk non-stop in a matter of hours. She sailed from Honolulu for Japan that night at ten o'clock. Japan these days after the war was all bucket discharging with the coal, but it was surprising the amount of coal they would shift even in this back-breaking way.

Once out in the Pacific there was no shortage of cargoes, as the fields of Australia and New Zealand had to be fertilised with phosphate from the Ocean and Christmas Islands, and there was guano and iron ore from Chile and Peru. After discharging these cargoes, other cargoes like sugar in Queensland and coal in New South Wales could be loaded for Japan or the west coast of South America. So it was a continuous sail round the Pacific for these tramps, picking up cargoes in isolated places where no regular traders ran to. All of the African, Indian and China coasts were served by such strong competition from regular runners that you were always sure if you saw a City boat in port you would see a Clan boat at the next berth. The British shipowners were the smartest in the world at this time, having had a long tradition behind them. They had people in offices who could tell at a glance whether shifting a cargo from one place to another a few thousand miles away would be an asset to their employer.

The same with Masters and chief stewards. If you were so bold as to gate-crash into their company ashore the conversation would always be about the price of cabbage, carrots etc., at such-and-such a place, because there were hard and fast rules laid on that everything bought had to be at a reasonable price. So the Master of a British tramp steamer had to be more than a seaman, as buying a pound of some commodity at an extortionate price would as much a misdemeanour in the eyes of his employer as being the guilty party in a collision.

Ships had to come home for Ministry of Transport surveys and cargoes had to be found for a U.K. port, usually from the west coast of Canada or the States. The colonies could be relied on if you were there at the time of the wool clip. Otherwise there was grain from the Spencer Gulf small ports, or that smelly stuff they used to load in Port Pierre for hardening steel. You could smell a ship with a cargo of it miles away. It was like rotten apples, worse than a whaler. Sometimes you wondered what the purpose was of all this shifting of stuff from one end of the world to the other, as the same stuff could be had nearer your discharging port, but the queerest shifting I ever heard of was a cargo of sand from home to Port Said during the war. It must have been destined for some country that was overrun by the enemy or else there was a slip of the pen by somebody, but there they were in the Bitter Lakes and all around them as far as the eye could see was sand, after having sailed with it for nearly three months around the Cape of Good Hope.

The Suez Canal was the hub of activity during those years from the middle of 1940 to the beginning of 1943. Everything that was needed, men and material, to keep the Desert Rats going had to be hauled around the Cape to there. If anybody was to ask me who were the smartest people I have met in this world I would say, as far as picking up languages and dialects goes, I would give top marks to the fellows who run the bumboats in Port Said. It is not that they were past masters at languages, but they would only have to have one squint at a ship's stern to see her port of registry and they were smattering away as if they had never been a day away from Plantation in Glasgow, Scotland Road, Liverpool, the Mildam in Shields or Stepney in London. They were smart at bargaining, but some of the fellows aboard ships were just as smart at it, like the time I saw a crew member lowering down what he said was some sugar in return for some article in the bumboat. The fellow had a sprinkling of sugar at the mouth of the bag all right, but that was only to barricade off the sand he had at the bottom. It was only after the deal was made and the fellow aboard ship had his article that the bumboat boy started excavating further into the bag and found the sand. It was then the cursing and swearing started. At last he got himself so worked up with the other bumboat boys laughing at him that he jumped out of the bumboat into the sea.

The town to a certain extent would be depending for its livelihood on traffic passing through the Canal, as the locals used to come aboard to see if there were any odd jobs for them to do, proudly showing off previous references as to their honesty and ability that had been given to them by crew members. They were smart enough at picking up languages, but to read them was beyond their capabilities, as some of the references would read, 'This is to certify that So-and-So is a bloody robber and any berth you are thinking of giving him make sure it's a wide one'. But they would invite you to their houses saying, 'Plenty of nice girls, lady doctors and school teachers, plenty fun, three men killed last night!'.

Of all the countries I have ever been to I think our own country is as good as any, especially when you have had humiliating experiences like all hands standing on deck and an army of policemen searching for stowaways everywhere from the truck of the mast to the keel, and one of them being last down the ladder, not trusting the pilot to be last.

People in this country take things like the freedom to travel so much for granted and are never thankful enough to the ones who laid down their lives in two world wars to give them that freedom. The ones alive today who survived these wartime years fighting are all trying to make ends meet now that they are of pensionable age. There are veterans taken into Erskine Hospital because they have no families to look after them or bury them. I have seen one of them being buried from our church without any representatives from any families around, just a few church members, some of whom do pall-bearing duties.

Before the war the Armed Services and the Merchant Navy were manned by some who knew no other home, ones from broken homes, orphanages etc., and anything happening to these people, like being taken prisoners of war, was all taken in their stride. Some fellows from the islands of Scotland never so much as had a glimpse of their parents from the day they left home. With large families there was not enough at home for all of them, so they were sailing from wherever there were ships for them, mostly Shields and the Bristol Channel. For some of them whose parents had died, their only contact with their birth place was through meeting others from home all over the world, as was the case with a friend of mine I sailed with, Donald Gillies 'Saite' from Barra.

With nearly all ships making for the Clyde with its big anchorage space in 1941, and it not getting the bombing as bad as English ports, Saite arrived in Glasgow on some ship. After spending his pay-off amongst his friends in Glasgow it was time to ship out again, but on the first day aboard he and the Mate collided, having sailed together before. 'Well', Saite says to the Mate, 'if you don't like me here you know what to do'.

'Yes', replies the Mate, 'just pack your bags and I'll pay you off right now'.

After Saite signs off he asks, 'Where is my month's wages?'

At that, an argument started, and the union was called in, with the result that, seeing the man was paid off through no fault of his own, he was entitled to a month's wages. The ship sailed and was lost with all hands, and as far as everybody knew Saite was still aboard, as people were getting to know that she was lost through word coming to the next of kin of others. That was Saite gone to meet his Maker, or so people thought. After people die in our islands their names are put on what is known as the Dead List, the names being called out in church for some time afterwards, and so Saite's name was here. Almost a year passed then word came from one of the boys who was in a prisoner of war camp in Germany that Saite was taken into the camp. No, they said, it could not be Saite, his name has been called in church every Sunday for a good while. So enquiries were made anyway and it turned out to be Saite back from the dead. 'How did it happen?' was the question, the answer being that after he got his month's wages he decided to give his haunts around Shields a visit, and on the money running out he shipped out from there. The next ship he joined was also sunk, but by a German Raider this time, who picked up the survivors, putting them aboard a supply ship which eventually managed to reach a port in German-occupied France from where they reached the camp in Germany.

After spending the rest of the war years as a prisoner of war he eventually arived home in Barra, and by the time I sailed with him he was married and settled down. One thing about him was he would always have various necessities of life in his kit bag, things like darning gear, boot polish etc. I believe he had been so long on his own in the world, having always had to look after himself, that he had got into this way of life. The boys aboard would always be after him when going ashore for a rub of his blackening for their shoes. During that year I was along with him Saite would shake his head and say, 'I am thinking it must have been from the poorhouse you fellows came to join her'. He was left on his own in his teens, his mother having died and his father getting drowned on the way over to Vatersay from Castlebay where they were staying.

Vatersay was not very lucky for them as they were not very long there when they all more or less lost their worldly possessions in one blow. It happened on 21 March 1921, when a severe hurricane came out of the blue. They lost their herring fleet, five lovely boats all newly-engined. The result was that with the island being newly settled it never seems to have got over it. I had a fairly good idea of their way of life, since nearly all of them were from the other Barra Head Islands which was my granny's territory, and I often heard from her about their ups and downs. The ones from this territory always visited her if over our way, and this was how I became acquainted with their way of life, as most of them were relations. Family fishing smacks engaged in some of the numerous fisheries around our shores were cradles that produced the men who were mostly the backbone of the Merchant Navy. You even had men there who, hard as it may be to believe, actually fished from carts and horses, something which caused laughter amongst others who fished from boats. This dangerous type of fishing was carried out for shrimps in Morecambe Bay where there is a rise and fall of thirty feet. When the tide starts flooding it is at the speed of a trotting horse. God help the poor horse if he is caught in quicksand, as there is nothing men can do but save their own lives by jumping into the nearest cart. It was mostly Mersey ships that were crewed with men from around these and Welsh coast areas, along with their own men.

Sometimes, with the depressed state of shipping between the wars, men from the big towns were forced to seek anything that was going in trawlers and drifters from Milfordhaven and Fleetwood. I have sailed with a deep sea Master who was forced to seek a cook and coiler's job in a Milford haven drifter, and a chief engineer from Liverpool I also sailed with got so fed up on the means test that he hitch-hiked to Fleetwood to see if he could get a job on a trawler. On enquiring around the offices he was told there was nothing doing, but then someone came along and said there was a Scots fishing boat looking for an engineer on a temporary basis. So he went aboard and got the job, but was mystified as to what kind of craft it was, as everywhere he looked aboard all he could see were baskets, lines and hooks. As he was a bit hampered by the language difficulty he did not ask too many questions. They sailed from Fleetwood anyway, and of course he thought the fishing grounds would be their next stop, but there were going to be two other stops before then.

First stop was Campbeltown, and he was wondering why, since all he had ever heard of Campbeltown was its name on a bottle of whisky. From what he saw of the crew they seemed to be a sober, inoffensive crowd, the kind who would not call for whisky, unlike trawler men. At last he seemed to catch on to what they were looking for, namely herring to bait their hooks, not drink. No herring could be had in Campbeltown so they sailed and proceeded to Downings in Ireland, where they got all the herring they wanted. After they got their bait it was Rockall they made for to catch the fish.

Once Rockall was reached the shooting and hauling of lines commenced, with the trawlers their biggest curse, trawling over their lines. One day this Fleetwood trawler was coming too close to their lines, and, of course, the shouting to keep clear began. The trawlermen shouted back some abuse: 'You burgoo scoffing b——s'. However they fished at Rockall till they had their fill, then made for Aberdeen, where the Scouser was paid off.

Sad to say, this depressing state of things must have hit the Mersey bad, as there was a big seagoing population around that area. It has been years since I was around there. At one time walking into the Bootle Arms was to an Isleman what walking into their local was to other people. If you did not see anyone you knew, the Burns girls would soon put you in the picture as to who was around. The Burnses knew them all by their Gaelic names, and they married men from the Isles eventually.

The great excitement in that area is loading in the Welsh quarries. I believe stones are still loaded there today, but with steel hatches it will be nothing compared to the old coasters with the wooden hatches. It was when the last hatch was loaded and the ship down to her marks, or what you thought were her marks, and waves breaking over you and men trying to catch the floating hatch covers to get the hatch battened down—that was the trouble. Well, I must say that since I left home over fifty years ago, of the various escapades I have had, both fishing and sailing, I would put the Welsh quarries down as one of my most hair-raising experiences.

Across country on the north east coast, the Tyne area, are the Geordies, another fine crowd of people. You would not be long there looking for a job in the heyday of the coal trade, until some smart Alex thought a better way to pay dividends was to build power houses up north, and so throw thousands out of work in the process. For the last thirty years you could see this unemployment coming, with better ideas of doing away with labour. It was only the contingent that never worked or who did not have any intention of ever working that was keeping it at bay. These Geordie collier men, annexed with men from the fishing cobles who used to sail in colliers if things were slack at the fishing, started feeling the pinch towards the end of the fifties. As with anything that is built to do a certain kind of work, and that work is taken away, other kinds of survival have to be found, thus putting people's livelihoods in danger. It was this sort of situation that faced the Geordie collier towards the late 'fifties and early 'sixties.

Coastal running between their own coal ports and southern ports was a great job for a Geordie with watch aboard and watch ashore, half of them going home on trips up north and the other half going the next trip. These runs were no good for strangers, but I happened to be relieving the mate of one of them loading up north once when it was his watch aboard. This time a young scullion from North Shields was doing the serving in the saloon. North Shields at that time had kippering houses and this young scullion's mother worked in one of them. As with all Geordies, the whole family, father and all, call the mother of the family the lass. So this was the situation one morning at breakast during the loading, with myself trying to get something down after having too many pints the night before. After I had breakfast and was finishing off my tea, the scullion came over to me and asked in a secretive sort of way as to how I had enjoyed the kippers for breakfast. I said they were very nice indeed. He then whispered to me, 'Our lass works in a kippering house and she gets them out inside her drawers'. I managed to make the toilet anyway until I heard the trimmers shouting to shift the ship. I went up to the fo'c'sle head and there was an old Irishman standing there who took one look at me and said, 'By heavens you look as if you've seen the Bhan Shee'.

I told him of the escapade at breakfast.

'Ah', he said, 'that's nothing, it will add a better flavour to them'.

This changeover for the Geordie collier from coastal to deep sea had to be done by sometimes using a different breed of seamen, who at times had to be bullied by the Pool to sail in them. Sometimes, as was once the case with me, people were destitute and had to take anything going. I was relieving in a wee oil tanker when her time came to go into dry dock. As I was surplus to requirements, I was paid off with a few measly pounds, after having spent my week's wages which I had received a few days beforehand. The Master, a man from my own islands, had come aboard with the news that I was being paid off. I told him that paying me off was making me destitute, and he said that I was not destitute as I had received money a few days ago. I told him that I had drunk that. Well then, he said, I had better ask Taffy the mate how to survive on that kind of money, as Taffy could have a fortnight's holiday in Butlins with it. He had warned me about Taffy on the first watch I had kept, when he had checked me for putting cigarette butts in an ashtray, as Taffy had the habit of collecting them for roll-your-own. I had said that he must be a hard-up bugger. 'He is not', replied the Master, mentioning the sum of money Taffy had been gifted on the day he was born. Anyway I said 'cheerio', put my belongings in the left luggage and made for the Pool.

'There's a good job for you here', they told me there, mentioning a collier's name. I said, 'No watch aboard, watch ashore job for me', then mumbled something about that carry-on being all right for Geordies who could get home on their watch ashore.

'Oh', the fellow replied, you're all right, this one is on deep sea articles going outside Home Trade limits, probably up the Baltic or down the Mediterranean.

'Well', I said, 'beggars can't be choosers', and so an engineer and myself went down to the boat. On the way I gathered from the engineer's conversation that he also was in financial difficulties. He mentioned that as we could not get an advance note—officers, being of the upper crust, could not ask for one—we would have to tackle the Old Man for a sub. I nodded, agreeing with him, and adding, 'Great minds think alike'.

We arrived aboard, and, looking around at the crowd coming and going, I had an idea before asking that something funny was going on. On enquiring we found out that she was bound for Canada, so before signing on we tackled the Old Man about the sub. He started mumbling that it was bad enough getting ratings from the workhouse, but now they were sending him officers from there. As I was looking around the accommodation I heard some words being passed between the chief mate and the Old Man. They were talking about the charts that had arrived aboard, which gave me another shock—we were going north about. The mate did not like it, but the Old Man had his orders from the office telling him to catch a tide on such a day at such a time or he would have to wait another fortnight for the tide to be in the same state. It looked good enough on paper, but tides in the Bay of Fundy can rise and fall over thirty feet. The C.P.R. (Canadian Pacific Railway) Beaver boats used to have a whole watch, with three men on during the night in St John's, New Brunswick for ropes and gangway. Going north about was also the shortest route for anything leaving the Tyne bound for any ports on the eastern seaboard of Canada or the United States. As with all shore wallahs, weather was never taken into consideration—the further north you go, the shorter the route, but the further you go, the better the weather.

I was once shanghaied into one of Curries of Leith's ships, thinking that she was on the Mediterranean run, but on going aboard I found that she was bound for Philadelphia. However, that was not too bad, as she was sailing from London south about. Being young at the time and just tramping around I did not think much of it, but for elderly men who had been on the same run all their lives this taking them away from all they held sacred was a hard pill to swallow. I could not help but feel pity for them rubbing the dust off their old Vernier Sextants, which probably had been lying in some attic for thirty years, and mumbling at noon sights, 'What have you got, second mate, what have you got, third mate?' This downward trek in the Merchant Navy started thirty years ago, with every run worth taking being taken over by foreigners, or some cheaper way being found to get things moving.

The Geordie collier sailed for Canada north about, and from the time we passed the Butt of Lewis until she reached the Bay of Fundy, I do not think the wind was under force 6, a whole month of it blowing from the west. People might say it is sad we have no ships any more, but we seem to be surviving without them, for it was a dog's life, especially crossing the Atlantic in any kind of craft. So there we were with the Geordie collier, diving into it for a whole month. One day, just for the sake of curiosity I started to count the miles she was west of Eriskay, when the Master arrived on the scene. 'You aren't wishing yourself on that rock', he said. 'That I am', I responded.

The Atlantic is much kinder coming back, as you more or less always have the prevailing westerly wind helping to drive you across. The sailing ship *Lancing* sailed once while under the Norwegian flag from Sandy Hook, New York, to Cape Wrath, in six days, eighteen hours. This flyer was sailing in the twenties as a timber drogher between Ardrossan and New Brunswick, carrying spool wood, and was chartered by Coats of Paisley. One wonders why a country whose seamen were world famous at one time had to have its commerce carried by strangers.

These bluenoses from the maritime provinces of Canada were the same breed of people as the ones they left behind in the rocky shores of Northern Scotland. They were all cleared from the straths and glens to make way for sheep, arriving in the New World with hardly any knowledge of how to build or sail a boat. Before the sailing ship era was to pass, their clippers were for forty years to sail the seven seas unchallenged. Their seamen, with no seafaring tradition behind them, were to sail these ships, sometimes very brutally, their seagoing way of life leaving much to be desired. While fishing in their dories their noses turned blue from rubbing their blue jerseys against them, hence the name bluenoses.

The MacKay family, who could build and sail these ships, were just one generation away from being cleared, for it was after 1800 that all these terrible clearances took place. One of the MacKay ships, built by themselves and commanded by one of the family, left on her maiden voyage bound for San Francisco. The *Flying Cloud* was going to suffer a dismasting by going on her beam ends off Cape Horn, but she still passed through the Golden Gate to make an east-to-west record not beaten to this day.

The changeover from wood to steel was not made by these bluenoses as they could see the writing on the wall themselves in the land of opportunity, not being able to compete with poorer nations. It was not for the lack of iron ore, as most of it for building in this country came from Wabana in Newfoundland, and as for coal they had plenty of it on Cape Breton Island. Some people think that because they are expert at doing some kind of work it is their intelligence which is superior. But Clyde Built, for example, was world famous, not because of their people being more intelligent than others, but because the crowd who owned the shipyards could quote lower prices by paying their workmen lower wages than other places.

By this time that I am talking about nearly all coastal trade out there was in the hands of strangers. Things were getting bad for weekly and monthly shipping at home, and where better to use these ships than around these creeks out there. Four seasons I was out there myself, trading anywhere between Labrador and Mexico. The seasons were usually finished in December because of the ice blocking up nearly all of Canada's eastern seaboard. It was the creeks around the maritime provinces that were home from home, as at that time there was plenty of Gaelic spoken there. One old Geordie Master I was with, who, like many Geordies was of Scots descent, could hardly believe it. He used to follow me around listening to me conversing in Gaelic with the natives. 'After all these years', he would gasp. But it was one day after hearing a Gaelic song coming from my room that he almost had a fit, as on looking round he just saw myself and a negro in the room, the negro singing away as if he were in one of the glens in Scotland.

Seemingly, at the time of the clearances from Scotland, slaves in the West Indies were given their freedom, and some of them landed around that area and with intermingling with the Scots they had come to know the language. On the west side of Canada, around Vancouver, are emigrants who went over after the First World War. They had gone to the prairies of Alberta but did not remain there for long. I have been to relations' homes out there where the wife had found her way from the prairies and the husband, having got fed up with his pound and pint and sloppy hash, had jumped ship.

The reason they kept the language in the Maritimes for so long was there were not so many people out there before them, as all small villages are named after villages in the Highlands of Scotland. The only curse out on that coast was the way the pound sterling was devalued from approximately four fifty to two dollars fifty in one jump. No wonder they wanted British ships out there—they would have to pay their own seamen in a week what they would give us in a month.

In all my time out on that seaboard it was always bulk cargoes from some mine or quarry, except once we had a cargo of old army trucks full of everything you could think of from a needle to an anchor. This cargo was loaded at Goose Bay in Labrador for Montreal by Yankee soldiers, telling us to help ourselves to anything we wanted, as some fellow in Montreal had bought the lot at next-to-nothing prices. I do not think there was a ship sailing with so much gear, spanners etc. and a crew so well-shod as ours before we were finished helping ourselves. Some fellows going on watch dressed as a generals, and took some stuff to sell in Montreal for beer money at Joe Beef's pub.

I have seen only one other cargo like it, which was loaded in New York for the Persian Gulf. This time it was Yankee gear—civilian cast-offs. All kinds of suits, coats and leather jackets were in that cargo, including evening and morning dress that big shots used to wear. We arrived in the Persian Gulf around July, and going ashore there with a suit on over the light clothing you would need for coming back was no mean feat. Some fellows were too greedy, putting two suits on and also carrying a heavy overcoat on their arms, telling the fellows at the dock gate it was going to rain by and by. We used to get the boys off the tankers in Abadan aboard to rig them out for their beer money. The poor souls could do with something as they had been out for quite a while.

My father's family and neighbours at Balla, Eriskay were some of the better-off ones in the years before the First World War. Nearly all of them were staying in stone-built two-storey houses and had three new zulu-built boats, all of then over fifty foot long, the *Mystical Rose*, the *Virgin* and our own family boat, the *Handy*.

It was not the money that was earned in these herring boats that was important but the way they were placed, so that nearly every day, despite the weather, they could take home a meal of fish from the Oitear, which their community was next door to. They were placed in this happy situation when others in days of oars and sail had to tack against head winds.

Money that was earned by the younger members in the herring boats was all frozen money kept in big sea boot stockings, none of it to be spent, as the older members were out in small boats after cod and ling, their innards, roe and liver, being theirs to take home, along with flounder, skate etc, which were unmarketable at this time.

Large ship-owning companies were started by communities like Balla Eriskay, where people clubbed together money earned from their small farms to send away younger members to buy at scrap value of a few thousand pounds a tramp ship laid up during the depression years.

Goodness knows how these ships were run by men whose only seagoing experience was sailing in small boats among their own islands, but they were fortunate they could employ men who were starving on the beaches and were glad to work as long as they got fed.

A man has told that he once saw, in a foreign port before the war, some crew members of one of these ships going on strike, climbing up and tying themselves to the masts, and the chief of police of that port offering for a sum of money to shoot them down. It was only the involvement of some consuls of more civilised countries that put a stop to them.

It was only tight-fisted meanness that stopped the older members of Balla putting any of the money that was in the big sea boot stockings to some use, but if they were put in the same situation as the owners of the above-mentioned ship, I believe they would have agreed with the chief of police to shoot them.

I believe some hard bargaining was done by ones from Balla but my father got the best bargain when one day in Canna he came across this man from Mull who had arrived in Canna to see about his uncle's property. His uncle, who had died some time recently, must have been a bit of a hermit. He was fishing lobsters there, this being a year after the First World War, and anybody working during the war had some money. The nephew must have been pleased with the money that was left, but to take all that stuff to Mull by way of Mallaig, then to Oban and back to Mull, was too much.

'Well', my father says, 'I only have one pound in my pocket.'

'Give it to me', says the nephew, 'and you can have the lot'.

'The lot?', says my father.

'Yes', says the nephew, 'the lot, and the house too if you can get it aboard your boat.'

So off to the boat my father went to tell them of the bargain. His two brothers were flitting to Glendale and his brother John was after building the shed, his family being named after it during their their lifetime, Clan e Sheat. They had the *Virgin II* with them, which they were after buying, but she needed a poop, and so the timber in the house would come in handy. There was also a stove, all sorts of cooking utensils, pots and pans etc., also hens, ducks and a nanny goat, and so most of what went in the new flitting was out of the Canna bargain.

Canna had the only decent harbour in the small inner isles of the Hebrides, and almost everything happening where all kinds of craft were gathering. It was one day there that that well-known Campbeltown man, Bob Robertson, known as the Hoodie, came into the harbour with two brand new ring netters, the *Falcon* and the *Frigate Bird*. He was looking for some boat crew who had enough courage to take him fishing to the outer isles. This no drift netter fisherman in his right mind would do, as all the islands at that time had drift net herring boats. These inner isles had no herring fleet, just enough workers staying in them working for the rich people who owned the islands. Drift net fishermen avoided Clyde ring net men like the plague at this time, but my father got talking to them and they started drawing him a rosy picture of how it would be if he could persuade his crew to take them to the outer isles, and how they would do the fishing, and those who had a bigger boat would carry the herring to the mainland markets. They finally got him to accept a ring net they had spare and put it in a place where they could get it aboard our own boat, the *Handy*, but on his going aboard and telling the others of the deal, they nearly killed him. Anyway the ring net went aboard the *Handy* and was hidden away somewhere.

Things must have been bad at the drift nets, when, one morning after hauling the nets at daybreak, some fish started playing around them. Thinking it was herring, and no other boats from their own community being near them except the *Virgin*, it was decided to try the ring net. All they knew about it was that it had to be shot in a ring with the one who had the net picking up the end. They did this with the *Virgin* towing her off, a thing they saw the ring net men doing. They found the ring full of coleys. How to get rid of them was the question, as they had no idea how to get them out of the ring or what to do with them after getting them out, when somebody mentioned Uisdean, a north Uist man who was shopkeeping and curing white fish in Castlebay, a price of a shilling each being mentioned for them. They got them aboard after a struggle, as they had no idea that the two boats had to be used, one with the cork rope and one with the net. They split the catch up between the two boats, hid the ring net below their drift nets, and off they went to Uisdean, telling him lies that they had caught them with hook and line. Everyone around Castlebay was amazed at the shot of coleys Uisdean had on his hands, over five hundred of them.

What I could gather about Uisdean was that he was very good at splitting fish, and would have a fish in the air before the one he had split hit the ground. Plenty of white fish used to be caught in herring nets. They tell me hake—the dearest fish on the market today—used to lie rotting, as it could not be salted and dried for export like cod and ling. This ring net that caught all these coleys the first time it was shot, was used in Eriskay when herring was drying itself in sounds and fords, where it could be seen swimming near the sandy bottom.

Half of Eriskay must have had a hand hauling that ring net, whichever boat was handy at the time the herring was seen. It was used through the years in the winter months, and I must say they used to catch some herring with it when the herring came inshore, but there was so much shouting about catching herring with ring nets that my folks had to stop using it.

There was a move afoot to stop trawling and ring netting in the Minch a few years before the war, called the Sea League. So for fourteen years there were no ring nets used by anybody from Eriskay. It was a few years after the war in 1949 that my father used a ring net again when we got the *Lady of Fatima*, which was built for ring netting. He was nine of these years without doing any fishing of any kind, as the family boat, the *Ocean Star*, was taken over for war service and he was in a salvage boat.

During all these years the Clyde men, and men from the west coast mainland ports like Mallaig and Kyle, kept fishing with ring nets. They must have made fortunes during the war years, and a few years after, as every food was scarce except fish.

The ring net lifetime lasted until the mid 'seventies when, with all the herring that was caught with new patents like mid-water trawling and purse netting, all herring fishing was banned altogether, or the seas would have been swept clean of it. By the time it was resumed people must have lost their taste for it, for I have seen myself a Dunure, Ayrshire fisherman, Bob MacCrutchon, trying to sell a few crans of it in Ayr and nobody wanting even a free meal of it, except myself, when I took a few of them to my caravan

Mary and myself on our wedding day, 26 June, 1971

in Prestwick. It went over a hundred pound a cran in Stornoway one day before the ban.

If there are two persons in this world I would like to thank, they are my mother's father and mother, who I was left with when my father and mother went on the second flitting when I was six years old. It was at the Castlebay fishing they first met my grandmother's family, after coming over from Berneray, Barra Head, to keep shop in the bank house which they built. Grandfather was shopkeeping in some shack put up like many others by folks from other islands, as it was the Castlebay herring fishing that was the only work available to people living at our end of the long island.

About one hundred years ago it was only big, strong, healthy families who were able to survive the hard work ones had to do to earn their living. The poor, unhealthy souls living without any means of survival, except what the ones shopkeeping would give them, fell to T.B. owing to unhealthy sanitation, this being the scourge of almost everywhere the poor lived.

My grandfather and grandmother and her father could not be put in the mean bracket, for they were both forced into bankruptcy while Castlebay fishing was still in its heyday. The younger members of grandmother's family were left without a home when the city wholesalers sold it to the bank to recover some of their debt. There wasn't much granny could offer them, as she was in the same boat herself, my grandfather working for a city merchant, Hamilton Bros., as a commercial traveller. The first help they got was when the oldest of the family, Eddie, got an ordinary seaman's job at the age of fifteen in the Clyde Shipping Company. I have seen them with tears in their eyes telling me how Eddie used to give ten shillings to grandfather, and would add another ten shillings to send granny a pound to help her bring up a young family. For four years Eddie sailed in the Clyde Shipping until he left to get time in deep sea so he could go and sit for a deep sea ticket.

After two years deep sea he managed to save enough money to go to school, get a second mate's ticket and get a job as third mate in one of Donaldson of Glasgow's ships called the *Cambotia*, one of the Allan Line boats which Donaldson bought over in 1913. He was only twenty-one years of age then. It was on the way back from Canada when they were one hundred miles north-west of Tory island that a submarine started following them on the surface using gunfire. The Master, thinking he would out-distance her, got more firemen in the stockhold. No gun being on her stern the submarine got within her range and started hitting her, forcing them to abandon ship at dusk.

With many of them injured going into the lifeboats, only a few survivors were picked up. Over thirty of them, including the Master and Eddie, were lost. After this a law came out that all ships of nations at war could have a gun on their stern to defend themselves. I don't think my gran ever got over that, especially when they lost another boy, Angus, a couple of years after that. He was also twenty-one. She also lost her brother called Joseph. There were only a couple of sisters left, who were lucky enough to train as nurses when the family still had the shop. My granny was also lucky that she could cook for lodgers, something she learned in a dough school after the family moved over from Berneray. She used to make lovely apple pies. I would have many friends around to get some of the peelings from the apples. Their diet in Berneray would leave much to be desired, as they ate mainly birds and fish. Anybody moving over to the main island of Barra would be treated very cruelly, especially in school, where the children would make bird sounds at them.

There was also the Canon, a brother of granny's, who came back wounded from the First World War, where he served as chaplain. Except for a few years in Dalibrog, South Uist, he was in Morar until he died and is buried there.

I heard my granny say that after they came over to Castlebay they left the Barra Head islands well populated till they all moved to Vatersay in 1910, and that their shop would be the one they would do most of their shopping in. Healthy young families able to work were all right but it was the old and the sick that her father used to refuse tick, and then go after them to their boats and take them back to the shop to give them what they wanted, him knowing what it was like living in these islands.

Not many folks could afford a holiday these days before the last war, so it was mostly ones on business, commercial travellers etc. and young students who came to visit the islands. One young fellow from the south of England who must have been working in a laboratory, sent back a bag full of brown powder which he said would cure rheumatism, an illness very common in the damp weather of the western isles. The dosage was what you could lift of the powder with a sixpence. It seemed to be curing them, too. The ones in these laboratories were trying out these remedies on the ones living in these out of the way places, using them as guinea pigs. They were the kind of people who used to stay in granny's home.

There were nearly always some strangers around the islands looking for a place to stay. Some of them rich ones, like the German who in 1933 managed to escape from the German Embassy in London after he was called back to Germany when Hitler and his party came to power in 1933. Doctor Kissling had a good idea he wasn't being called back to Germany for the good of his health, and so, with the help of some British friends from his Eton days, he got away. He stayed in granny's house for about six weeks, collecting all sorts of old stories, and taking pictures with a cine camera, the first on the island, which pictures were made into a proper video by Grampian Television recently.

People were against anything German at this time, as ones had fresh memories of the First World War and ones that were killed, injured or gassed, but Doctor Kissling was a nice man of noble birth who wasn't able to go back to Germany until after the war. His brother had to commit suicide when he was involved in the 1944 attempt on Hitler's life. Doctor Kissling died in Dumfries when he was eighty-eighty years of age. His estate, which was in Russian-occupied east Germany, went out of his family.

Doctor Kissling wasn't the first German granny had to feed. Germans

The four Eriskay men who crewed the Virgo *in 1996-97, when she was the highest earner for the north west of Scotland*

buying herring used to stay in the bank house in Castlebay when they were shopkeeping in it. One, in particular, used to eat six eggs for breakfast, the leg of the biggest ram they could find for his dinner, and seven salt herring for his tea. He would then go to the bar next door with his own two-pint mug and drink beer. When the Barra folks would see him coming in, the cry would be, '*Tha fhearr iad air na seachd e cuir leathe eadal'*, meaning, 'That one is after eating his seven'.

Eriskay where I was born and brought up is today down to a sixth of the population of what it was when I first knew it in the late twenties and early thirties. Its sixteen boats, all engine-powered, were owned by the islanders with the help of the best financier and gentleman a community could have— Donald Ferguson of South Lochboisdale, whose help was always called for when any disaster or want came your way.

Donald was to all communities around our area the prince of finance, as there was no buying or selling of any property involving a large sum of money that he did not have a hand in. The place just could not have survived without him, as he knew who wanted to sell or buy a boat between the Harris border and Eriskay. I have yet to hear of a refusal from him to anyone wanting to buy gear or property for a start in life. God bless him, it is very rarely he would use strong-arm tactics, only if property he had a hand in buying was left to rot on the beach. This is what happened one day when he, with a couple of flunkies, went to lift a boat Domnal Ian Mhac e Tailler had lying rotting on the shore near to his house at Harbour, Eriskay. As usual Ferguson had a hand in buying the boat, but when Domnal Ian saw she was going to be lifted he went berserk and started chasing Ferguson and his flunkies with a sickle. This must have been a bit hair-raising for Ferguson, who was at the tail-end of the chase, the flunkies being only young boys out of school who could run faster.

Domnal Ian was never tackled again about the boat. She just rotted away there. He had some queer ideas on how to survive in this world, never starting tilling his land until mid-summer and never castrating any male animals. Seeing ghosts was his specialty. He was another one who must have been seeing more of the dead than of the living. His other one was his habit to threaten anyone who dared to say 'boo' to him with a relative who was a policeman.

Donald must have had a great brain, knowing all the families personally. In Scalpay and Eriskay especially, it was thanks to him that the herring fishing kept going, and was able, after he was not with us any more, to keep going, never losing the expert seamanship that was needed in order to make a living at herring fishing. Scalpay, near Harris, was another island Donald had dealings with. They were using the barrel type of nets, as they had hard ground at the mouth of Loch Seaforth. Big boats they were, some of them big enough to work spring, as they had plenty of room down below at the stern for coiling. One of them, the *Daffodil*, had a steam capstan in her when she was bought from the east coast after the First World War. But that was their stumbling block, the hard ground, so all the boats working these kinds of nets in our place landed up there. Donald Ferguson, his folks coming from the Harris area originally, always had a market for any old boat there. Some of these boats lasted them a long time. *Jasper, Virgin, Agate* and *Industry* were there after the Second World War. Their iron man must have done some turning, its purpose being to haul the boat along with the cork rope.

These two islands of Scalpay and Eriskay were blessed in not having a drinking den, the scourge of the Highlands and Islands. It was only recently that bars came their way. It was to Donald Ferguson that people looked in their hour of need. Even when young children met him in his shops or on the road he was never too busy to have a word with them and find out who they were. I believe the worst thing that happened to him was when his son Donnie disappeared overboard while crossing from the north to the south side of the loch. I don't think he ever got over it, especially when his body was never found. There was a nice song composed by a minister to his memory, a song that is sung plenty on the radio these days.

There is only one boat crew of four men fishing out of Eriskay today, working a boat that is not even their own, but thanks to their early training they had the highest money-making record for the north west of Scotland fishing fleet for 1996-97, not bad for Eriskay, fifty percent of whose population are old-age pensioners or incomers.

Eriskay was first settled by a population who had gone through three flittings in ten years, first from the west coast of South Uist where they were used by the Laird for making kelp from tangles and seaweed. For the next ten years they must have gone through hell on earth, with another couple of flittings, first to the back of Ben Mhor, then to Bhaigh Hartabhaigh and Bun Struth, and then to Eriskay. It was only after they reached Eriskay that they realised the sea was to be kinder to them—indeed it was going to be their saviour. It was a hard life to survive there, as everything like peats and seaweed had to be ferried by boats from the mainland island or off-shore rocks. It bred a hard-working race of people, men who could hold their own aboard anything afloat, women whose life besides croft work was a hard one, from the time they would go away to the herring gutting in May till the new year, following the herring around Britain. In this book I hope I have given people an idea of their way of life from the cradle to the grave, as it was older ones, married women and school children, who had to do the hard work around crofts. To the ones lying buried facing the western ocean in its two graveyards, the ones in foreign graveyards far from their folks, and the ones with no known graveyards except the seas, I have dedicated this book, along with my three songs composed by myself and another by my father, to the memory of the population of the island of Eriskay who are not with us any more.

Four songs of Eriskay and the sea

NA REITEAN AN EIRISGEIDH NUAIR BHA MI OG

1. Tha'n t-earrach ma-riagh san oitear arrachd
   Sen aon chail as an latha son beo-slàint
   Tha ràmh cho sàraicait 'e gaoth n iar tràigheadh
   Ri fuachd a mhairt falus blath tighinn rompha

2. Gath sgeir is bàt innt crann na àirde
   Air esgorraidh dainge muir tràigh an comhnaidh
   An fheamain geàrtadh se cliabh ais gràbha
   Se linn tha cràmh siad mar geàrr a copadh.

3. Samhradh blàth nuaur bhios crioch air àiteach
   Chùtag mà rinn feur fàs is neoinean
   Gach te air airleas fear na bhàta
   An ceitein tràth a cuir gàir nan còmhradh.

4. Deoine tapaidh bham Bagh a Chaisteal
   'G-isciagh sgadain a' cosnadh lòin ann
   Nuair thig an uair ach a' dhol gu cruadail
   Siad supailt subhaich cuir bhuap Muldonaich.

5. Nuair bhios a ghrian a dol sios san iar oirnn
   Air feasgar briagha se sealladh boideach
   Na daoine tha crianadh an diugh san t-siarach
   Bhiodh cuir na lion tuath san iar air Gunna.

SONG OF THE CROFTER FISHERMEN OF ERISKAY
1. Spring with us, small line fishing/The only way to earn a living/The oars so hard with west wind and ebb tide/With the cold March wind, hot sweat pouring through them 2. Every rock with a boat and mast up/Upright, firm and low tide with us/Seaweed cut, creel and fork to carry/Generation that's dead like hares frothing at the mouth 3. Summer with us and croft work finished/Cuckoo with us, grass and daisies growing/Every woman on retainers, man in the boat/Early May putting a laugh in their conversation 4. Smart men who were in Castlebay/Fishing herring, earning a livelihood/When the hour comes for hardship/Them lively and smart sailing from Muldoanich (an island off Castlebay, Barra) 5. When the sun goes down in the west/On a nice summer evening, lovely scenery/People who are dead today/Shooting their drift nets north west of Gunna between Coll and Tiree

6. Moch mhaduinn tràth sa mhor sluagh nan tàmh ann
   Bith gach làmh dhol a sàs an òrdugh
   Sgadan briagha tighinn innt 'nan ceudan
   Èrigh grian a cuir blinn na sòlas.

7. Clann càs ruisgte leum gu sunndach
   Ruith nan caorach, crodh laoigh, siad còmhla
   Tarb feadh achaidh is bo ri casgadh
   Na h-eich s na làraichean tarruing mhòine.

8. Thigh foghar milteach bi barr fo dhiltean
   Sgadan iosal dol mach a orden
   Mh'oin cho sàraichte toirt thar sàile
   Am Bun Struth a tha I ait mi comhairteal.

9. Na daoine laidir tapaidh gradach
   Bhan Erisgeidh nuair a bha mi og ann
   Iad mach lem bata san dudlachd ghrannda
   Treabhad saile gach la ach Domhnach.

10. Ceud mile failte gach mullach arde
    Sios gu tràigh glaic s bagh 's geodh ann
    Na thug a bàs bhuain 's ùir e tamh iad
    Sluagh cho càirdeal bhann a' comhnaidh.

---

6. Early morning when most of the world's population is asleep/All hands are awake hauling nets/Lovely herring coming aboard in hundreds/Rising sun putting a glow in their happiness 7. Children barefoot running wild/Chasing sheep and cows with calves/Bull around fields and cows being herded by children/Horses and mares carrying peats 8. Autumn with us and the crops under rain and wind/Herring spent out of order/Peat so hard taking her over water/Bun Struth on South Uist, a wild place to load peat into boats 9. The strong, lively, holy people /In Eriskay when I was young/Them out in boats in rough December/Ploughing the seas every day but Sunday 10. A thousand welcomes to its highest top/Down to its shore, valley and bay/Those death took from us in its soil and them that's drowned/ The nice population that's staying there

ORAN NA SEOLADEARAIR

1. Ga Gearradh geal ais smud mha gruaidh
   Dhol ma cuairt Cape Saint Vincent
   Scapaidh e mhuir tiugh cluas
   Cursa gan tuath fuachd ais fionnachd

2. E-gilla tha fiare ard se cuach
   Cridhean fuachd reothaidh minach
   Trusgan cumadh mu e fuachd
   Air e suaip son droch dibhe

3. Mile molachd gan deoch grann
   Se canal aig na cinneach
   Balachd iad leth ruiste ga grain
   Gan droch aite leis na mionnin

4. Gillean son bi sibh fo grauim
   Gu bheil e auir aig u tighinn
   Nuair hi sibh tigh-osd aig clar
   Geibhach ard son gach dibhe

5. Gun thig sinn cuairt gan Mason's Arms
   Railway Bar suas gan Eastern
   Charlie Brown se Bootle Arms
   E Black Man Morven Dick's Bar

6. Gur ann a tir na Gaelig tuath
   Bha part sluagh bha gha sgioba
   Balaich tapaidh subaity cruaidh
   Modhal subach na grinneas.

7. Chud u dhuit e tamh se uaigh
   Na bheil bhuaindhol nas sine
   Erisgeidh cha marach oig
   Ais bha dorlach dhu tighinn

SAILORS' SONG
1. Rounding Cape St Vincent, Spain and heading north into cold and miserable weather. 2. Look out, crow's nest. No warm clothing, clothing bartered for plonk. 3. Suez Canal. 'Changie for changie'. With bumboats for plonk. Boys half naked, cursing them to hell with swear words. 4. Pay-off days, into the pubs. Plenty money. At the pub table shouting loud for all drinks. 5. London, Liverpool and Glasgow pubs frequented by island seamen. 6. All Gaelic-speaking island seamen who manned these cargo steamers, boys who were strong and healthy, good-living in their way. 7. To all seamen alive and dead in their graves in Eriskay, where some came from, including me.

ORAN NA CUTEIRAN

Chorus:
Meudal air e dh fhearr nach gluas
Chron na acaidcha thigbuaidh
Sa thoirt fasgadhh go cuid sluagh
An deidh e cuairt air aineol ais

1. Cuitearain gab riomh mi dhuain
   Calleagain bha subhailt cruadh
   S theidh e suile deas ais tuath
   Lineadh suas na barral gean

2. Mios e ceitean saltuin tuath
   S gadan snamh gu deas gu luath
   Mha thig crioch gan dulaich fhuair
   Bi chursa tuath gun na-blianda

3. Nuiar e thig e am re thin
   Fad e saile ach e gan tir
   Eilean araich iad fon cìoch
   Eibh on chridhe ga bennache

4. Mile bennacha ais ceud failte
   Dhionsaigh tir ais gilla traigh
   Erisgeidh le geo se bhàigh
   Thoirt teurtuinteas go mairaichean

5. Mhaduin samhraidh cuin ais blàth
   Ceol na eun ais geum no bà
   Haltain cuir siul an ard
   Fuam na ràmh ga fann ache

6. Na dha kil tha gin e crabh
   Anns gach tìr nach th-eil iad slàin
   Cuid u tha s'gruin nach tràigh
   Fois shiarraidh baigh gan anamin ach

SONG OF THE GUTTERS
Chorus: Love to the one that won't move/No moans or agony from it/Giving shelter to its people/After their roving around the world 1. Gutters that I have made the song for/Girls that were supple and hard/They would go south and north/Filling up the barrels 2. The month of May Shetland north/Herring swimming fast south/Till the end of cold December/Its course north till next year 3. When the time comes/The length of their heel of the place/Their birth-place from breast feeding/Shout from their heart, blessing it 4. A thousand blessings a hundred welcomes/To the place of white sands/Eriskay with its coves and bays/Giving safety to its mariners 5. Summer morning nice and warm/Birds singing, cows bellowing/Halliards heaving sails up/Oars making sounds rowing them 6. In its two graveyards are they buried/All over the world where they didn't come back/And in the ocean that won't dry/God's blessing to their souls

ORAN REINN M'ATHEIR GAM MAIGHEIR

1. O san tha mo gaol na Haun
    Ann e Erisgeidh fad thall
    Eilean gregach sgorrach lom
    Thruigh nach robh mi ann e fanail
    O san tha mho gaol na Haun

2. Mhar tha mise duigh cho truigh
    Bho di Saturine gu di Luain
    Margarita trebaidh chuain
    Se ma cuirt air aois e pension
    O san tha mho gaol na Haun

3. Ach ma greibh mi gu brath
    Nas gan *Handy* sgaoth mo grath
    Mi gun deanaidh innte tamh
    Cha dh-fhag me e gu brath leum maireann
    O san tha mho gaol na Haun

4. Eather tapaidh laidir srien
    Le mhuir gairbhe bharr na sinnte
    Ais seol cartach set gu deane
    Air e susie air cruin fallain
    O san tha mho gaol na Haun

5. Erisgeidh ais gille traigh
    Na bi agaim fad mu saile
    Luibh mo duinne luichd mo gradh
    Tha e deanna tama aig balla ann
    O san tha mho gaol na Haun

6. Balla ais biodhe dearsa grian
    Aghaidh air e cuain en iar
    Boidhchach ailach se dha kil
    Sluagh nach maireann sinnte fo th-alla
    O san tha mho gaol na Haun

    (Repeat first verse)

[FATHER'S SONG, MADE IN 1923] 1. O my love is at the Haun/In Eriskay far away/Rocky bare island/Pity I wasn't there/O my love is at the Haun 2. O how unhappy I am today/From Saturday to Monday/*Margarita* ploughing the ocean/And her around pension age/O my love is at the Haun 3. If I ever get back/In the *Handy*, my own boat/I will stay in her evermore/I will never leave her/O my love is at the Haun 4. Boat that's strong, smart and fast/In heavy seas in bad weather/With her barked sails set for safety/Them set on healthy masts/O my love is at the Haun 5. Eriskay of the white sands/If I had the length of my soles of it/Among my folks, my dear ones/That's staying at its village/O my love is at the Haun 6. The village that's nice under sun/Facing the western ocean/Its nice scenery with two graveyards/The folks that are dead lying there/O my love is at the Haun